WITHDRAWN

D0301634

LIVERPOOL
JOHN MOORES UNIVERSITY
AVRIL ROBARTS LRC
TITHEBARN STREET
LIVERPOOL L2 2ER
TEL. 0151 231 4022

GROUP INTERACTION IN HIGH RISK ENVIRONMENTS

Group Interaction in High Risk Environments

Edited by
RAINER DIETRICH
with TRACI MICHELLE CHILDRESS

Written by
The GIHRE Project

LIVERPOOL
JOHN MOORES UNIVERSITY
AVRIL ROBARTS LRC
TITHEBARN STREET
LIVERPOOL L2 2ER
TEL. 0151 231 4022

ASHGATE

© Rainer Dietrich and Traci Michelle Childress 2004

All rights reserved. No part of this publication may be reproduced, stored in a retrieval system, or transmitted in any form or by any means, electronic, mechanical, photocopying, recording or otherwise without the prior permission of the publisher.

Rainer Dietrich and Traci Michelle Childress have asserted their right under the Copyright, Designs and Patents Act, 1988, to be identified as the editors of this work.

Published by
Ashgate Publishing Limited
Gower House
Croft Road
Aldershot
Hampshire GU11 3HR
England

Ashgate Publishing Company
Suite 420
101 Cherry Street
Burlington, VT 05401-4405
USA

Ashgate website: http://www.ashgate.com

British Library Cataloguing in Publication Data
Group interaction in high risk environments
    1. Teams in the workplace 2. Hazardous occupations 3. Language
    in the workplace 4. Industrial safety - Management
    5. Communication in management
    I. Dietrich, Rainer II. Childress, Traci Michelle III. GIHRE
    Project
    658.4'022

Library of Congress Cataloging-in-Publication Data
Group interaction in high risk environments / by Rainer Dietrich with Traci Michelle Childress.
        p. cm.
    Results from The Ladenburg Collegium Group Interaction in High Risk Environments' (including linguists, psycholinguists, psychologists and
specialists) 1999 - 2004 study of four representative workplaces: the cockpit of a commercial airliner, a hospital operating room, a hospital intensive care unit, and the control room of a nuclear power plant.
    Includes bibliographical references and index.
    ISBN 0-7546-4011-6
    1. Teams in the workplace--Case studies. 2. Hazardous occupations--Case studies. 3. Stress (Psychology) --Case studies. 4. Miscommunication--Case studies. 5. Group decision making--Case studies. I. Dietrich, Rainer. II. Childress, Traci Michelle, 1977-

HD66.G746 2004
658.4'036--dc22

2004010338

ISBN 0 7546 4011 6

Printed and bound in Great Britain by MPG Books Ltd, Bodmin, Cornwall

Contents

Foreword

The Ladenburg Collegium 'Group Interaction in High Risk Environments' initiated joint research between linguists, psycholinguists, psychologists and specialists from the fields of aviation, surgery, intensive care and nuclear reactor safety to work on a common project from 1999 to 2004. Guided by Professor Rainer Dietrich at the Humboldt University in Berlin, the experts have investigated how teams operating in the above areas should work together to best deal with crisis situations. The participants came from Europe and the USA.

The Gottlieb Daimler and Karl Benz Foundation was the Collegium's main sponsor. The Foundation supports interdisciplinary research into the interrelationship between humanity, environment and technology. The topic suggested by Professor Dietrich in this context raised an extremely interesting question: what governs the way in which people work together and handle technology in high risk environments? The results have more than fulfilled the Foundation's expectation of helping to improve general safety and security in our high-tech world. The Foundation expresses its gratitude to Professor Rainer Dietrich, the project managers and all members of the group for their fascinating work.

The research results could not have been obtained without the participation and sponsorship of numerous companies and institutions to whom the Foundation is also extremely grateful. A full tribute to the valuable support they have provided is found in the Foreword. We mention here only the Lufthansa City Line and the Training Center of the former Swissair, Zurich, as examples. Both of these institutions made their flight simulators available for the investigations.

Prof. Dr. Dr. h.c. mult. Gisbert Freiherr zu Putlitz
Dr.-Ing. Diethard Schade
The Board of the Gottlieb Daimler and Karl Benz Foundation

Ladenburg, April 2004

Preface

This book is about teams. It has also been produced by a team, the interdisciplinary research project 'Group Interaction in High Risk Environments' (GIHRE). The collective task of this Collegium of the Gottlieb Daimler and Karl Benz Foundation was to investigate and analyze the behavior of professional groups working in high risk environments. Four representative workplaces were investigated in three broad settings: in aviation, the cockpit of a commercial airliner; in medicine, the operating room and the intensive care unit of a hospital; in nuclear power, the control room of a nuclear power plant. The international and interdisciplinary composition of the Collegium brought different methodological and conceptual approaches to bear on a problem of both theoretical and practical significance. The research team as a whole was comprised of experts from the sample-settings, as well as experts in cognitive psychology, experimental psychology, social psychology, work and organizational psychology, psycholinguists and linguists (see Appendix I). The goals of the project were not only to increase understanding of group behaviour in these circumstances but also to develop practical suggestions for enhancing performance in such settings. The Collegium was made up of seven research projects in Germany, Switzerland and in the United States, tied together by their complementary aims and objectives, methods and shared data bases. The individual projects are described in the first section of the book, which is made up of Chapters 1-7. For the sake of maintaining a sense of continuity, the bibliographies for each chapter appear together at the end of the book. A glossary of terms can be found in Appendix II.

This book could not have been realised without the Gottlieb Daimler and Karl Benz Foundation's support or without the generous co-operation of a large number of institutions and companies, including the Computer Simulation and Training Center (CST) in Berlin Schönefeld and its director Raymund Neuhold, the Lufthansa City Line, the Training Center of the former Swissair Group, Zurich, the University Hospitals of the Humboldt-University Charité and Buch, the University Hospital of Zurich, the University of Texas Center of Excellence and the nuclear power plant operators of the German nuclear power plant Kernkraftwerk Gundremmingen GmbH. The authors would especially like to acknowledge the co-operation of the pilots, nurses, doctors, surgeons and patients who volunteered numerous hours to the data collection sessions. The editors would like to thank Guido Kiecker at the Humboldt University for his technical support.

Rainer Dietrich, Traci M. Childress and members of The GIHRE Project

Introduction

Rainer Dietrich and Traci M. Childress

The Research Question

This book deals with conditions and aspects of high task load management by small groups of professionals working in high risk environments such as in the cockpit of an airplane, an operating room, an intensive care unit and a nuclear power plant control room. It focuses on team interaction, especially on group communication, and on the predictability of team performance on the basis of team interaction indicators. The general scientific aim is to describe the interrelation between conditions of high task load and threat, as well as team members' behaviour in such situations. There is also a practical aim, which is to examine if suggestions for the improvement of existing behaviour routines and, perhaps, of technical equipment, can be derived from the findings.

High risk environments are environments in which there is a more than normal chance for damage to one's own life, the life of others or to material property. Working in high risk environments is inherently stressful. Individuals working under high risk are subject to the cognitive and physiological changes imposed by external stressors. While there are some positive effects associated with stress – induced arousal, including enhanced vigilance and reactivity (Janis, 1976) – the overall sequelae of stress are negative. Negative effects include impaired concentration and decision making, memory deficits and reduced ability to cope with multiple, simultaneous task requirements (multi-tasking: Waller, 1994). The latter effect is often referred to as 'the tunnel vision of stress' and refers to a narrowing of cognitive attention induced by stress (Dirkin, 1983; Janis & Mann, 1979).

The last fifty years have seen tremendous efforts to improve safety in human-machine systems. Better education, more real-life oriented training of personnel and the development of more sophisticated control systems have increased security in all fields that utilize high technology. One of the most visible measures in the training arena has been the development of real-life oriented training methods that consider the team to be a functional unit. Consider, for instance, the successful design of *Crew Resource Management* (CRM) in the training of cockpit crews (Orlady & Foushee, 1987). Coming out of practical experience, CRM has proven to be in accordance with many scientific perspectives on the issue. Both empirical and theoretical research by social psychologists (Helmreich, 1987; Hackman, 1987; Helmreich & Foushee, 1993; Janis & Mann,

LIVERPOOL
JOHN MOORES UNIVERSITY
AVRIL ROBARTS LRC
TEL. 0151 231 4022

1977), linguists (Cushing, 1994) and sociologists (Palmer, Lack & Lynch, 1995) have revealed that the study of individuals' behavior in teams is a core issue in interactionist psychology.

Research populations in this study consist of professionals who are all strongly motivated to perform successfully and to maintain high standards of safety. Given that these research populations each work in occupations that have high qualification standards and entry gates, it can be assumed that they all meet basic standards of professional proficiency.[1] Thus, a central focus of this book is how groups in these professions deal with the factors that can threaten the safety and effectiveness of their task performance. These factors can be in the environment or in the team itself. For example, unexpected severe weather or a mechanical failure in an aircraft can place a flight at risk, as can breakdowns in communication between crew members. Similarly, unexpected reactions to drugs or disagreement between members of a surgical team can threaten the safety of a patient and reduce the quality of medical care given. Overconfidence in team capabilities can also lead to serious accidents, as in Chernobyl, for instance. Urban et al. (1996) investigated the effect of the hierarchical vs. non-hierarchical structure of the team on the team's decision making and communication under time pressure. A major effect of the *hierarchical structuring* factor was revealed in communication concerning the allocation of resources.

Linguistic analyses of the verbal interaction proved that the misunderstanding of phonetically, structurally or semantically ambiguous utterances can lead to trouble, danger and disasters; compare the study of Stephen Cushing (1994). Another potential source of danger was pointed out by Palmer, Lack and Lynch (1995), namely, communication conflicts caused by over generalization of status roles; see also Orasanu (2003). The relevance of personality factors to team interaction was shown in a classic study from Helmreich (1987), which laid the groundwork for the social psychology of the Crew Resource Management (CRM) program; see also the more recent findings of Kivimaki et al. (1997) and Berg, Retzlaff & King (2002). As early as the mid-fifties, sociologists undertook quantitative analyses of human behaviour in disaster (Chapman 1954); social psychological experiments intending to investigate the individual behaviour in (non-professional) small groups under sudden danger and time pressure followed some ten years later; see, for instance, Kelley et al (1965). This latter project yielded a number of expected as well as unexpected results. It proved, for instance, the correspondence between fear and success in escaping. Clear evidence was gained that demonstrated the importance of the time element. Given that there is a constant chance of escape, there is, in general, a significant decrease in the likelihood of escape success when time begins to run short. There

---

[1] This is certainly true of pilots, air traffic controllers and power plant operators. The situation in medicine is more problematic since much of the actual training comes from on-the-job experience. Residents see a procedure conducted on a patient and are then expected to perform it. The level of mentoring associated with this practice varies greatly as a function of the individual physician. There is on-the-job training in air traffic control and commercial aviation, but it is much more highly controlled and supervised than in medicine.

is, however, also evidence suggesting a non-linear correspondence between success rate and the amount of time remaining for escape: people who feel that time is running extremely short show better success rates in simple tasks than those under medium time pressure. This is explained by time dependent behaviour differences during times of trouble. Attitudes seem to affect behaviour in different ways during different phases of a hazardous situation. This assumption was confirmed by questionnaire data from the field of disaster research, especially by the NORC studies of human behaviour in disaster (Fritz & Marks, 1954). These studies show that 'death losses and injury losses were actually *higher* for the group that had had brief forewarning than for *either* the group with no forewarning or the group with more extensive forewarning.' (Fritz & Marks, 1954: 38).

Although more than forty years old, the NORC studies are still relevant today, since one of the general findings was 'that the immediate problem in a disaster situation is neither uncontrolled behaviour nor intense emotional reaction but deficiencies of co-ordination and organization, complicated by people acting upon individual (and, often conflicting) definitions of the situation' (Fritz & Marks, 1954, p. 33). Situation awareness is a key concept in decision making in high risk settings (Janis & Mann, 1977). At present, the understanding of decision making, communication and other dimensions of team interaction within aircrews and other teams in highly stressful situations is based on a large number of individual studies. However, until now, there has not been an integrated interdisciplinary account of the dynamics and the main explanatory factors of team interaction under high workload. The present book presents the work and the results of such an endeavour. The research team was comprised of experts in aviation, medicine and nuclear power plant technology, in cognitive psychology, experimental psychology, social psychology, psycholinguistics and linguistics. The sample settings were chosen because they differ in respect to a number of major parameters determining the teams' behaviour, as for instance, size of team, general degree of risk and personal risk in the event of a worst-case scenario. This is expanded upon in more detail in the following sketches:

Operating room

Medium sized teams; in the worst possible case there is relatively minor damage (low risk); in a national framework, the chance for damage per year is great; in the case of a breakdown the team is not endangered; hierarchically structured; face-to-face interaction; shared focus of attention within the shared work; communication is not highly regulated.

Cockpit

Small team; in the worst possible outcome, middle damage to people and things (middle risk); in a national framework, there is relatively low damage per year; in a breakdown, the team is endangered; team is strongly hierarchically structured; face-to-face interaction; separate focus of attention within the shared work; communication is highly regulated.

Nuclear power plant control room

Medium size team; in the worst possible outcome, there is the chance for very large damage to human life, landscape and material property; in a national framework, there is relatively minor damage per year; in a breakdown, the team is endangered; not hierarchically structured; communication is highly procedural but not standardized.

The GIHRE project's seven subprojects[2] are defined by two categories of conditions and are interconnected. The two categories are 1) framework conditions for interaction and 2) dimensions of interaction. This taxonomy determines the content and the structure of the book. This chapter introduces the leading question of research (see above). Part I, Chapters 1-7, presents brief descriptions of the seven perspectives that were taken in the analysis as well as the specific issues, methods and types of data that form the empirical basis of the findings. Chapter 8, the first chapter in Part II, gives a general account of conditions under which group interaction in high risk environments takes place and also introduces the Threat and Error Management Model, a conceptual model that serves as a reference frame in the presentation of the results, which are represented in the remainder of Part II, Chapters 9-12. The linear ordering of the chapters reflects a sort of zooming in on the components of interaction. It begins with the effects of institutional framework conditions on interaction behaviour and outcome such as structures, regulations and company culture, Chapter 8. A treaty follows this on the structural features of language and language use, Chapter 9. Chapter 10 focuses on leadership and co-ordination within and between groups as systematically affected by the setting parameters. A detailed reconstruction of the determining factors of communication and interaction, i.e. the so-called setting parameters of interaction behavior are found in Chapter 11. Detailed linguistic and microstructural processes that influence the individual's communication and decision making behavior are described in Chapter 12. Table 0.1 provides an overview of the workplaces.

---

[2] Throughout the book, GIHRE subprojects will be referred to as follows (the name of the primary investigator follows in parenthesis): *Threat/Error Group* (Robert Helmreich), *Behavioral Markers Group* (Werner Naef), *Process Control Group* (Oliver Sträter and Ryoko Fukuda), *Linguistic Factors Group* (Manfred Krifka), *Co-ordination Group* (Gudela Grote), *Language Processing Group* (Rainer Dietrich) and *Microstructure Group* (Werner Sommer).

Table 0.1 Overview of workplaces, features and research groups that make up GIHRE

Features	Workplaces			
	Operating Room	ICU	Cockpit	Nuclear Power Plant Control Room
Relative Size of the Team	Middle	Large	Small	Middle
Outcome in Terms of Fatalities and Damage in Worst Case	1 person	1 person	Hundreds of fatalities and middle damage to material property and landscape	National catastrophe
Life/Health Threat to Team Members	None	None	Death	Death
Social Structuring	Strong	Strong (Change of positions possible)	Strong	Flat
Communica-tion Channel	Face to face	Multiple channels	Face to face; separate focus of attention	Face to face; separate focus of attention
Degree of Standardiza-tion of Interaction	Low	Low	High	Low
Research Group (see footnote 2 above)	Threat/Error Co-ordination Language Processing	Threat/Error	Threat/Error Behavioural markers Co-ordination Linguistic Factors Language Processing Micro-structure	Process Control

PART I:
Seven Perspectives on Teamwork

Chapter 1

Group Interaction under Threat and High Workload

Robert L. Helmreich and J. Bryan Sexton

Introduction

The University of Texas at Austin project, Group Interaction under Threat and High Workload – referred to in this book as the *Threat/Error Group* – focused on the attitudes and behaviour of front-line personnel. The focus of investigation was how team members perceived and managed threats to safety and errors in their work environment. This research bridges the disciplines of social psychology and human factors, investigating the interplay between individual attributes and situational factors that affect behaviour in group contexts and the interactions between humans and technology.

The types of data collected by within this project included communicative behaviour (through linguistic coding and content coding), behavioural indicators (markers) of flightcrew performance and surveys of pilots and healthcare professionals. The aviation data on communicative behaviors is presented first, showing the links between language use, pilot performance, workload and cockpit position. Next, the factor structure of aircrew performance using behavioural markers is described. Then the linkage between pilot perceptions of safety and performance is described. Finally, the chapter describes the development and validation of an attitude assessment tool for healthcare providers, and demonstrates the linkage between attitudes and healthcare outcomes following an intervention designed to improve attitudes regarding safety related behaviour.

Verbal Behaviour: How and What Pilots Communicate

Historically, the role of language use in communication processes has been neglected, but researchers are recognizing the need for a deeper understanding of its behavioural implications and characteristics (Orasanu & Fischer, 1991; Cushing, 1997). There is a growing body of Cockpit Voice Recorder (CVR) data from high fidelity simulations and from investigations of aviation accidents – both of which detail the verbal interactions of crews. Coding of interactions in flight simulations and accident transcripts has provided valuable insights into communication processes (e.g., Orasanu & Fischer, 1991; Predmore, 1991). As part of this research into threat and error management processes, the *Threat/ Error Group* undertook an archival investigation[3] of how and what pilots communicate as a function of crew position (captain, first officer, and flight engineer), workload (low vs. high), and expert-rated performance (low, middle, and high). For additional insights into the role of language and communicative behaviour, see Part I, Chapters 5 and.6, and Chapters 9 and 11 in Part II.

How Pilots Communicate: Linguistic Factors

Research conducted by Professor James Pennebaker at The University of Texas at Austin has shown that linguistic styles can be considered individual difference markers, i.e., individuals appear to have a distinct 'language-use fingerprint' which is relatively stable across time and situations (Pennebaker & King, 1999). Pennebaker has identified language dimensions as being internally consistent, and modestly correlated to objective and self-reported health and performance measures at rates comparable to or greater than traditional trait markers of personality such as the 'big five' (McCrae & Costa, 1987).

In order to provide an efficient and practical method for studying the emotional, cognitive, structural and process components present in individuals' language use, Pennebaker and Francis developed and validated a computer-based text analysis program called Linguistic Inquiry and Word Count (LIWC: Francis & Pennebaker, 1993; Pennebaker & Francis, 1999). LIWC analyzes written or transcribed verbal text files by looking for dictionary matches to words in the text file. LIWC does this on a word-by-word basis by calculating the percentage of words in the text that match a particular dimension of language. Standard linguistic dimensions include categories such as word count, sentence punctuation, first person plural (we, our, us), negations (no, never, not), and assents (yes, OK, mmhmm). Dimensions of psychological processes include categories such as positive emotions (happy, pretty, good), anger (hate, resent, pissed), and cognitive

---

[3] The 727 Simulator Study: The cockpit communication data discussed here were collected at the NASA-Ames Research Center during an investigation into the effects of captain personality on crew performance (see Chidester, Kanki, Foushee, Dickinson and Bowles, 1990 for a detailed description). These data came from three person crews (captains, first officers, and second officers) flying a Boeing 727 simulator on a 5 segment trip completed over two days. Transcripts were made available for 12 crews across the last four flight segments (A, B, C and D), and for 14 crews for the last two flight segments (C and D). Segments A and C were routine (low workload), and segments B and D were abnormal (high workload). As part of the data collection process in the original simulator study, an expert pilot observer was present in the simulator. Flight outcome data regarding individual performance, individual errors and individual communication skill were recorded for each pilot on each segment.

processes (cause, know, effect, maybe, would, should). Other categories include swear words, nonfluencies (uh, er, um), and fillers (you know, I mean).

In the archival simulator study (Sexton & Helmreich, 2000; Sexton & Helmreich 2003), it was found that specific language variables were correlated with individual performance, individual error rates and individual communication ratings. Also, as shown in Figure 1.1, language use was found to vary as a function of crew position and level of workload during the flight.

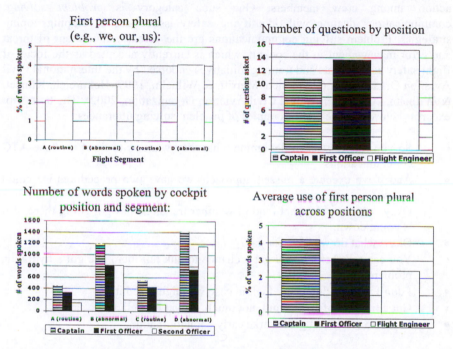

Figure 1.1 How pilots use language over time, across positions and as a function of workload

Use of the first person plural (we, our, us) increases over the life of a flightcrew, presumably as a marker of familiarity. Captains speak more in the first person plural than first officers or second officers, and captains ask fewer questions, indicating a linkage between linguistic factors such as using the first person or inquiry and one's place in the decision making hierarchy. Also, language use in initial flights was associated with performance and error in subsequent flights, which may indicate the importance of setting a 'linguistic tone' as the team is forming and individuals are becoming more familiar with one another. The notion of 'setting the tone' is consistent with other sources of data, which demonstrate the linkage between successfully establishing the team and subsequent performance measures (Ginnette, 1988; Hines, 1996). The next step was to try to compliment this investigation of *how pilots communicate* with one of w*hat pilots communicate*, using a content-coding method of communication analysis.

What Pilots Communicate: Content-Coding Factors

In addition to using LIWC, micro-coding of content was conducted using a method pioneered by The University of Texas Human Factors Research Project (Predmore, 1991; Helmreich, 1994). Using the micro-coding technique, individual utterances were classified into action-decision sequences (ADS), which are task-related communication categories centred on events and issues requiring co-ordinated action among crew members. One such category is *problem solving*: communications dealing with identifying safety issues and developing coping strategies. Problem solving communications are the verbal embodiment of threat and error management in the cockpit, which is currently accepted as the focus of flight safety assessments and training initiatives endorsed by the International Civil Aviation Organization (Helmreich, Merritt, & Wilhelm, 1999; Helmreich, Klinect, & Wilhelm, 2002; International Civil Aviation Organization, 2002). The transcript excerpts below provide eight examples of problem solving utterances:

- So you might want to determine what they want us to do if we lose ATC communications.
- And if we execute a missed approach, we have two procedures we could follow.
- Okay, ask him, uh, what kind of weather trends he has got going there, if it is going down.
- Okay, what do we have for gas?
- You can tell them, if you get a chance to talk tell them, we got a hydraulic problem.
- I don't want to dump any fuel, in case we might need it.
- Got a little bit of cross wind, not much, 240 at 8 I believe he said.
- I want to see if that gear works early enough, though.

As the above examples illustrate, *problem solving* communications are task-related communications regarding the management of threats and errors during a flight. Perhaps not surprisingly, flights with higher workload appeared to have more problems that needed to be 'solved,' as reflected in many more problem solving utterances during abnormal flights than during routine flights.

There were important differences in the use of problem solving utterances as a function of pilot performance. It is important not only to identify what ineffective crews do poorly, but also what high performing crews do well. Problem solving communications are a prime example of what distinguishes superior from substandard performance. For example, captains of high performing crews used problem solving utterances seven to eight times more often than their low performing counterparts. Furthermore, there were no differences in how *high performing* captains used problem solving utterances as a function of workload. High performing captains consistently devoted a third of their utterances to problem solving, whether it was a routine or an abnormal flight. In fact, the more frequent use of problem solving utterances was not unique to outstanding captains

– outstanding first officers and second officers used problem solving utterances in approximately one third of their overall communications (see Figure 1.2e). This pattern of results is striking in that there is a substantial difference in the use of problem solving utterances between outstanding pilots and both average and poor pilots. The best pilots simply talk more about their task related problems and how to solve them – the essence of threat and error management.

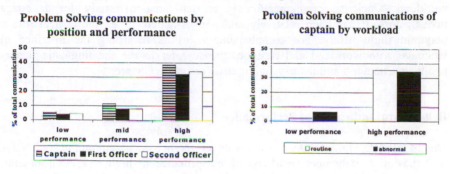

Figure 1.2 Number of problem solving utterances by position, performance and workload

Linguistic and Problem Solving Results

Language is a coping mechanism in that it helps individuals lessen and manage both the causes and the effects of stress. Language use is dynamic, as it is sensitive to both workload and position and varies systematically with flight outcome measures. Research into language use has the potential to yield a clearer understanding of thought processes involved *during* communication.

Without making a causal statement, it is important to consider the potential implications that language use could have for training. Perhaps the use of more effective language styles is trainable. The findings of Siegel & Federman (1973) indicate that it is possible to isolate aspects of effective communication and to train those aspects successfully (in this case using anti-submarine helicopter crews). Chidester, Helmreich, Gregorich & Geis (1990) have assessed the trainability of specific behaviour and have found that human factors training produces measurable improvements in communication skills and practices.

The performance of cockpit crews is determined by multiple group processes of which language use is just one. The results of this exploratory study indicated that the language use of pilots varied as a function of who is talking (captain, first officer or second officer) and as a function of workload. The relationships between the LIWC/problem solving categories and flight outcome measures of safety such as performance, error and communication skill serve as a form of convergent validity for the utility of linguistic and content analyses. The problem solving results also indicate that the current human factors emphasis on threat and error management is a valuable initiative.

The linguistic and content coding results replicated findings of previous research and provided additional levels of insight into *how* pilots use language and *what* they communicate relative to their performance, position and workload. These results are important because poor communication is commonly associated with authoritarian captains and/or unassertive first officers, while the current study demonstrates specific aspects of language use relevant to flight outcome and to workload. Cockpit communication is a rich area of study for language investigators. It has been relatively under-investigated, given the critical role it plays in flight safety. For complementary results regarding the interface of language with workload and position, please refer to the the linguistic factors results in Chapter 5 and the psycholinguistic results in Chapter 6.

Behavioural Indicators of Performance

One of GIHRE's initial tasks was to create a reference document on the application of behavioural indicators (markers) of performance in high risk environments. Behavioural markers are critical non-technical skills associated with effective and safe job performance. The GIHRE Project, together with an international and interdisciplinary group of behavioural markers researchers and industrial practitioners produced the consensus document on behavioural markers, highlighting their functionality, application, measurement and research and regulatory issues including the qualification and training of evaluators (see Klampfer, Flin, et al. 2001). One of the contributions to this effort, made possible by GIHRE, was the development of a model of aircrew performance using behavioural markers.

Using data from eight major airlines, 3,241 observations of crew behaviour were analyzed as part of an effort to create a two-factor structural equation model of behavioural markers (Sexton, 1999). This model empirically corroborates current thinking in the literature about behavioural markers of cockpit crew performance, namely that there are two principle components of behaviour, an interpersonal factor (i.e. quality of crew member interactions) and a taskwork factor (i.e. the ability of the team to prepare effectively for contingencies).

This model relates markers of crew behaviour to overall observations of technical proficiency and crew effectiveness, as well as three measures of technical performance (error indices). See Appendix III for a table of how frequently each behavioural marker is observable. The taskwork factor is a good predictor of overall technical proficiency and of the three technical markers dealing with checklist compliance, altitude and terrain awareness, and adherence to sterile cockpit procedures. Moreover, the taskwork factor becomes an even better predictor of these technical markers under conditions of high operational complexity, further underscoring its relevance to flight safety.[4] The taskwork factor is highly correlated with the teamwork factor, indicating that the ability of a cockpit crew to manage interpersonal interactions is strongly related to its ability to manage the technical aspects of flying. The two-factor model is a superior fit to the data within each of the four phases of flight (predeparture, take-off & climb, cruise, and descent/approach/land) as well as overall, using a mean of each variable across the four phases.

These data led to a new model of observable crew behaviour (Figure 1.3). The model may prove useful for the aviation research community, trainers, curriculum developers in aviation and simulator instructors – all of whom are currently functioning without an empirically derived model of crew behaviour. Currently, work by James Klinect is underway at the University of Texas Human Factors Research Project exploring the relationships between behavioural markers and threat and error management data collected during LOSA (Line Operations Safety Audit). In addition, work by Eric Thomas at the University of Texas Center of Excellence for Patient Safety Research and Practice, has found that seven of these ten behavioural markers are important in medical settings, are reliably observable and are related to error management in neonatal resuscitations (Thomas, Sexton and Helmreich, under review).

In recent years, there has been growing interest in safety climate (also referred to as safety *culture*), particularly in safety critical industries such as nuclear power generation, petro-chemical plants, spaceflight, medicine and aviation. For further insights into structures, regulations and company culture, please see Chapter 5. Safety climate is typically assessed through structured interviews, focus groups, and most commonly, through attitudinal surveys.[5] Relative to focus groups and structured interviews, surveys provide an efficient and economical means of collecting data across a large cross-section of an organization. Surveys can be used to diagnose organizational strengths and weaknesses, evaluate the effects of organizational changes, improve communication with employees and provide context for important organizational variables such as absenteeism and turnover.

---

[4] Observers indicate the level of operational complexity (i.e. workload) during their observation of crew behavioural markers. Applying the model to crews performing under varying levels of operational complexity demonstrated that the relationships between behavioural markers, overall markers and technical markers (error indices) were strongest in the high workload situations. In fact, the taskwork factor accounted for half of the variance found in technical markers (altitude awareness, sterile cockpit and checklist compliance) for crews in high workload environments.

[5] What is measured, however, is not necessarily the same thing across settings and researchers. Unfortunately, it has the authors' experience (though anecdotally) that many individuals who have a sophisticated understanding of safety climate are the ones who work at the front-lines of operations and don't generally pause to write academic pieces that summarize their findings and insights.

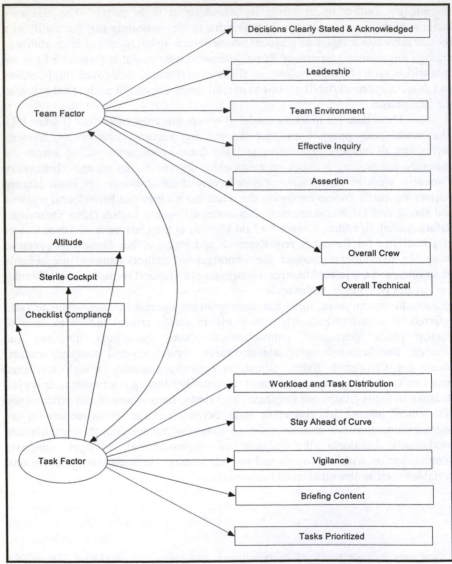

Figure 1.3   Model of crew behavior – safety climate in commercial aviation

Is a happy worker a safe worker? Job attitudes, such as morale and job satisfaction have been studied extensively. Meta-analyses have demonstrated that there is a consistent (albeit modest) correlation between job attitudes and performance (Iaffaldano & Muchinsky, 1985; Petty, McGee & Cavender, 1984). Although thousands of investigations have examined the link between job attitudes and productivity for the past 70 years, the specific notion of safety climate is relatively new. Safety climate has been studied in numerous doctoral dissertations, but there is relatively little mention of it in the peer-reviewed literature.

Pilots are a vital source of safety-related information in aviation. They are in a critical position to see aspects of flight operations as they unfold. By tapping into pilots' perceptions of their role in the safety of a flight, as well as the extent to which they feel that their organization has a genuine commitment to flight safety, it is possible to measure safety climate as a reliable construct. The *Threat/Error Group* has created a scale designed to assess safety climate. Within this research group, safety climate has been defined as *the extent to which individuals perceive a genuine and proactive commitment to safety by their organization*. The safety climate scale has face validity, internal reliability and has been used to detect differences between and within airlines (Sexton, Wilhelm, Helmreich, Merritt and Klinect, 2001). Recently, Sexton & Klinect (2001) administered the safety climate scale to crews flying regularly scheduled revenue flights that were observed as part of a Line Operations Safety Audit (LOSA). The crews were observed by trained and calibrated (to reliabilities of .80 or higher) expert observers who collected data on pilot behavior and threat and error management during the flight.

Crews consisting of pilots with positive perceptions of safety climate trapped more errors, managed threats better, committed fewer violations and had better CRM ratings than crews with negative perceptions of safety climate[6] (see Figure 1.4).

Attitudes about safety climate reflect the relative importance placed on safety and crew member practices relevant to safety. Safety climate, when poor, may set the preconditions for poor threat and error management during a flight, and in this sense, poor safety climate can be a latent threat (see TEMM-model, Figure 8.6). Conversely, an excellent safety climate may act as a buffer against threats and errors. The causal mechanisms at work are still under investigation, but two likely mechanisms are conformity and learned helplessness. In any high reliability organization, management's role is to create and maintain optimal work conditions, remove obstacles from the paths of the workers and foster an environment in which safety is valued and safe practices are endorsed and widely followed. If the workers perceive management to be accomplishing this task, they can be motivated to conform to the norm of *being safe*. If workers perceive management to place new obstacles in their path, it can be demotivating, and may cause workers to feel that their efforts to be safe are undermined by the actions of their superiors, leaving them unwilling to adhere to safe practices (a form of learned helplessness). Simply stated, it appears to be the case that a happy pilot is indeed a safer pilot.

---

[6] The differences between crews with positive vs. negative attitudes were generally a standard deviation or more. Consequential errors are defined as those that lead to an undesired aircraft state or resulted in another error.

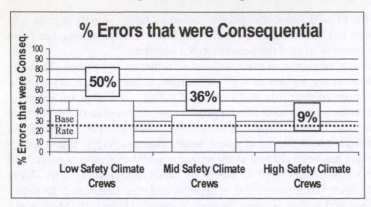

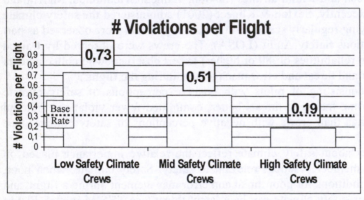

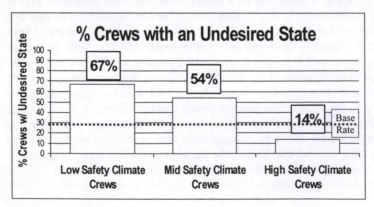

Figure 1.4   Safety climate and observed outcomes

The Safety Attitudes Questionnaire: Climate in Medicine

Research at the University of Texas into job attitudes and safety climate in commercial aviation led to the GIHRE supported development of a conceptually parallel assessment tool for medicine: the Safety Attitudes Questionnaire (SAQ: Sexton, 2002; Sexton, Helmreich, et al., under editorial review). In addition to retaining aviation attitudinal items for use in the SAQ, new survey items were generated by focus groups of health-care providers, review of the literature and round-table discussions with subject-matter experts. This generated a pool of over 100 new items covering four themes: safety climate, teamwork climate, stress recognition and organizational climate. These targeted themes were based on prior research in the aviation industry and in medicine (Gregorich, Helmreich and Wilhelm, 1990; Helmreich, Merritt, Sherman, Gregorich and Wiener, 1993; Helmreich, 1984; Helmreich and Merritt, 1998; Itoh, Andersen, Tanaka and Seki, 2000; Maurino, Reason, Johnston and Lee, 1995; Shortell, Denise, Rouseau, Gillies, Devers and Simons, 1991; Thomas, Sexton and Helmreich, 2003). Items were evaluated through pilot testing and exploratory factor analyses. This phase of survey development yielded six factor-analytically derived attitudinal domains containing 40 items. Three of the targeted themes, safety climate, teamwork climate, and stress recognition, emerged as factors. The fourth, organizational climate, consistently emerged as three distinct but related factors, perceptions of management, working conditions and job satisfaction. An additional 20 items were retained as individually diagnostic items because they were deemed interesting and valuable to the unit managers and senior hospital leadership to whom the results of the pilot studies were reported.

The SAQ has been adapted for use in intensive care units (ICU), operating rooms (OR), general inpatient settings (Medical Ward, Surgical Ward, etc.) and Ambulatory Clinics. For each version of the SAQ, item content is the same, with minor modifications to reflect the clinical area. For example, 'in this ICU, it is difficult to discuss mistakes,' vs. 'in the ORs here, it is difficult to discuss mistakes.' The SAQ elicits caregiver attitudes through the six factor analytically derived scales: teamwork climate; job satisfaction; perceptions of management; safety climate; working conditions; and stress recognition (Figure 1.5.).

The SAQ consists of 60 multiple-choice questions plus demographics information (age, sex, experience and nationality). The questionnaire takes approximately 10 to 15 minutes to complete. Each of the 60 items is answered using a five-point Likert scale (Disagree Strongly, Disagree Slightly, Neutral, Agree Slightly, Agree Strongly). Some items are negatively worded. There is also an open-ended section for comments: 'what are your top three recommendations for improving patient safety in this clinical area.'

Factor: Definition	Example Items
Teamwork climate: perceived quality of collaboration between personnel	–Disagreements in the ICU are appropriately resolved (i.e., what is best for the patient) –Our doctors and nurses work together as a well co-ordinated team
Job satisfaction: positivity about the work experience	–I like my job –This hospital is a good place to work
Perceptions of management: approval of managerial action	–Hospital management supports my daily efforts in the ICU –Hospital management is doing a good job
Safety climate: perceptions of a strong and proactive organizational commitment to safety	–I would feel perfectly safe being treated in this ICU –ICU personnel frequently disregard rules or guidelines developed for our ICU
Working conditions: perceived quality of the ICU work environment and logistical support (staffing, equipment etc.)	–Our levels of staffing are sufficient to handle the number of patients –The ICU equipment in our hospital is adequate
Stress recognition: acknowledgement of how performance is influenced by stressors	–I am less effective at work when fatigued –When my workload becomes excessive, my performance is impaired

Figure 1.5   SAQ Factor definitions and example items

The SAQ is a psychometrically sound instrument for assessing the safety-related attitudes and perceptions of front-line healthcare providers (Sexton, 2002). It has been administered in more than 200 hospitals. Results show significant variability in teamwork climate, safety climate, job satisfaction and working conditions. For example, the per cent of respondents reporting high levels of teamwork with their colleagues varied 10-fold, from seven per cent to 74 per cent across 200 clinical areas (Figure 1.6).

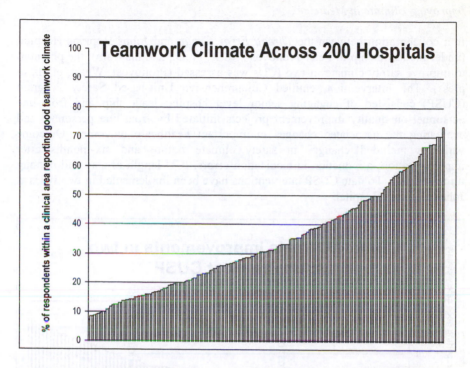

Figure 1.6 Teamwork climate across 200 sites: each bar represents the per cent of respondents reporting positive teamwork in their work unit

In work environments with low teamwork climate scores, fewer than one out of four respondents reported that nurse input was well received, that conflicts were appropriately resolved and that physicians and nurses worked together as a well co-ordinated team. Providing healthcare in such uncommunicative and information-poor settings is a formidable task, given the multi-disciplinary and interpersonal nature of modern care delivery (e.g. involving nurses, physicians, pharmacists, respiratory therapists, technicians, etc.). Poor climates such as these provide the preconditions for threat and error to snowball into undesirable outcomes, and are therefore defined as latent threats in the TEMM-model proposed in Chapter 8.

A large archive of SAQ data has been established for use in benchmarking and comparison with future administrations. Given the psychometric properties, wide use and reference data collected, it could be used to fulfill some of the demand for survey assessments of climate and culture in medicine.

Improving Climate in Medicine

In a collaboration between the *Threat/ Error Group* and Johns Hopkins Hospital (under the leadership of Peter Pronovost, M.D., Ph.D., and his team), the potential to improve safety climate in two ICUs was assessed (Pronovost, Weast, et al., in press). The intervention, entitled Comprehensive Unit-based Safety Program (CUSP) consisted of engaging senior level hospital leadership and front-line personnel on quality improvement projects initiated by front-line personnel and evaluating the associated changes in important healthcare outcomes. Outcome variables included changes in safety climate before and six-months after implementation, a reduction in medication errors, ICU length of stay and nursing turnover rates. To date CUSP interventions have been implemented in two ICUs at Johns Hopkins Hospital.

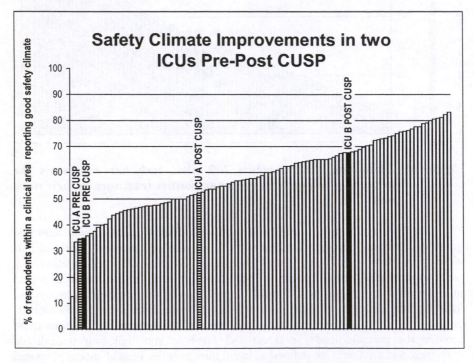

Figure 1.7 Safety climate scores before and after CUSP at Johns Hopkins Hospital

Identifying safety concerns and partnering with leadership led to the implementation of patient transport teams, maintaining a pharmacist's presence in ICUs, incorporation of medication reconciliation at time of discharge, use of short-term goal sheets and relabeling equipment (specifically Buretrol and epidural catheters). Medication reconciliation identified 134 preventable errors over 16 weeks at a time of unit transfer. Medication errors in patient transfer orders decreased remarkably from 94 per cent of patients having an error to zero. One year after CUSP implementation, length of stay dropped from an average of 2.2 days to 1.1 days and nursing turnover decreased from 9.0 per cent to 1.9 per cent.

These results highlight two important points. First, improvements in safety climate are associated with declines in medication error rates, length of stay and nurse turnover rates – each of which has tremendous impact upon patient safety and the fiscal performance of a hospital.[7] Secondly, these results demonstrated that safety climate is a malleable construct, receptive to targeted interventions and tractable over time. With further replication and validation, safety climate could become a new 'vital sign' for ICUs and other hospital settings. These preliminary data suggest that a poor safety climate could be improved to become a positive one, changing from a latent threat to a buffer against unsafe practices.

Summary and Conclusions

This project overview has looked at how pilots communicate linguistically using a computerized language analysis program. Relationships between language use, pilot workload, pilot position and performance were discussed. Through the content coding of action decision sequences, the relationships between problem solving communications and workload and performance have been demonstrated. For further insights into language use in safety critical industries, refer to Chapters 4, 5 and 6, and the Language Processing and Communicative Behaviors chapters. For additional findings relevant to workload, see Chapter 7 on task load and the microstructure of cognition.

A model of behavioral indicators in aviation has been presented here; their relationships with workload and error indices has been described through a structural equation model using data from over 3,000 flight crew behavioral observations. For additional insights into pilot behavior in aviation, please see the seminal cockpit simulator work conducted by the *Behavioral Markers Group* in Chapter 2. Finally, the importance of climate research in safety critical industries has been emphasized, and the safety climate results from aviation and the Safety Attitudes Questionnaire in medicine have been presented. Ongoing research is investigating further linkages between climate and outcomes in both aviation and medicine.

---

[7] This is a clear example of how 'safer is cheaper,' demonstrating the return on investment in safety – a critical issue in the contemporary healthcare environment, where budgets are lean and hospital administrators too often pay more attention to their fiscal bottom line than to the quality of the care they provide to patients.

Chapter 2

Behavioral Markers in Analyzing Team Performance of Cockpit Crews

Ruth Häusler, Barbara Klampfer, Andrea Amacher and Werner Naef

Introduction

The significance in aviation of the relation between effective teamwork and safety is well documented in accident and incident reports, which show breakdowns in teamwork and failures to communicate. The term Crew Resource Management (CRM) was coined to denote non-technical skills that enhance the effective utilization of all available resources (e.g. crew members, airplane systems and other supporting groups). CRM training was first introduced as an effort to change attitudes that impair safe teamwork and the best use of available resources. Among these are self-perceptions that deny human limitations such as constricted capacity to process information or impairments caused by exposure to high levels of stress or lack of recovery from fatigue that results from intense work shifts. However, changes in attitude do not always lead to a change in behavior (Ajzen & Fishbein, 1980). Therefore, CRM training advanced in the direction of practical skill training in simulators.

The concept comprises aspects of teamwork within the cockpit crew and interactions between the crew and other groups such as cabin crew, air traffic control (ATC) or dispatchers who collaborate with cockpit crews in order to ensure safe and efficient flight operation. CRM covers topics identified as crew behaviors that contribute to accidents and incidents such as inadequate leadership, lack of task assignment, insufficient prioritization of tasks, lack of monitoring, failed communication and so on, as well as countermeasures for threat and error management.

Cockpit crews operate in a high risk environment that can force team members into situations with little time available for communication or co-ordination and that presents the risk of severe consequences from system failure like injury or death to team members and others (Caldwell, 1997). Therefore, the ability to cope with high task load situations is vital to cockpit crews.

The work of the *Behavioral Markers Group* is first to investigate the impact of task load on the team performance of cockpit crews. To this end, CRM performance of crews was analyzed in situations with different levels of task load.

The question of whether team performance is resistant to high levels of task load is obviously of great practical relevance.

A second part of the study is dedicated to the stability of CRM performance across different situations: are teamwork skills consistent, trait-like characteristics of a person or is CRM performance strongly influenced by situational properties? The first assumption suggests that CRM performance will be stable across different situations, whereas the second expects variability.

A third aspect of the study concerns the comparison of two behavioral marker systems that measure CRM performance: LOSA (Line Operations Safety Audit; Klinect, Wilhelm & Helmreich, 1999) and NOTECHS (NOn TECHnical Skills: Avermaete & Kruijsen, 1998). Behavioral markers specify observable behavior that is relevant to the safety and effectiveness of flight operation (Klampfer, Flin, Helmreich et al., 2001). Their application can improve communication of performance standards, improvement of individual performance by means of feedback, competence assessment, evaluation of training (e.g. for AQP),[8] assessment of training needs and organizational diagnosis (e.g. safety audits). They have been applied in professional fields such as aviation and medicine, especially in the operating room. They contain a standard set of behaviors that are applied following specific rules.

Further questions still under investigation address the relationship between CRM performance and technical performance and the effect of adaptation to specific task and situational demands on team performance.

Analysis with behavioral markers is a methodology that the *Behavioral Markers Group* shares with other GIHRE groups: the *Threat/Error Group* and the *Co-ordination Group*. Recommendations on the use of behavioral markers have been published by an international and interdisciplinary group of researchers and practitioners (Klampfer et al., 2001).

Method

A simulator study was conducted at the training center of former Swissair. Data were collected during the annual recurrent training session of the Airbus A320 fleet. A built-in camera filmed crews from behind. Moreover, flight data (altitude, speed, heading, pitch, bank, power setting and indications of localizer and glide slope deviation during approach) were displayed on the bottom of the screen (cf. Figure 2. 1). Simulator instructors acted as ATC, cabin crew and other supporting groups that were in contact with the crew (e.g. dispatch, maintenance). At the end of the simulator session, pilots and flight instructors filled out questionnaires.

---

[8] The Advanced Qualification Program is a voluntary, alternative program for the fulfillment of training, evaluation, certification and qualification requirements of flight crew members, instructors, evaluators and other operations personnel.

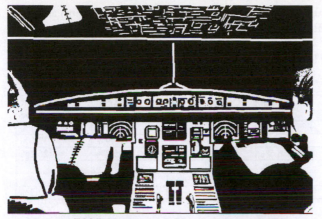

Alt.   : 7695.33 Pitch : 3.22 Loc Dev : 0.000
Speed :   248.7 Bank : 0.04 GP Dev : 0.000
Head. : 332.07   PWR Setting : 35.87

Figure 2.1   Screen presentation for video analysis

Design

The study is designed as a quasi-experiment. All crews flew three scenarios, and different levels of task load were analyzed: two high task load and one moderate task load scenario. High task load was generated by technical failures. The order of the three scenarios was not counterbalanced; therefore effects of learning from the first to the second and third scenario could not be controlled. However, a study from Prince, Brannick, Prince and Salas (1997) with counterbalanced presentation of the scenarios did not find evidence for such an effect. Pilots were assigned to crews according to the scheduling practice of the training department, which can be expected to be random.

Subjects

A total number of 81 crews voluntarily participated in the study. This corresponds to a response rate of 60 per cent. After exclusion of deficient videotapes (missing scenarios, missing tone or flight data), data from 46 crews were analyzed.

At the time of the data collection, the majority of the captains (76.1 per cent) in the sample are aged between 36 and 45 years. Most of the first officers (65.2 per cent) were between 26 and 35 years old. On average, captains had been in their actual position as captain for 3.4 years (SD= 2.83, N= 46) and first officers for 2.5 years (SD= 2.68, N= 46). 26 per cent of the captains worked as check pilot or instructor, whereas only one first officer was also an instructor. The flight experience of the crews is shown in Table 2.1 with the majority of the captains having 5,000 to 10,000 hours of total flight experience (71.7 per cent) and 1,000 to 5,000 hours experience on the specific aircraft type (56.5 per cent). Most first officers have 500 to 5,000 hours of total flight experience (69.6 per cent) and up to 1,000 hours on the aircraft type (71.7 per cent).[9]

Table 2.1   Total flying hours and hours on type

	Captains		First officers	
	Total	On aircraft type	Total	On aircraft type
up to 500 hours		26.1%	15.2%	39.1%
up to 1,000 hours		17.4%	23.9%	32.6%
up to 5,000 hours	6.5%	56.5%	45.7%	26.1%
up to 10,000 hours	71.7%		15.2%	
More than 10,000 hours	21.8%			
Missing				2.2%

Scenarios

The first two scenarios imply high levels of task load; the third scenario implies moderate task load. Scenario one is called *handling problem*. After the occurrence of several severe technical failures (loss of flight control computers), the crew has to control the aircraft with rudder, pitch trim and power only.[10] An emergency landing with ILS approach is flown in manual back up law, which is a non-certified emergency procedure. The problem itself is well defined and the required actions are obvious to the crew. Workload is especially high in regards to psychomotor flying skills. The captain is the pilot flying. The mean duration of scenario one is 33 minutes (SD= 6 min. 14 sec.).

Scenario two is called *diagnosis problem*. Several technical failures occur in the Air Data Unit of the ADIRU systems. The crew needs to interrupt their flight and land at an alternate airport. An ILS approach has to be performed in direct law.[11] In this scenario, the crew must strive to accurately diagnose the complex technical problem. They must decide what recovery actions need to be taken, which is complicated by misleading guidance from the ECAM system.[12] Good system knowledge and a systematic approach to problem solving are crucial. The first officer is the pilot flying. Problem analysis is primarily carried out by the captain as pilot non-flying. The mean duration of scenario two is 41.5 minutes (SD= 7min. 36 sec.).

Scenario three is considered to be of moderate task load. It is called *difficult approach* and requires a non-precision (NDB) approach with subsequent

---

[9] The latter figure shows that the A320 is the initial start up aircraft on which young first officers start their career in this commercial airline.

[10] This leaves the crew with extremely limited steering capability of an otherwise uncontrollable aircraft. The emergency procedure for these failures is only designed for a limited period of time in order to restore normal control ability. But in this scenario, the crew has to land in this state.

[11] In this state the computer-based flight envelope protection is reduced. The protection is designed to avoid e.g. undesired or extreme aircraft attitude due to inappropriate pilot input.

[12] ECAM stands for Electronic Centralized Aircraft Monitoring.

circling to the opposite side of the runway. In this scenario no technical failures occur. However, this kind of approach is rarely flown and can be especially demanding for inexperienced pilots. This approach requires good planning and a timely execution of sub-tasks. Good use of automation facilitates the task. The first officer is the pilot flying in this scenario. The mean duration of scenario three is 17.5 minutes (SD= 4 min. 40 sec.).

Variables

Several measures of crew performance and an indicator for subjective workload were recorded in the study.

CRM performance CRM performance was measured using two behavioral marker systems: LOSA and NOTECHS. They measure CRM performance by observing cockpit crews' communicative behavior and actions. Aspects of team performance such as leadership are observed by focusing on what is said (e.g. assigning tasks, giving orders, etc.) and on when and how it is said (e.g. in an authoritarian way vs. collaboratively, etc.).

LOSA (Line Operations Safety Audit; Klinect, Wilhelm & Helmreich, 1999) consists of three parts: the Human Factors Checklist, the External Threat Management Worksheet and the Flight Crew Error Management Worksheet. The Human Factors Checklist comprises eleven behavioral markers that are rated in each phase of flight with six overall markers (cf. Table 2.2). The unit of analysis is the crew.

Table 2.2   LOSA behavioral markers (Human Factors Checklist)

PLANNING:	EXECUTION:	REVIEW/MODIFY PLANS:
• Briefing • Contingency management • Workload assignment • Plans stated	• Monitor/cross-check • Workload management • Vigilance • Automation management	• Evaluation of plans • Inquiry • Assertiveness

OVERALL MARKERS:	
• Communication environment • Leadership • Flight attendant briefing on first leg	• Captain contribution to crew effectiveness • First officer contribution to crew effectiveness • Overall crew effectiveness

NOTECHS (NOn-TECHnical Skills; Avermaete & Kruijsen, 1998) includes four main categories (co-operation, leadership and managerial skills, situation awareness and decision making) that are each linked to three or four behavioral elements (cf. Table 2.3). The unit of analysis is the individual pilot. For reasons of comparability all NOTECHS elements were rated for each flight phase in the present study (for normal practice see Avermaete & Kruijsen, 1998).

Table 2.3   NOTECHS categories and behavioral elements

CO-OPERATION:	LEADERSHIP & MANAGERIAL SKILLS:
• Team building and maintaining • Consideration of others • Support of others • Conflict solving	• Use of authority and assertiveness • Providing and maintaining standards • Planning and co-ordination • Workload management
SITUATION AWARENESS:	DECISION MAKING:
• Awareness of aircraft systems • Awareness of external environment • Awareness of time	• Problem definition and diagnosis • Option generation • Risk assessment and option selection • Outcome review

There are several differences between LOSA and NOTECHS (cf. Klampfer, Haeusler & Naef, 2003), the most important being the difference of purpose of application. LOSA is used for safety audits and research and is applied in normal flight operation. In contrast, NOTECHS assesses the CRM performance of individual pilots for training and possibly for qualification purposes.

Three project observers with aviation and psychology background (one of them being a captain) served as external observers. They had received formal training for LOSA and NOTECHS and showed good inter-rater agreement (for both instruments average r_{wg} was above .80; James, Demaree & Wolf, 1984; 1993). To assure the quality of the CRM judgments, several inter-rater calibrations were run and regular expert consultations were scheduled. In addition, subject matter experts reviewed all crews that were rated *poor* or *very poor* on overall ratings. To prevent any systematic influence of possible rater bias, each scenario was observed for LOSA and NOTECHS by a different rater and a systematic variation of raters and scenarios was carried out (for more detailed description of rating procedure see Appendix IV).

Risk index The risk index is an additional measure of CRM performance, derived from ratings of the behavioral markers. It is an aggregate measure of substandard CRM performance and corresponds to the total number of instances in which observed behavioral markers were rated *poor* or *very poor* for NOTECHS and *poor* or *marginal* for LOSA. The risk index is an indicator of the degree to which crew behaviors compromise the safety of the flight.

Subjective workload Workload is generally defined as the effort invested by a human into task performance (e.g. Eggemeier, 1988; Wickens, 1992). The NASA Task Load indeX (TLX; Hart & Staveland, 1988) is known as a globally sensitive instrument (Wierwille & Eggemeier, 1993). It measures subjective workload with six subscales: physical demands, mental demands, temporal demands, performance, effort and frustration. Each of these aspects of workload is rated on a continuum ranging from zero (low) to 100 (high). For the analysis in this study, all six rating scales were weighted identically.[13] Crew members indicated the workload they experienced in each of the three scenarios on the TLX scales.

Results

Impact of Task Load on CRM Performance

To test the manipulation of the task load level, the perceived workload of crew members was compared across the scenarios. It was expected that the two scenarios with technical failures (S1 and S2) would lead to higher subjective workload ratings than the scenario with normal operation (S3). Table 2.4 shows the mean workload ratings of captains and first officers for the three scenarios.

Table 2.4   Descriptives for perceived mental workload

		Task load level	Mean subjective Workload	N	Std. Deviation
Capt.	**Scenario 1**	**High**	75.22	45	18.15
	Scenario 2	high	73.33	42	19.87
	Scenario 3	moderate	57.73	44	21.95
F/O	Scenario 1	high	67.21	43	19.71
	Scenario 2	**high**	**73.78**	**45**	**17.09**
	Scenario 3	**moderate**	**60.44**	**45**	**20.44**

Means for the subscale mental demands of the NASA Task Load indeX (ranging from 0 to 100)
Bold letters indicate cockpit position as pilot flying in a specific scenario.

The assumed differences in task load level of the three scenarios are fully confirmed by the captains' ratings of mental workload: on average, workload ratings for the two high task load scenarios are rated significantly higher than for scenario three (S1 vs. S3: t= 4.874; p= .000 S2 vs. S3: t= 3.352; p= .002; results for paired-samples t-tests are shown in Appendix IV). In contrast, first officers do not show as much workload in high task load scenario one as expected. This can partly be explained by their role as pilot non-flying. The manual handling of the airplane is the demanding part of this scenario, which is the captain's responsibility. In this way, for first officers, scenario one was similar to moderate task load scenario three (t= 1.692; p= .980) and produced significantly lower subjective workload ratings than scenario two (t= -2.425; p= .020). As was expected, first officers perceived workload in scenario two as being significantly higher than in scenario three (t= 3.608; p= .001).

Changes in the level of performance can be seen as an indicator for workload in response to high task demands (e.g. Eggmeier, 1988). With higher workload, performance is expected to increase first and then to continuously degrade with increasing overload (cf. Yerkes & Dodson, 1908). The risk index is

---

[13] According to Nygen's conclusions (1991), the original weighting procedure of the NASA TLX was not used.

considered to be a sensitive measure of crew performance for different levels of task load, as it represents the total number of ratings below an acceptable level of performance that a crew received across all behavioral markers observed in one scenario. An increase in the number of crews showing substandard CRM performance under higher task load would indicate vulnerability of crew performance to high task load. Table 2.5 shows the proportion of crews with risk index higher than zero for all three scenarios.

Table 2.5   Frequencies of crews with risk index equal to zero or higher than zero

	S1: high TL (handling problem)		S2: high TL (diagnosis problem)		S3: moderate TL (difficult approach)	
	Frequency	Per cent	Frequency	Per cent	Frequency	Per cent
Risk Index = 0	23	51.1%	33	73.3%	40	88.9%
Risk Index > 0	**22**	**48.9%**	**12**	**26.7%**	**5**	**11.1%**
Total	45	100%	45	100%	45	100%

Risk Index includes *very poor* and *poor* ratings from observations of NOTECHS behavioral markers summed up for the captain and the first officer of a crew. Bold letters highlight substandard performance.
S: Scenario; TL: Task load

The comparison of the proportion of crews with a risk index higher than zero across the three scenarios shows that under high task load (S1 and S2) more crews show substandard team performance compared to scenario three which has moderate task load. In high task load scenario one – the handling problem – almost half of the crews (48.9 per cent) evidence difficulties in teamwork. It is an extreme emergency situation with severely degraded control facilities. To test the expectation that more crews show difficulties in their teamwork (risk index higher than zero) under conditions of high task load compared to moderate task load, McNemar tests were performed (tables with ratios can be found in the Appendix IV).

Comparison of scenarios with high and moderate task load The proportion of crews with teamwork difficulties (risk index higher than zero) is significantly higher in high task load scenario one than in moderate task load scenario three (48 per cent[14] vs. 11 per cent; p= .000; N= 44). This confirms the assumption that under high task load team performance deteriorates. The comparison of high task load scenario two and moderate task load scenario three did not yield a significant

---

[14] The indicated percentage of crews with risk index > 0 in the comparisons of two scenarios can deviate from figures in Table 2.5 (see Appendix IV) due to single missing data in one scenario.

difference in the proportion of crews with risk index higher than zero (25 per cent vs. 11 per cent, p= .146; N= 44). Although the difference points in the expected direction, both scenarios have a high proportion of crews with a risk index equal to zero. More than 70 per cent of the crews handle the high task load scenario two without any difficulties in teamwork.

Comparison of the two high task load scenarios In scenario one the proportion of crews with a risk index higher than zero is significantly higher than in scenario two (50 per cent vs. 27.3 per cent; p= .041, N= 44). This indicates that the two scenarios with high task load are not equivalent in the difficulties they raise for teamwork, which was not necessarily expected.

Stability of CRM Performance

Analyses in this section include results on the general stability of CRM performance across three scenarios for the full sample. These are followed by a description of characteristics for two subsamples.

Trans-situational consistency Even though CRM performance is dependent on task load, crews might still be consistent in their CRM performance if the performance level, in comparison to the sample, is similar in all three scenarios (e.g. a crew that is amoung the top 25 per cent highest performing crews in all three scenarios, even if CRM performance is somewhat lower in the high task load scenarios). Table 2.6 gives an overview of correlations of CRM markers across the three scenarios (detailed results in Appendix IV).

Table 2.6   Summary of the stability analysis

		Range of correlations	Mean correlation
Correlations across all three scenarios (S1xS2; S1xS3; S2xS3)	LOSA behavioral markers	-.38 to .22	.01
	NOTECHS categories captain	-.06 to .34	.14
	NOTECHS categories first officer	-.12 to .21	.06
	LOSA risk index crew	.01 to .11	.06
	NOTECHS risk index captain	-.11 to -.05	-.08
	NOTECHS risk index first officer	-.01 to .07	.05

Spearman correlations (one-tailed) for behavioral markers and categories
Pearson correlations (one-tailed) for risk indices

In general, CRM markers rated in one scenario do not strongly relate to ratings from other scenarios. For LOSA behavioral markers, NOTECHS categories and risk indices, most of the correlations are statistically non-significant. The low correlations for both instruments (LOSA and NOTECHS) indicate that CRM performance varies across the different scenarios. This is not only the case for ratings of specific behaviors, but also for measures on a more abstract level, such as categories or risk indices. This suggests that properties of the situation might have a stronger effect on team behavior than relatively stable characteristics of the team or individuals. Brannick, Prince, Prince and Salas (1995) reported similar results from a validation study for team performance measures. In their study, they used two similar scenarios and found average correlations of r= .31 within behavioral markers across two scenarios. The lower or even negative correlations in the present study can be partly attributed to the use of three very distinct scenarios (differing in the level of task load, the kinds of demands and the cockpit position – pilot flying/pilot non-flying – across scenarios). Results indicate that measures taken in one scenario cannot be generalized to other scenarios, especially if the scenarios differ widely.

Characteristics of high and low performing crews   Two subgroups are characterized in Table 2.7, showing the strengths of excellent crews and deficiencies of ineffective crews. An explanation follows.

Table 2.7   Strengths and deficiencies

		STRENGTHS of excellent crews	DEFICIENCIES of ineffective crews
S1	**NOTECHS**: Captain	Authority / assertiveness Planning / co-ordination Awareness of time	Maintaining standards Workload management Awareness of A/C systems Awareness of environment
	NOTECHS: First officer		Support of others
	LOSA	Contingency management	Briefing
S2	**NOTECHS**: Captain	Authority / assertiveness Awareness of A/C systems Problem definition Option generation	Authority / assertiveness Maintaining standards Planning / co-ordination Awareness of A/C systems Problem definition Option generation Risk assessment
	NOTECHS: First officer	Support of others	Awareness of A/C systems
	LOSA	Plans stated Workload assignment Contingency management Monitoring, cross-check Inquiry	Briefing Plans stated Vigilance Automation management Evaluation of plans
S3	**NOTECHS**: Captain	Authority / assertiveness	Support of others Authority/ assertiveness Maintaining standards Awareness of A/C systems Awareness of environment
	NOTECHS: First officer	Planning / co-ordination	Maintaining standards Planning / co-ordination Awareness of A/C systems Awareness of environment Awareness of time
	LOSA		Briefing Vigilance Evaluation of plans

Despite the general inconsistency of CRM performance across the three scenarios, crews vary in their consistency of CRM performance. Two subgroups with stable performance patterns were identified on both sides of the performance spectrum: *excellent crews* (N=8) received only good and outstanding CRM ratings in all three scenarios. *Ineffective crews* (N=9) were characterized by an accumulation of poor and very poor ratings in all three scenarios. The strengths shown above (Table 2.7) for excellent crews correspond to areas in which the majority of these crews had outstanding ratings. The deficiencies of ineffective crews are shown when the majority of them had marginal or poor ratings on specific behavioral markers.

Excellent crews showed particular strengths in aspects of planning (including anticipation and contingency management), leadership and situation awareness. In the scenario with the diagnosis problem (S2), decision making behavior (problem definition, option generation) was highly adequate. In general, ineffective crews showed deficiencies in their briefing behavior, in aspects of situation awareness and leadership. The pattern of insufficient briefing, poor situation awareness and lack of evaluation of plans seems characteristic, which might lead to poor adaptation to situational requirements. Ineffective crews often failed to fulfill and maintain standards. In scenario two, the diagnosis problem, they also failed to make decisions in a well-structured and appropriate way (problem definition, option generation, risk assessment).

Comparison of LOSA and NOTECHS

Two different observers for each scenario used NOTECHS and LOSA independently. Besides differences that predominantly concern the way and the purpose for which the two systems are used and the subject they focus on (individual pilot vs. crew), they comprise similar constructs. Table 2.8 gives an overview of the relationship between similar constructs of LOSA and NOTECHS (detailed results in Appendix IV).

When one takes into account that LOSA behavioral markers are correlated with NOTECHS categories, which are a more abstract level of CRM measurement including several elements, the two behavioral marker systems have moderate to high correlation on similar constructs despite their differing focuses (crew vs. individual pilot rating). Additionally, the relationships between LOSA and NOTECHS risk indices are highly statistically significant ($r= .87^{**}$, $r= .50^{**}$ and $r= .88^{**}$ for S1, S2 and S3; N=45 crews). This indicates that CRM assessments with LOSA markers and NOTECHS elements correspond well overall and also on a more concrete level of measurement.

Table 2.8   Correlations between similar LOSA and NOTECHS constructs

	Range of correlations for captain	Range of correlation for first officer
LOSA Leadership x NOTECHS Leadership[15]	.568*** to .650***	.294[+] to .332*
LOSA Vigilance x NOTECHS Situation Awareness	.382** to .564***	.214 to .571***
LOSA Communication Environment x NOTECHS Co-operation	.309* to .572***	.352* to .612***

Spearman correlations (one-tailed) across all three scenarios (S1xS2; S1xS3; S2xS3); N= 43-45
[+] p< .1; * p< .05; ** p< .01; *** p< .001

Summary and Conclusions

CRM Performance under Different Levels of Task Load

To a certain extent, CRM performance seems to be vulnerable under high task load. When task load becomes exceedingly high, as in emergency scenario one, many crews show substandard CRM performance. Svensson and Wilson (2002) report performance decrements in pilots with increasing workload, whereby, the decline in performance is slower than the increase of workload. They attribute this protective effect to active coping with situational demands. Although in the present study more crews showed substandard performance under high task load, a subsample of eight crews ('excellent crews') coped very well with both high task load scenarios. Further analyses of the mechanisms that protect these crews from performance degradation are in progress.

Trans-situational Consistency

In general, consistency of CRM performance across the three different scenarios is very low. This suggests that situational characteristics have a strong influence on CRM performance and points to the importance of adaptation to specific task and situational requirements for adequate CRM performance. Especially in the case of non-normal situations (as in scenario one and two), CRM performance in one situation is not expected to be predictive for other situations. As a practical implication for training and performance review, it seems necessary to include different scenarios with various kinds of situational and task demands for the reliable measurement of CRM performance and for appropriate training of these skills, as they do not seem to be generic across different situations.

On the other hand, the low consistency might also express the differential meaning of certain CRM behaviors for performance in specific situations.

---

[15] Leadership is defined as 'captain showed leadership and co-ordinated flight deck activities.' Therefore, higher correlations are expected for captains than for first officers.

Situations vary in the opportunities they offer to observe certain CRM behaviors (Prince et al., 1997). For a more reliable measurement of CRM aspects it might be necessary to select those behavioral markers that are relevant for coping with the events of a specific scenario. This would also lessen the workload of the observer, who is most frequently a simulator instructor having additional duties to accomplish in parellel. Methodologies that pursue this event-based selection approach are already in use (e.g. Fowlkes, Lane, Dwyer, Willis & Oser, 1994).

Comparison of LOSA and NOTECHS

The independent use of both behavioral marker systems offered the opportunity to cross-validate the two. Results show a high correlation between similar construct and between overall indices of CRM performance. The choice of the best system to be used depends on the purpose: for training of individual teamwork skills it is necessary to give personal feedback, which calls for individual pilot ratings. For the assessment of a company's training needs or as a basis for safety guidelines, crew ratings might be more appropriate.

Chapter 3

The Effects of Different Forms of Co-ordination on Coping with Workload[16]

Gudela Grote, Enikö Zala-Mezö and Patrick Grommes

Introduction

In general, much of the literature in the organization sciences, and in relation to the make-up of safe organizations in particular, is concerned with analyzing and designing adequate mechanisms of co-ordination within and between parts of an organization. A key issue in this respect is the degree of standardization of such co-ordination. Usually, the more routine work processes are the more standardized and have the more formalized co-ordination, while work processes requiring action in novel situations are less prescribed (e.g. Kieser & Kubicek, 1992; Thompson, 1967).

In high risk environments in particular there have been strong efforts to increase the level of standardization in order to make the system's behavior more predictable and controllable. At the same time there are major disadvantages to high levels of standardization that are mainly related to reducing the system's capability to adequately act in the face of requirements stemming from internal and external disturbances of normal operation (e.g. Perrow, 1984; Grote, 1997).

The present study aimed at analyzing work teams that operate under varying degrees of standardization as well as varying degrees of task load. Cockpit crews were compared to anaesthesia teams, with aviation being a highly standardized environment and medicine usually having fewer and more local rules (see Chapter 8). The co-ordination behaviors of these teams were studied in order to learn about the influences of standardization on effective co-ordination and to support decisions in organizations about the adequate degree and kind of standardization in terms of the amount and types of rules used.

---

[16] The authors would like to thank the *Behavioral Marker Group* for providing the data for the aviation scenario and especially Werner Naef for his support in analyzing the data, Johannes Wacker and Carsten Engelmann for their support in obtaining the data in the medical setting and making sense of them, and Barbara Künzle for assistance in the project and analyzing the interview data from her diploma thesis.

Background

In this study, team co-ordination was analyzed using concepts from psychology and linguistics in order to obtain a more complete picture of team behaviors. As co-ordination is a crucial notion in the understanding of team interaction in both disciplines, it was also of interest to determine whether or not definitions of good or successful co-ordination could be operationalized from a psychological perspective in linguistic terms and vice versa.

Psychological Concepts of Team Co-ordination

As a basis for analyzing team processes, the definition of a team by Salas, Dickinson, Converse and Tannenbaum (1992, p. 4) was used: 'a distinguishable set of two or more people who interact dynamically, interdependently, and adaptively toward a common and valued goal or mission, who have been assigned specific roles or functions to perform, and who have a limited life-span of membership.' This definition stresses the importance of the interdependence of the team members and the dynamic nature of team work. Task characteristics, degree and type of division of labor and specialization require different amounts and kinds of co-ordination. Crucial in this respect is the type of interdependence created by the chosen division of labor in combination with the general demands of the task and the task environment. According to the classification of the interdependence of work processes (Van de Ven & Ferry, 1980; Thompson, 1967), cockpit crews and anaesthesia teams can be considered *intensive work arrangements* as work flow is poly-directional, flexible and very intensive, especially when the teams face novel situations with new problems, which have to be diagnosed and solved within the team. In these teams, co-ordination is not the only factor but is one of the most crucial ones for teams to perform well (Zaccaro, Rittman & Marks, 2001).

Demands on co-ordination are also affected by workload. In cockpit crews it has been frequently observed that appropriate co-ordination and communication styles change in phases with different workload levels (e.g. Orasanu, 1990; cited in Kanki & Palmer, 1993). Serfaty, Entin and Johnston (1998) describe two co-ordination forms: explicit co-ordination is based on communication as the means to co-ordinate action, involving, for instance, the transfer of information in response to an information request; implicit co-ordination, on the other hand, relies much more on a pre-existing common understanding of the situation, thereby requiring less communication, with team members communicating e.g. not upon request but through anticipation of the information needs of the other team members. Implicit co-ordination is less time consuming and less resource intensive, but it requires an accurate common mental representation of the situation.

One powerful mechanism for forming a common framework for action is standardization. Standard operating procedures help teams to develop a shared mental model (Mathieu, Heffner, Goodwin, Salas & Cannon-Bowers, 2000) of the situation and of the actions required by each team member. It allows them to act routinely and quickly, without using additional resources for co-ordination.

However, the danger of high levels of standardization is that teams lose the ability to switch to a more conscious and deliberate action mode when something unexpected happens (see Chapter 8 for a more detailed description of the reasons for and effects of standardization). As Zaccaro et al. (2001, p. 475) suggests, '...regulatory mechanisms (should) have "built-in" operating procedures that promote adaptability.' This suggestion has been taken up by a number of authors who, instead of arguing for or against standard operating procedures, have begun to study different types of rules in order to specify better what kinds of rules are needed to ensure safe and efficient co-ordination and work processes under different conditions (Hale & Swuste, 1998; Leplat, 1998; Rasmussen, 1997).

When studying team interaction, it is also relevant to analyze the roles that different team members have in co-ordinating the team. In hierarchically structured teams, the role of the leader is formally assigned so that problem solving or complex work processes may require the entire team, while final decisions are to be made by the leader who is also held responsible for team success and failure. However, impersonal co-ordination mechanisms, i.e. standardization, can serve as a powerful and efficient substitute for personal leadership (Kerr & Jermier, 1978). Therefore, it is important to analyze leadership in the context of other co-ordination forces that change requirements for appropriate leadership. This point has been stressed by Zaccaro at el. (2001, p. 454-455) in their concept of functional leadership: 'functional leadership is not defined by a specific set of behaviors but rather by generic responses that are prescribed for and will vary by different problem situations. A critical task for researchers in team leadership, then, becomes the definition and validation of the contextual influences that enhance the efficacy of some leadership actions and diminishes some others.'

As an overarching concept for effective team co-ordination, Weick and Roberts (1993) have introduced the notion of *heedful interrelating*, which requires all team members, regardless of their formally assigned role '[...] (to) construct their actions (contribute) while envisaging a social system of joint actions (represent), and interrelate that constructed action with the system that is envisaged (subordinate)' (Weick & Roberts, 1993. p. 363). Heedful interrelating represents a very autonomous, dynamic way of interacting, in which every team member feels equally responsible for team performance and tries to match his/her own behavior to the behavior of others in order to achieve success. In particular, in unexpected situations, and more generally under high workload conditions, it can be assumed that heedful interrelating is needed in order to complement standardized co-ordination and formally assigned leadership.

Linguistic Concepts of Team Co-ordination

Communication or, to be more precise, verbal interaction plays a double role with respect to co-ordination in the settings studied. According to Clark (1996, p. 59) one may assume that 'there is co-ordination of both *content*, what the participants intend to do, and *processes*, the physical and mental systems they recruit in carrying out those intentions.' Thus, verbal interaction provides processes with which to co-ordinate non-linguistic team activities, i.e. to promote the achievement of their shared goal, which is to successfully solve the task at hand. But, at the same time, these processes, themselves, have to be co-ordinated. Thus, successful co-ordination at the linguistic level can be understood as a prerequisite for successful co-ordination on any other level of action. Very briefly, the requirements for successful co-ordination of linguistic actions are that for any contribution to conversation there should be some relation to the previous contribution(s), and the type of contribution should fit its predecessor's type. Successful discourse depends on the juxtaposition of the right type of utterances and on connecting them by appropriate means, the result of which is a coherent sequence of utterances. Recognizing the fitting type of utterance and applying suitable means of coherence is the co-ordination task that the participants of a discourse have to solve.

A way to understand how language users solve this task is to think of utterances as verbalizations of a mental representation of a situation. The perception of a situation – and of its constituting elements: events, processes or states, persons, objects and spatial, temporal and modal relations (see Levelt, 1989) – may lead a person to recognize that any desired change of this situation can only be achieved via verbal interaction. In this case she/he develops a communicative task that can be seen as the mental representation of an abstract question that the speaker is setting out to answer – a so-called *quaestio* (Stutterheim & Klein, 1989; Stutterheim, 1997). This quaestio then sets constraints as to which elements of the situation have to be referred to linguistically and in which order. Obeying these constraints leads to coherent texts.

This approach to coherence does not so much focus on the discourse as a product but on the mental planning that speakers have to perform in the preparation of speech production. For the purpose of the present research, this approach, which was originally developed for the analysis of monological speech production, has been adapted for the analysis of dialogue. The assumption is that each contribution to a dialogue answers a quaestio and that subsequent speakers may accept or refuse to plan their utterance in relation to the constraints of the foregoing quaestio. Thus, any contribution that follows next may or may not be related to and coherent with the preceding one. Only in the former case does discourse become co-ordinated in the end. For well-formed dialogue sequences, one would expect a linear and delimited series of related quaestiones that do not simply fade out but become formally closed by utterances that display mutual agreement on the topic discussed up to the given point.

There is an obvious relationship between verbal interaction and the psychologically founded co-ordination mechanisms. In regards to *standardization*, the linguistic co-ordination task can be approached in a rather strict manner, as in aviation. The high degree of standardization in this field is not only reflected in prescribed wordings, but in some cases, also in script-like rules. These can be understood as pre-formulated coherent sequences. *Leadership* includes the right to allocate speaker's rights and to set a content frame for a discourse. The relationship between communication and *heedful interrelating* is subtler. Being coherent in one's verbal actions means, in essence, heedfully relating them to any other verbal actions and facilitating understanding of the utterances, as well as of the more abstract message that they convey on the recipient's side, i.e. allowing him/her to build a coherent representation of the discourse and, as a consequence, of the situation in his/her mind.

Study Design

The overall design of the study is presented in Figure 3.1. The effects of varying task load and varying degrees and types of standardization on co-ordinating behavior and indirectly on team performance were analyzed in two settings: the cockpit and the anaesthesia induction area.

There are two independent variables in this design: degree of standardization and task load. The degree of standardization varies between professional teams (cockpit teams and anaesthesia teams) and within teams during different work phases. In both settings, there are phases with more and with fewer rules, even though there are fewer overall rules in the medical setting. Task load varies between different work phases. Task load was defined as situational demands placed on the team based on expert rating and cannot be considered equivalent to workload, which depends on the relationship between the resources of the individual and the demands of the situation (Norman & Bobrow, 1975). This relationship is influenced, among other things, by practice, which enhances resource efficiency and thereby reduces workload (cf. e.g. Bowers, Braun & Morgan, 1997). As workload very much depends on the individual's resources, it is difficult to define workload for a team. Therefore, task load as an objective account of situational demands, was taken as an approximation to team workload (see Chapter 8 for a more detailed account of task load and workload).

Co-ordination behavior in teams was rated based on videotapes using psychological and linguistic categories and was linked to performance measures based on expert ratings. As standardization varied between and within settings, analyses were carried out comparing aviation with medicine and also comparing different work phases within aviation and medicine.

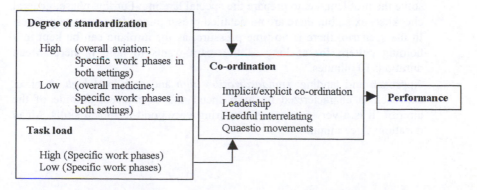

Figure 3.1   Study Design

Methods

In both professional fields, video recordings were used. The aviation data stem from simulator sessions, which were part of a training day. The *Behavioral Markers Group* collected data from four scenarios and provided access to the data from the fourth scenario (for a more detailed description of the data collection procedure see the methods section Chapter 2). Tapes from 42 teams consisting of two individuals, captain and first officer, were analyzed. The data of 23 anaesthesia teams were recorded from live inductions in an emergency department of a university hospital. In addition to the video recordings, interviews were carried out with the relevant staff of the hospital department, i.e. anaesthesiologists, residents, nurse anaesthetists and surgical personnel, in order to obtain background information on working conditions, written and unwritten rules and perceptions of relevant influences on team performance. In both settings, different work phases could be distinguished regarding standardization and task load.

Aviation

In the simulator scenario, teams take off for a flight from Turin to Zurich but are called back to Turin. When preparing for the approach to Turin, they discover that flaps and slats are jammed which requires a so-called clean approach.

The work phases during the flight (level of standardization and task load as assessed by expert ratings) are as follows:

- Normal take-off: *standardization high* and *task load low*. After an uneventful take-off, the team, because of weather conditions, gets the order to go back to Turin and to reduce speed. As they try to reduce speed they realize that the flaps and slats on the wings are jammed. Mean duration: three minutes.
- Problem solving: *standardization low* and *task load low*. This phase starts when the crew realizes what the problem is and lasts as long as they need to solve the problem, i.e. to prepare the special landing. For this phase, general checklists exist, but there are no detailed prescriptions for action sequences. In the scenario, there is no time pressure, as the airplane can be kept in a holding pattern for as long as the team wants to hold it there. Mean duration: 10 minutes.
- Approach and landing: *standardization high* and *task load high*. A clean approach is characterized by high speed and an unusual attitude of the aircraft. It is a very rare event, requiring very good technical skills. Mean duration: three minutes.

Medicine

The work phases during induction were as follows (level of standardization and task load as assessed by expert ratings; 51 rules were relevant for the five phases, eight per cent of which concerned all phases – see content analysis of rules below):

- Preparation: preparation of monitoring (electrocardiogram, blood pressure, oxygen saturation of the blood); patient gets an intravenous drip, through which the drugs will be administered. *Task load low* and *standardization high* (41 per cent of all rules concern this phase). Mean duration: 11 minutes.
- Preintubation: starts with the administration of the first drug and ends when the patient has a complete neuromuscular blockage. *Task load moderate* as the main task is monitoring; *standardization moderate* (19.5 per cent of the rules apply to this phase). Mean duration: seven and a half minutes.
- Tracheal intubation: the anesthetist inserts an endotracheal tube into the trachea through the mouth. The phase ends, when the anesthetist confirms correct tube position, connects the tube to the ventilator and fixes it to the patient's face. *Task load high* and *standardization moderate* (19.5 per cent of the rules apply to this phase). Mean duration: three minutes.
- Additional preparation: the repositioning of the patient with the ventilator; sometimes the monitoring has to be disconnected. Good co-ordination and especially good leadership are vital for this process, during which the anesthesia team has to work together with the surgical team. *Task load high* and *standardization low* (12 per cent of the rules apply to this phase). Mean duration: 12 minutes.
- Transport: after anesthesia induction and monitoring the team wheels the patient to the operating room. Ventilator and monitoring are regularly disconnected, so time is of crucial importance, but this task is also highly routinized. *Task load low* and *no standardization* (no rules for this phase). Mean duration: two minutes.

Observational Categories – Psychology

The video recordings were rated based on a number of observational categories. Three main groups of categories were developed that were driven by both theoretical and practical considerations. Two behavioral marker systems for the evaluation of crew resource management, LOSA (Helmreich et al., 1999) and NOTECHS (Avermate & Kruijsen, 1998) were used as references. While LOSA and NOTECHS provide overall ratings of individual and/or team performance in cockpit crews on a number of quite general characteristics, categories had to enable the coding of all utterances in the two settings. Therefore, more specific categories were developed within each of the content areas covered by LOSA and NOTECHS.

The first set of categories concerned the information flow on a general level without much reference to the content of the information. The aim was to create mutually exclusive categories covering all utterances and to be able to differentiate between elements of explicit and implicit co-ordination (Serfaty et al., 1998).

Information flow - explicit co-ordination contains categories such as (for the entire list of observational categories see Appendix V):

- Provide information
- Request information.

Information flow – implicit co-ordination contains categories such as:

- Provide unsolicited information
- Offer assistance.

All utterances were either assigned to categories under explicit or under implicit co-ordination such that the frequencies for these two types of communication add up to the total amount of communication. The information flow categories also provide a general quantitative account of the observed communication, concerning e.g. speaker dominance and proportion of standard versus non-standard information exchange.

The other two groups of categories are not fully exclusive and do not cover all utterances. *Leadership* contains categories such as:

- Make plans
- Assign task.

The third group of categories contains elements of heedful interrelating such as:

- Consider others
- Question decisions.

Observational Categories – Linguistics

The categories for the linguistic analysis were developed under the premises of the quaestio model of dialogue production as described above. In Grommes and Dietrich (2002, 199) a set of possible reactions to quaestiones – so called quaestio movements – has been presented. Grommes (in preparation) extended this set of possible reactions as follows:

* New: a speaker signals the perception of a new communicative task;
* Shift: a speaker takes up the quaestio of the preceding speaker and constructs on this basis a related quaestio that offers additional information to come closer to the communicative goal;
* B(ack)shift/Restoration: a speaker takes up a quaestio in the same manner as above, but this time it is not the quaestio of the immediately preceding contribution, but of an earlier one;
* Maintenance: a speaker has no further information to add. At this point – at the latest – a sequence is expected to be closed.

For the analysis of the aviation data all verbal activities were coded according to these types of quaestio movements. In this way, it is possible to describe who initiates discourse activities, how complex the resulting sequences are and whether or not they are constructed and concluded jointly. Therefore, it is possible to qualitatively assess the coherence of discourse and, thus, whether or not co-ordination is a success or failure at the linguistic level.

Performance Measure

In the aviation setting, performance was rated on a scale from one to six by an instructor who had conducted the session and observed the teams. Additional observation, based on the video recordings, answered the question of whether or not the teams had carried out all the compulsory tasks and had obeyed all the rules relevant to the situation, resulting in ratings on a scale from one to four. These two scales were combined into a performance index ranging from one to ten.

In the anaesthesia setting, an experienced anaesthesia resident watched the video recordings and rated team performance on a scale from one to ten. An additional scale based on rule violations was not used, as teams rarely disobeyed rules. Such a measure would therefore not have differentiated between teams.

Quantitative Content Analysis of Rules

Documents were collected from both the national airline and the university hospital that described rules and standard procedures relevant to the tasks studied. These documents were analyzed using the following main categories: the *content* of the rule can prescribe a goal, a process to be followed to define an action or a concrete action (Hale & Swuste, 1998). Also, the degree of *strictness* of a rule (order versus advice; amount of scope provided) and whether exceptions to the rules and reasons for the rule are mentioned were analyzed.

Hypotheses

The basic assumption was that good co-ordination means different things in different situations. If a process were well known and/or highly standardized, one would expect mostly implicit co-ordination and only few leadership behaviors. If all team members know their job and have a shared model of the situation, they can operate according to this model and do not need to devote additional resources to co-ordinating their actions. On the other hand, in unexpected complex situations, teams need to establish a common understanding of the task. Explicit co-ordination helps teams to form a shared mental model and good leadership enables smooth and rapid co-ordination.

Task load (as the objective task-dependent component of the subjectively experienced workload) results in a limited capacity to process information. The consequence is a possible switch to more efficient forms in the information exchange process, like implicit co-ordination (e.g. anticipating the information needs of other team members and providing that information without being requested to do so).

Because communication is not only subject to co-ordination but is in itself a tool for co-ordination, discourse success is assumed to be correlated with at least some other co-ordination mechanisms, especially to heedful interrelating and to standardization. With respect to the latter, different patterns of conversational organization were expected within the aviation dataset for the first and third flight phase, which are highly standardized as compared to the second flight phase, and possibly to some less prescribed parts of the approach briefing in phase three. In the more standardized phases, the quaestio movement should show only a few restorations, and sequences should often be ended by at least one maintenance move because of the procedural requirement to explicitly acknowledge that information has been received. In the other phases, teams are freer in their conversational organization, and they have to rely on different means for co-ordination, such as heedful interrelating. Teams that interrelate heedfully should show better linguistic co-ordination in the sense that they will produce either undisrupted linear structures or complex quaestio movements in cases in which information transfer or task co-ordination would otherwise be insufficient. Less heedful teams should show less well-formed structures; i.e. missing maintenances or an imbalance of shifts and maintenances or restorations (bshifts) that can be, e.g. related back to misunderstandings. Overall, linguistic breakdowns were expected to indicate general problems of action.

Results

Aviation Data

Table 3.1 shows the results of the comparison between different work phases in the aviation scenario. The percentages were calculated based on the sum of observations in a given category during the given phase. This was then divided by all interactions in that phase.

Table 3.1   Co-ordination patterns during different work phases in the aviation setting

	Flight phase		
	1	2	3
	Take-off	Preparation Clean approach	Approach and Landing
Average duration (min.)	3	10	3
Task load	Low	Low	High
Standardization	High	Low	High
Communication units (CU) overall	840	3514	1429
CU standardized communication	52%	9%	28%
CU explicit	66%	81%	60%
CU implicit	34%	19%	40%
CU leadership	2%	14%	3%
CU Heedful interrelating	2%	18%	19%

Generally speaking, in the first, highly standardized, low task load phase, standards are sufficient as a co-ordination tool. Teams need comparatively less explicit co-ordination and leadership behavior, and they show very few acts of heedful interrelating.

In the second flight phase, during which the teams have to figure out how to carry out the landing under the special conditions (flaps and slats are jammed; clean approach), explicit co-ordination, leadership and heedful interrelating play an important role in team co-ordination. This phase is less standardized as teams, for instance, have to decide on the division of work themselves. Task load is rather low, since there is no time pressure and the task to be accomplished is clear. Explicit co-ordination is crucial, as team members have to create a common picture of the situation and plan the difficult landing in the next phase. Leadership behavior such as planning and assigning tasks is important in order to perform well during the actual phase, as well as to prepare for the next phase. Heedful interrelating as a non-hierarchical form of co-ordination is also important in order to make optimal use of all team members' resources.

The last phase, the clean approach and landing, is characterized by high standardization and high task load. There was generally more communication observed in this phase than in the first phase, as there was more uncertainty in the situation even though both phases are highly standardized. As expected based on the findings by Serfaty et al. (1998), more implicit co-ordination was found, corresponding to the high task load, which calls for a less resource intensive co-ordination. Few leadership actions were found, also as expected, as this kind of co-ordination tool is more useful in the planning (second) phase (Orasanu, 1993). Heedful interrelating occurred most frequently in this phase – even though there was only a minor increase when compared to phase two. Yet again, this non-hierarchical way of co-ordination helps to make use of all resources in the team, in this phase in particular, in order to support the pilot flying during the highly demanding clean approach and landing.

Linguistic Analysis of the Aviation Data

The linguistic analysis shows some qualitative, though no statistically significant, interrelations with the psychological analysis (For more details see Grote, Zala-Mezö and Gromees, 2003). The overall picture shows that the first and third flight phases are structurally similar for all crews. This was expected because, in both phases, the crews are obliged to use a large amount of standard communication (see also Table 3.1 for frequencies of standardized communication units). Only at the beginning of the third phase, when the approach briefing is carried out, is there some space for less regulated interaction. This briefing is obligatory, but its form is not prescribed. Thus, some crews use this opportunity to clarify some last important points regarding the landing. This often results in sequences that are longer than average. In one simulation, e.g. the pilot in command (PIC) repeats most of the discussion from the second phase during the approach briefing and, thus, initiates sequences of an average length of 6.7 turns of talk, while the average for all crews is 3.0. There are also some quaestio restorations, but these are less complex than in the second phase.

In the second phase, one can identify clear differences in how the crews organize their problem-oriented interaction. The technical problem appears at a point in time when crews perform the last steps of standardized activities. Some crews have problems co-ordinating the switch from standard-based to problem-oriented task accomplishment. When the crews have finally entered the problem solution part of phase two, some of them use the handbooks as a guideline to structure their discussion – as the linguistic analysis shows – while others read them like a script. The former approach provides space for individual co-ordination strategies. Thus, the linguistic structure of the crew's conversation that takes the more liberal approach might be more complex and less straightforward than in the other cases. But these complex structures are often employed to build a shared mental model of the situation, and they reflect the effort of the interlocutors to share and provide crucial information. For an illustration, consider the following table.

Table 3.2   Linguistic evaluation related to results from psychological analysis of phase two

Team	Linguistic evaluation	Percentage of heedful interactions relative to all interaction units
B10	Task-oriented conversation organization by PIC, complex structures employed to update mental model of the situation of F/O.	22%
B40	Structural complexity due to difficulties to enter problem solving phase, otherwise inconspicuous, passive behavior by F/O.	5%
B46	Initially difficulties of PIC to order the tasks, but F/O minimizes resulting complexity of structures, otherwise inconspicuous.	12%
Mean		16%

Table 3.2 shows a relationship between the linguistic and the psychological analysis. Team B10 can be rated as the best on the linguistic level. This team also shows a high value for heedfulness in this phase. This means that this team makes good use of the low degree of regulation for this situation. The opposite can be stated for crew B40. Thus, linguistically well-performing – and co-ordinating – teams seem to also obtain better results in the psychological analysis. It is, however, important to mention that these results only hold true for this phase and that they do not account for the full paradigm of behavioral factors on which the observational analyses are based. Considering all of these factors might alter the overall evaluation of the outcome of team processes. In other words, linguistically well co-ordinated interaction might fail due to non-linguistic factors. Nevertheless, one can easily see that conspicuous linguistic structures indicate possible problematic behaviors. An additional factor that becomes visible through the linguistic analysis – and that has been illustrated in the table for crew B40 – is a possible imbalance in the amount of information crew members contribute to the problem solution process. It is especially noticeable that some of the first officers participate almost equally in the communication; they produce shifts and maintenances in similar numbers, while others remain very passive, which is apparent because maintenance-moves clearly outnumber quaestio shifts.

In summary, it is possible to state that the less regulated situation allows the crews to employ linguistic co-ordination tools but not all crews make equal use of them. Contrary to the hypotheses, it is not possible to clearly relate inconspicuous linguistic structures to positive incidents of heedful interrelating or to other co-ordination behavior. It is, however, possible to show that structural complexities or disruptions are related to some behavioral factors. The linguistic analysis also makes it possible to identify sequences in verbal interaction in which co-ordination strategies come into conflict as, for example, when the crews have to master the transition from following normal flight procedures to diagnosing and solving a problem.

Medical Data

The *anaesthesia teams* that were observed show differences in co-ordination between the phases as well. Table 3.3 shows the summary of the results. Percentages are calculated in the same way as they were for the aviation data.

Table 3.3   Co-ordination patterns in the anesthesia teams

	Explicit co-ordination	Implicit co-ordination	Leadership behavior	Heedful interrelating
Phase 1: Preparation Low task load; High standardization	59%	41%	10%	6%
Phase 2: Preintubation Medium task load; Medium standardization	68%	32%	15%	10%
Phase 3: Intubation High task load; Medium standardization	71%	29%	16%	12%
Phase 4: Additional preparation High task load; Low standardization	74%	26%	17%	10%
Phase 5: Transport Low task load; No standardization	70%	30%	22%	15%

In the first four phases, the fewer rules available, the more explicit co-ordination can be observed. The most explicit co-ordination occurs during phase four, when teams have to reposition the patient. In this phase, team size increases as new team members join the team, and, therefore, co-ordination needs increase. The main task becomes establishing a shared mental model of the situation, so that every team member knows what he/she should do.

In the last phase, during which teams transport the patients to the operating room, there are no written rules available. However, there are certainly some unwritten rules about the process and labor division. In this phase the highest share of leadership behavior is observed, presumably enforcing the unwritten rules.

The amount of heedful interrelating is generally rather low. Even in the high task load situations there is little support provided through this non-hierarchical form of co-ordination. Especially in phase four, this is also due to the fact that the team cannot operate from a shared mental model of the situation, which is crucial for both implicit co-ordination and heedful interrelating.

Co-ordination and Performance – Comparisons of the Two Professional Fields

For the aviation data, a statistically significant positive relationship was found between the overall amount of explicit co-ordination and performance ($r=.37$, $p \leq .05$). For leadership, work phase specific results were found in the aviation data. There was a positive relationship ($r=.31$, $p \leq .05$) with performance during the low standardization phase (phase 2 in aviation and negative relationships for the two high standardization phases (for phase 1 $r=-.42$, $p \leq .05$; for phase 3 $r=-.24$, n. s.). These findings support the hypothesis that standardization can be a substitute for leadership behaviour (Kerr & Jermier, 1978) and that too much leadership in situations in which team members can work on their own, without needing much direction, can have a negative effect on team performance. For the other co-ordination forms no statistically significant relationships with performance were found. In the medical data, no significant correlations were found with the performance measure.

Thus, there is partial support for the hypotheses related to the psychological categories and the general assumption that adaptive co-ordination is needed for successful performance. Reasons for not finding more extensive evidence for the effectiveness of certain types of co-ordination lie in the generally low variance in the performance measures – basically all teams could be considered quite good teams – and especially for the anaesthesia teams in the rather global nature of the performance rating. More specific reference to technical details of the anaesthesia process in each team would have been necessary to derive more detailed performance assessments. Another possible explanation for the generally weak relationship between performance and co-ordination behaviour of the teams is that good co-ordination or, generally speaking, good team work might make little difference until the workload is extremely high, which was not the case in the settings studied here. Teams have many possibilities to compensate for bad co-ordination. They have time to correct mistakes. Even one person might manage a task alone, at least for some of time.

No support was found for the assumption that the generally lower level of standardization in medicine would be associated with less implicit co-ordination by comparing the two professional fields. Overall, there was more implicit co-ordination in the anaesthesia teams. Possible explanations include the co-ordination force of the shared visual field and the higher familiarity in anaesthesia teams, which overcompensates for the lack of common ground through standardization. Also, there was more leadership and less heedful interrelating in the anaesthesia teams, which corresponds to the higher degree of hierarchical structure in those teams when they are compared to cockpit crews. More detailed comparisons will be presented in Chapter 10.

The linguistic analyses have proven to be a very important complement to the psychological analyses, as behavioral problems can be related back to unsuccessful co-ordination on the linguistic level. Yet again, more detailed findings will be discussed in the Leadership and Co-ordination chapter.

Chapter 4

Communication in Nuclear Power Plants (NPP)

Ryoko Fukuda and Oliver Sträter

Aims and Objectives

Safety in nuclear power plants (NPP) is a paramount issue, since accidents in NPP have the potential to cause tremendous damage to people and things. Although many automated operation technologies have been introduced, NPP safety still depends on humans. 20 – 70 per cent of all system failures in NPP, including Three-Mile Island or Chernobyl, are caused by human error (Fleishman and Buffardi, 1999).

One important aspect of human behaviour in NPP is group interaction. In NPP, many people are working together in various work places (in the control room, local control stations, on the spot, etc.). Therefore, operating a NPP involves the co-ordination of several people between and within workplaces. In addition to spatially distributed communication, communication has to compensate for the temporal gap of crews between shifts. Former studies have confirmed the importance of communication both during normal operations and abnormal events. For instance, field studies by Mumaw et al. (2000) and Vicente et al. (2001) showed that in addition to the control room indicators and alarms, the information obtained via communication with local operators is an important source of information for controlling a plant. If the controlling demands are too high, an operator can pass the workload on to another operator by asking him/her to supervise some indicators or alarm screens in order to decrease his/her own memory and attentional demands.

Therefore, the importance of communication in NPP is obvious and important for the safe operation of the plants. On the other hand, communication issues are difficult to investigate because of the variety of technological solutions and staff organizations. Therefore, the GIHRE *Process Control Group* investigated the communication issue in NPP operation using two approaches. It started with investigating safety-related events regarding communication problems and their contributing factors. Event reports provide plenty of information about the causes of each event and reflect on the safety relevance of the issue in several existing plants. With special focus on the communication problem, the importance of communication in events can be clarified. Based on the findings from incidents, the second approach aims at detailed investigation into the cognitive aspects, which may lead to the observed communication problems. In order to better understand the communication behaviour observed in the incidents, a simulator study was carried out. The cognitive processes were analyzed using eye tracking, protocol recording, behaviour observation and an interview with video confrontation. Overall, both steps provide a valid and reliable way to investigate communication problems in NPP by integrating incident data and experimental studies.

Former Studies on NPP Safety Issues and the Objective of this Investigation

In order to secure safety in NPP, many studies have already been carried out. They may be roughly divided into two groups: event analysis and empirical studies.

Event Analysis

Operational feedback programs are essential for the safe operation of systems. The nuclear industry has developed this important safety management feature quite far. Event analysis is important in order to become aware of safety trends (recent technological or human problems that need to be addressed) and to find holes in the safety system (because no safety engineer can imagine all possible events which may occur). Nuclear industry developed an exhaustive classification of events, the INES (International Nuclear Event Scale) system, with which to judge the safety relevance of nuclear plants (IAEA/NEA, 1998). The INES system is more or less compatible with national event-classification systems. Events are usually distinguished as follows: normal occurrences (abnormal plant behaviour with minor safety relevance), transients (abnormal plant behaviour with the potential to   have developed into an event with higher safety relevance), incidents (release of radioactivity within the plant) and accidents (major release of radioactivity outside of the plant).

  In Germany, data from all events beyond a certain safety criteria have been collected and analyzed since around 1969 by GRS (Gesellschaft für Anlagen- und Reaktorsicherheit), which is part of the German nuclear regulatory body. Normally, event protocols include a short description of the transition of the system status, the reasons for the event and the executed measures. Critics often point out that human factor issues and, in particular, communication and organizational factors are not sufficiently described in these reports. However, a study by Sträter (1997) showed that event records are providing useful insights into human errors and organizational aspects though the quality of these aspects could be improved. Therefore, there is no reason to leave this information source aside. However, nothing comparable to a flight data recorder has been established within the plants. It would be difficult to realize such a system due to the fact that people are not working at a fixed place, as in a cockpit. The analysis of communication behaviour during abnormal states of real operation is, therefore, dependant on the events that have taken place.

Empirical Studies

Empirical studies focus on gaining a deeper understanding of the cognitive and contextual aspects of human behaviour. Empirical studies can be further divided into field studies and simulator studies. The advantage of field studies is, of course, the opportunity to gain a realistic view of the full complexity of the work environment (Mumaw, 2000) and, thereby, provide better face-validity than experimental studies. However, field studies are often lacking sufficient reliability because it is not possible to manipulate variables such as system status or task load. As serious NPP events are relatively rare, field studies are also lacking information about the behaviour of the operators in an abnormal event. Consequently, the majority of field studies report on human behaviour in normal operation. In addition, the accomplishment of such field studies is sometimes difficult due to political backgrounds. Field studies in normal operations have revealed, as mentioned before, that communication is an important means in NPP operation and is needed in addition to various system indicators in order to guarantee safe operation. Communication during shift hand over is of great importance as well (Guerlain and Bullemer, 1996; Vicente, et al., 2001).

Communication is important for safety to study human behavior in abnormal situations in NPPs. In principle, empirical studies of such situations are only possible with simulator studies. The conditions can be freely manipulated in simulations according to the aim of the studies. In addition, simulator studies are easier to accomplish than field studies because they can be performed more independently from political constrains than field studies. Additionally, some physiological measurements are also applicable and therefore allow detailed analysis of cognitive aspects. However, it is uncertain whether or not the behaviour observed in experimental studies can be validly transferred to real life situations.

Simulation technology is applied not only for the simulation of various transients (on the system side), but also for the simulation of human operator behaviour (on the human side). For instance, the skills extracted from such simulations with an advanced knowledge-based system can be applied for generating training standards for computer aided operator support systems (Furuta and Kondo, 1993; Takano et al., 2000).

Another major issue is the development and improvement of the support system for operation. Many indicators are required for the operation of NPP. In a conventional control room, there are hard-wired indicators that are directly combined with each device. The main reason that plants still have conventional technology is that these systems remain safer than computerized systems. Large overview instruments are only utilized in the most essential systems, such as the reactor protection system. However, the tasks may vary and the information available may, at times, be better arranged. Introducing a computerized control room technology can eradicate the disadvantage of conventional systems, that is the difficulty of having a task or situation related overview of the system. Typically, the most important information is integrated by computers and presented on screens. Additionally, help for the diagnosis can be integrated in such systems. The effectiveness has already been confirmed in former studies (e.g. Sassen, et al.,

1994; Roth et al., 1998). In order to facilitate effective communication, large overview screens, which would be visible to all operators in the control room, can be introduced. This type of overview screen facilitates the maintenance of the shared information and shared situational awareness among the operators. The above mentioned studies are still lacking the analysis of the communication aspect.

Approach of the Process Control Group

The approach chosen in this study provides a complementary approach from incident data and experimental studies to provide valid as well as reliable statements about this issue.

With regards to event analysis, the data of GRS is appropriate for the analysis of communication in various events. The GRS database provides written event descriptions about technical and human failures. The descriptions can be used quite well for investigating communication failures because they contain the circumstances under which the communication failed in the real event (detailed discussion in Sträter, 1997 & 2002). On the other hand, written event descriptions do not usually include very detailed descriptions of the communication processes that took place during the event (like cognitive aspects). For some events, interviewing the appropriate personnel at the plant can compensate for this lack of information. Therefore, it should be considered that this data source has its specific limitations (as other data sources or approaches have as well). Based on this consideration, the *Process Control Group* seeks deeper insight into human failure and communication problems in NPP operation by complementing incident data with an experimental study.

In the empirical study, the communication behaviour of operators is observed in detail. The study is designed in such a way that the experimental layout and the hypotheses are based on the experiences gained from the analysis of incidents. The advantage of the experiment is that measurements of the cognitive states and processes can be derived, which is not possible from incident descriptions. In particular, eye tracking can provide very meaningful data with which to understand the cognitive state of operators as the basis (or background) of each procedural and/or communication behaviour. Its effectiveness has already been confirmed (e.g. Kirwan et al., 1995), and it has been applied in various areas such as in the evaluation of user interfaces and the analysis of driving behavior but only rarely for the analysis of the behavior of NPP operators. In one of the examples from Follesø et al. (1995), the effects of scenario complexity on operators' diagnostic behaviour were investigated using eye tracking. The results showed that the number of underlying faults is not the dominant factor determining complexity. The performance of operators is different according to the place of work (in which plant they are working) and diagnostic strategies did not vary systematically with respect to either subject pools or performance measures. Another example from Drøivoldsmo et al. (1998) investigated situation awareness and workload in NPP simulation based on eye tracking data. The result shows that higher situation awareness corresponds to shorter total monitoring of specific indicators critical for solving scenarios when operators are most active in their problem solving. Furthermore, it indicates longer dwell time[17] as a function of higher workload. These studies provide some important suggestions for understanding operator behaviour. However, the communication issue was not investigated. Drøivoldsmo et al. (1998) only pointed out the possibility of combining the verbal component with the eye movement data.

Eye tracking data provides a further advantage for the accurate analysis of verbal protocol, especially in the case of unclear or incomplete sentences. The lack of explicit objects or subjects (e.g. use of pronouns instead of nouns) makes the interpretation difficult (Kaarstad et al., 1994). With eye tracking, an accurate interpretation is possible, because the object that is the focus at a certain moment can be identified. Eye tracking data can also facilitate a verbal retrospection (also called video-confronting method). Sometimes the verbal retrospection is necessary to clarify the reason for a particular behaviour. The eye movement recording is a powerful tool for supporting verbal retrospection (Hansen, 1991). For these reasons, eye tracking is carried out in combination with verbal communication data in the *Process Control Group's* simulation study.

Event Analysis: Communication Aspects

In the first step, event reports of German NPPs are analyzed using the CAHR-Method in order to clarify to what extent communication problems were related to the observed events (Sträter, 1997; 2002).

Applied Data

The GRS database used for this investigation contained approximately 5000 events from German NPPs when this study started. 232 events were selected for detailed analysis regarding communication problems. These events were further broken down into 439 sub-events.

CAHR-Method

For the investigation of events concerning human failures in connection with communication aspects and cognitive aspects, the Connectionism Assessment of Human Reliability (CAHR) method was employed. Figure 4.1 provides a general overview of the event analysis procedure.

This method enables the combination of event analysis and assessment and, therefore, the human reliability assessment can be based on past experience (Sträter and Bubb, 1999). The basic idea of approach for event evaluation and data collection is a detailed analysis of information flows that are important in an event, followed by a detailed analysis of each sub-event regarding the human behaviour, the errors that occurred and the situational conditions contributing to the error. The

---

[17] Dwell time is a group of fixations representing the minimum gaze necessary to encode a single information unit during problem solving (Hauland, 1996).

MMS (Man Machine System) offers a general approach for detailed analysis. In addition to ergonomic and organizational aspects, this framework also enables investigation into the communication aspect using the items task-order (informaton sending) and task-dispatch (information receiving).

A collection of several event analyses is then analysed using a connectionism network (Figure 4.2). The network compiles with the event information in such a way that statistical statements about the collection can be made without loosing the specific interrelations represented in each single event.

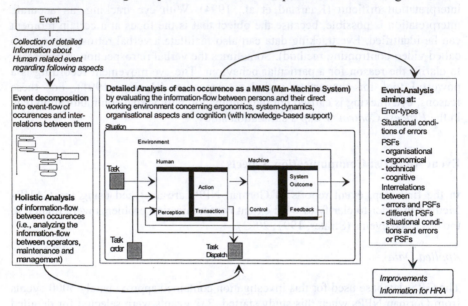

Figure 4.1   CAHR-Method event analysis (adapted from Sträter, 2003)

The connectionism approach described in Figure 4.2 represents a kind of language retention and production system. It contains language elements and represents different semantic elements on various syntactic layers. This means that the CAHR-model represents a language recognition system in which each syntactic rule is implemented as one level within the network. The network permits any connections between the levels so that linguistic interconnections materialise by virtue of the frequency with which certain relations are used. The correct reproduction of learned knowledge is then ensured by propagation and back propagation through the network. The network allows one to derive statements that take all of the collected events into account, but it also makes it possible to trace a statistical figure back to single events that contribute to the figure.

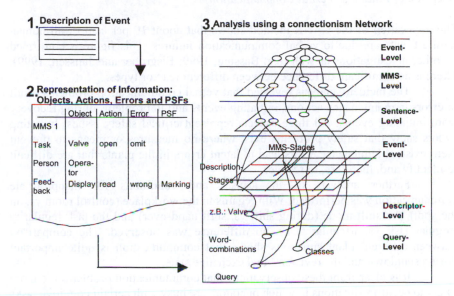

Figure 4.2 Overview of Semantic Processing of Event Information within CAHR (adapted from Sträter, 2003)

Verbal vs. Procedural Communication

Communication in NPP operation is classified into verbal communication and procedural communication. Verbal communication is defined as all direct communication activities like face-to-face communication or phone calls. Procedural communication includes every interaction in which paper based material is used. Procedures, ad hoc procedures, checklists, work permission forms etc. are examples of procedural communication. Verbal communication, in particular, is usually used in operational phases, whereas procedural communication is more connected to maintenance and work control processes.

The difference between verbal and procedural communication was further analyzed in regards to situational conditions and Performance Shaping Factor (PSF). The result indicates that verbal communication is always problematic if the communication partners are exposed to a certain degree of pressure (time pressure or situational pressure, task demands, task organization or preparation). On the contrary, procedural communication tends to fail more often due to ergonomic problems, like imcompleteness of information in procedures, labeling of equipment or others. Hence, verbal communication is clearly linked to a much greater extent to mental capacity and mechanisms used to cope with situations than to procedure-based communication. Within the scope of GIHRE, the results presented focus on verbal communication (for the results on procedural information see Sträter, 2002).

Overview of Findings: Verbal Communication

The application of the CAHR method shows that about 10 per cent of all human failure events are due to verbal communication failures. This figure is confirmed by other investigations as well (e.g. Bassing, 1999; Eisgruber and Janssen, 1999). There is no significant difference between different reactor types.

The incident analysis revealed that verbal communication problems result in errors in maintenance actions, initiating events and in problems during recovery from initiating events. All three aspects represent critical safety issues. Initiating events show that safety problems exist where no measures or means to prevent them exists. Maintenance errors lead to latent errors in the plants that are difficult to identify and, therefore, to recover.

Further analysis of the causes and conditions for inappropriate communication was performed. With regards to the workplace (control room vs. on the spot), the shift-mode (during shift vs. shift hand-over) and the task regularity (regular task vs. irregular task), no difference was observed. The comparison between different plant situations shows that communication is quite important during shutdown and the revision / fuel exchange state.

It is clear from these observations that communication problems are more likely to occur in situations in which operators are busy with certain cognitive tasks in the system rather than being open to receiving or sending information (like during checking or work-control processes).

Cognitive Aspects of Communication Behavior

The link between cognitive aspects and communication behaviour is known from many basic psychological research activities (see detailed discussions in Chapter 12). Communication becomes more difficult if the cognitive demands of the situation are high. In addition, the results also show that not only perceptual aspects (like precision of task or clarity of instructions), but also attitudes (like willingness to send or openness to receiving information in the situation at hand) are important factors for communication (goal reduction, processing of information).

Evaluation of the cognitive activities during events when communication errors occurred revealed that the importance of communication differs among various cognitive activities. Figure 4.3 shows the importance of communication in various cognitive activities. Within this figure, the relative importance is defined as the ratio of the frequency of a certain cognitive activity, given that communication was inappropriate, divided by the frequency of the cognitive activity observed in all events. If – for instance – 107 sub-events were observed in the control room and 10 of them were observed with inappropriate verbal communication, the importance for verbal communication under the condition of control room activity is $10/107 = 9.3$ per cent. This measure ensures that the statements are not biased by the absolute number of observations but are seen in their relative importance (cf. Sträter & Bubb, 1998).

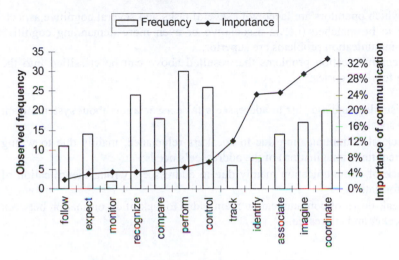

Figure 4.3 Importance of communication for cognitive activities

The importance of cognitive activities for communication increases in different cognitive activities from *follow* to *co-ordinate*. The different cognitive activities can be distinguished into the following groups and are to be understood as follows (for further discussion of cognitive activities see Sträter & Bubb; 2002):

- Follow and monitor: Activities of perceiving external information in a more topographic cognitive behaviour according to Rasmussen (1986);
- Expect, recognize and compare: activities of perceiving external information in a more symptomatic cognitive behaviour according to Rasmussen (1986);
- Perform and control: more open loop active inputs of operators into the system;
- Track: more closed loop active inputs of operators into the system
- Identify and associate: combining external information with internal representations;
- Imagine and co-ordinate: run one respectively several internal representations in the mind.

The importance of communication is obviously high in cognitive activities like co-ordinating, imagining, associating and identifying. Verbal communication problems occur less frequently in *open loop activities* like following, expecting, etc. Therefore, it can be concluded that in *open loop* situations in which the operators are usually also receptive to information from outside, communication problems are much less common than when compared to *closed loop* situations in which the operators are busy with applying their own way of thinking to a situation. The more items considered during a closed loop situation, the more difficult it is to get information from outside into the cognitive loop. In cognitive states in which operators are faced with several tasks and several cognitive aspects that have to be matched (i.e. in associative or even more demanding cognitive states), communication problems are superior.

The communication problems that resulted above can be classified into the following four categories:

- Misunderstandings due to addressee's false association about system meant by speaker;
- Lack of communication due to speakers reluctance, mainly due to wrong perception (imagination) of the addressee's needs;
- Lack of communication mainly due to addressee's wrong identification of information.
- Break-down of communication mainly due to lack of co-ordination between speaker and addressee.

Conclusions: Event Analysis and Motivation for Simulator Study

The findings from the incident analyses suggest that communication problems can be looked at from a cognitive perspective: human beings collect information constantly from the outside world and compare it with their own internal representations ('Cognitive mill' by Neisser, 1976). This process also holds true for the role of communication. The event analysis revealed that communication in NPP is heavily dependant on factors such as workload and situational pressure. On the other hand, operators do communicate extraordinarily well if they have to resolve a common problem, have to accomplish a common task or have to reach a common goal – even under very high workload and in situations of serious disturbance. This contradiction could be explained, if the following hypotheses are true:

- Communication is always an added task that is to be performed in addition to the operational task for plant control. This means that there are always two sub-tasks for an operator in any situation: one operational and one communicative;
- Communication is a disturbing/disruptive additional task for the addressee if the information he/she obtains disturbs the sub-task at hand. On the other hand, communication is a disturbing/disruptive additional task for the speaker if the information requirement of the other is not seen as part of his/her own task. This disturbing situation is referred to as an incongruent situation in this text;
- Communication is a congruent additional sub-task for the addressee if he/she requires the information for his/her sub-task at hand. On the side of the speaker, if the information requirement of the other is seen as part of his/her own or of a common task, communication is a congruent additional

sub-task. Congruent tasks are less prone to communication problems even in situations with high demands or high workload.

In order to confirm the hypotheses derived from the event analyses, the following simulator study was carried out.

Empirical Study on Communication in Nuclear Power Plants

All tasks in NPP operation are ultimately accomplished based on the cognitive status of the operators. Therefore, it is necessary to observe the cognitive status in order to investigate whether or not the context of communication (message from the other operator) and that of the operational task at hand are the same. For this purpose, the eye tracking method was employed.

Task Oriented Approach to Eye Tracking

In the eye tracking analysis, the frequency of fixation for certain parts of displays are often focused. This is still not sufficient for obtaining detailed information on the operators' cognitive status. For this, the fixation sequence should be traced with consideration of Areas of Interest (AOI). A similar method has been applied in former studies in various areas such as plant operation, flight simulation etc. Information collection is investigated in detail in order to solve the given task. However, in these analyses, interaction with the verbal communication task is not focused. This point is important in the analysis of human behaviour in task accomplishment in a team. Task and communication focused eye movement analysis provides a new component. Eye tracking can then be used to judge the detailed cognitive processes during decisions, dynamic event evolutions or problems with interfaces (Fukuda, 2003).

Subjects

Eight professional operators of one NPP (= professional), eight individuals from a research institute on nuclear safety and seven students of mechanical engineering in Germany (= novice) took part in this experiment. All the novices possess basic knowledge about how a NPP works.

Experimental Method

Figure 4.4 shows the experimental set-up. In the experiment, the transient 'loss of feed water supply' in a boiling water reactor (BWR) was simulated.

The task, to stop the falling of the reactor pressure vessel (RPV) level by checking the system status and executing appropriate measures, has to be performed by the subjects (from now on called operator A). For this purpose, two screens are available for operator A.

LIVERPOOL JOHN MOORES UNIVERSITY
LEARNING SERVICES

Figure 4.4   Experimental set-up: operator A is sitting on the left wearing eye-tracking equipment with operator B as communication partner on the right. The system overview picture is presented on the left large screen and the checklist or measure module table (describing the procedure to proceed) on the right large screen

On the left screen, the user interface of the simulator is provided. The system overview screen (Figure 4.5) offers important system values, a graphic display of the system status, warning signals (indicators of several automatic measures), an indicator of feed water supply and the simulation time.

Trend diagrams of all of the system values are also available by clicking on them with a mouse. To execute a manual measure, operator A has to click on a corresponding button (Figure 4.6). On the right screen, parts of the operation handbook, namely two checklists and five measure modules are available (one example is shown in Figure 4.7).

Warning signals (if they are activated, they turn into yellow)

System value

Indicator of feed water supply (enough: green, lacking: red)

Graphical display of system values

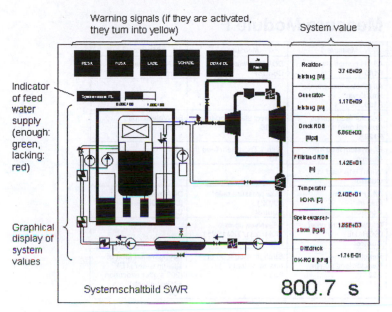

Figure 4.5   System overview screen: the screenshot contains the general cooling circuit of a boiling water reactor

Buttons to execute each measure (if a measure is executed by click on the corresponding button, it turns into yellow)

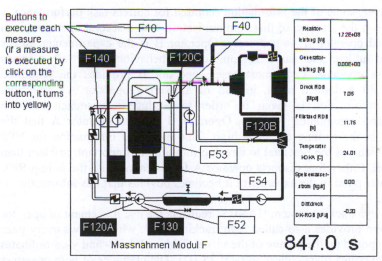

Figure 4.6   Module screen (module F): if necessary, it is displayed over the system summary screen and used for the execution of a manual measure

Measure Module F

Critical value	Measure 1	Measure 2	Measure 3
Fill level RPV > 15.60 m	All TH pumps shut down F140	DDA-feed water Control	DDA-main steam Control
Fill level RPV > 15.45 m	All reactor feed pumps shut down F130		
Fill level RPV > 15.28 m	Reactor feed pumps (except one) shut down F120A	Redirect station open F120B	S/E-Valves open F120C
Fill level RPV < 13.00 m	RL-System feed in? Control	With 1 THSystem feed in F10	
Fill level RPV < 11.80 m	With TH14 feed in Control		
Fill level RPV < 11.00 m	All TH-System feed in Control	Slow pressure relief (LADE) Control	DDA-main steam (DDA-FDL) Control
Fill level RPV < 11.00 m and duration > 200s	Quick pressure relief (SCHADE) Control	S/E-valves open TK41S231/ TK41S211 F40	
Fill level RPV < 11.00 m and duration > 500s	Reactivate Reactor feed pumps F52	Strengthened feed of rinsing water (YT) F53	Strengthened feed of sealing water (TE) (200 s after execution it takes effect!) F54

Figure 4.7   Measure module table. The procedure describes how to deal with inappropriate RPV levels (translated from German)

However, some of the information required for correct task performance is not available on the screens, so that communication with a second operator (from now on called operator B) is necessary. Operator B is the experimenter and is instructed to utilize the same communication behaviour with all subjects performing as operator A. In most cases, operator B provides the requested information. At a defined point, instead of answering operator A's question, incongruent information is given in order to produce a mismatch between operational and communicative tasks. Operator B informs operator A that the radioactivity in the cooling circuit is high. This is critical information for NPP operation, which has the potential to develop into a more important problem than the RPV level. It therefore distracts operator A from dealing with the falling RPV level. At a later point in the experiment it becomes obvious that this information is a false alarm.

The eye tracking system 'JANUS' registers the eye movement of operator A. This system provides a so-called 'eye tracking film', which shows every gaze point superimposed on the picture of the visual field, and the x- and y-co-ordinates of all the gaze points (data collection rate: 25 Hz). The utterance of both operators and operator A's gaze is recorded on the eye tracking film. The operator's observation is also recorded seperately on video for later video confronting.

The transient is considered successfully solved and the simulation finished, if the RPV level rises again. The experiment consisted of the following experimental phases, listed chronologically:

- Normal operation (without any trouble)
- Check of system status using a checklist (directly after the recognition of the transient = detection of decreasing RPV level) by operator A
- Check of system status using a second checklist (in order to decide the measure module to work) by operator Ad
- Dealing with the decreasing RPV level by operator A
- Dealing with additional information on radioactivity provided by operator B
- Identifying that the information on radioactivity is a false alarm generated by the system (notified by operator B)
- Successful accomplishment of the measures to prevent RPV from decreasing by operator A.

An interview is carried out after the simulation in which the recorded eye tracking film is presented to operator A (video confronting method). During the interview, the subjects are asked in particular about the background of behaviour that deviates from the prescription.

The results of this study are presented below. In Chapter 12, further results from this study can be found. For a complete overview of the study see Fukuda & Voggenberger (2004).

Utterance and Behavior towards Incongruent Information

The analysis of utterance and behaviour data shows the mismatch between the current operational task and the information given by communication in 11 per cent of all communication behaviour on the average for both subjects groups.

Subjects reacted to such 'incongruent' information in various manners. As shown in Figure 4.8, in most of the cases, subjects reacted to the given incongruent information immediately both verbally and with related handling. This tendency is especially strong in the case of novices. In contrast, professional operators execute the corresponding procedure more often without saying anything ((3) in Figure 4.8). In the most problematic cases, the subjects reacted neither verbally nor with corresponding handling. Such seeming disregard of given information is observed in 6.79 per cent of the cases with novice subjects and 14.48 per cent of the cases with professional operators ((9) in Figure 4.8). In most of these cases, the subject concentrated on his/her own task, such as handling on the user interface of the simulator, or operator A and operator B spoke simultaneously and unco-ordinatedly.

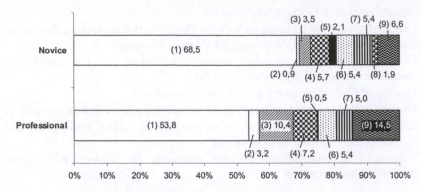

(1) Verbally reacted, correspondingly behaved (immediately)
(2) Verbal reacted, correspondingly behaved with some delay
(3) No verbal reaction, but correspondingly behaved
(4) Verbally reacted, but based on own opinion differently behaved
(5) Given information understood correctly, but difficulty with handling in corresponding procedure
(6) Given information understood correctly, but difficulty with the planning of the corresponding procedures
(7) Given information misunderstood, therefore differently behaved than the expectation based on the regulation
(8) Due to acoustic difficulty requested the information once more
(9) Given information disregarded, continued own task.

Figure 4.8 Observed reaction to incongruent information

With regard to the *produced* incongruent notification of the high radioactivity in the cooling circuit, most of the subjects reacted verbally. Without saying anything, three subjects continued to work on measures to prevent the RPV level from falling. After operator B's repeated suggestion, these subjects finally dealt with the additional task of the radioactivity. Some subjects required a rather long time to perform the corresponding measure, because the given information was completely incongruent with the current task at hand. In these cases, the subjects asked operator B what they should do or argued to continue working on the falling level of RPV before shifting the task. Therefore, they needed more time to deal with the additional problem.

Influence of Incongruent Information on Visual Information Perception

Eye movement data show different patterns depending on the congruence of the given information to the current attention or operational task (see also Chapter 12 for further discussion and related figures on eye tracking). If the information given by a communication partner is congruent with the current operational task, the gaze point stays on the relevant information and the reaction is made quickly. A very quick reaction from subjects was also observed in some cases when there was a mismatch between the utterance and behaviour data. The detailed analysis of eye tracking data shows that a fast reaction was possible in these cases because the gazed information and information given by communication match to a common problem space but do not require a shift to a completely different goal. The fit between the two types of information encourages smooth and quick communication.

In most cases, if incongruent information is given, the gaze point moves to the corresponding element on the screen. For example, if subjects are asked for the current level of RPV after the execution of the corresponding measure, the gaze point moves from the measure module table to the variable indicator or to the trend diagram of the RPV level. The latency for such eye movements varies depending on the handled information or the currently fixated element. The shift of attention can be seen as additional eye movements, which lead to the delayed reaction of operator A.

One further question is whether or not the shift of attention is also observed in cases of seeming disregard for the given information. In fact, the gaze point does not move in many of these cases. Subjects still gaze at the information relevant to their task at a given moment. However, in several cases, the subjects glanced at the relevant information for the new task for a short time. This was observed more frequently in the cases with professional operators. The interview after the experiment clarified that this is a matter of prioritization. If subjects judge their own task at hand as more important than the given information, they continue working on their current task. In such cases, operator B had to remind operator A by repeatedly giving the incongruent information.

Relationship between Communication and Workload

In the experiment, the pupil dilation of the subjects is used as an indicator of the analysis of workload. It has already been confirmed in various studies that pupil dilation increases as the complexity or difficulty of tasks and mental workload increases (Rößger et al., 1993; Hyönä et al., 1995; Van Orden et al., 2001). In particular, no specific influence of light changes may impair the quality of this measure for workload in computerized control room settings (e.g., Rößger et al., 1993, Low, 2003). A comparison of the experimental phases reveals clear differences in pupil dilation. The most prominent difference is observed before and after the recognition of the transient. In this situation, the difference in task load is obvious: before the recognition of the transient, it is normal operation. After the recognition of the transient, corresponding measures that are in accordance with the operational handbook (realized as the measure module table) should be accomplished, and this results in higher task load than in normal operation. In addition, the situational pressure becomes higher in this situation. Therefore, the subjects have higher workload after the recognition of a transient. A similar effect is also demonstrated by the fact that the notification of high radioactivity in the cooling circuit means the assignment of an additional task. In this experimental phase, the effect is clearly shown by novice subjects but not by professional operators. It can be concluded that the experience obviously influences the workload.

The increased workload decreases again in the course of time. The subjects become accustomed to the new situation, and the workload gradually diminishes.

Essential Issues: Communication Problems in NPP Operation

The analysis of utterance, behaviour and eye tracking data revealed the influence of congruence between the operational task and the communicative task on the quality of group interaction. The mismatch or incongruence between two types of information requires additional demand in cognition and communication and also leads to the delay in the corresponding handling.

What is more critical is the disregard of information by the communication partner. If the addressee concentrates on his/her own task, or if two or more people speak simultaneously, the given information is often not regarded by the addressee. If the crucial information for the handling of the transient is disregarded, it can lead to serious trouble. This is apparently related to the limited resources for information processing. In order to avoid such situations, the timing of communication should be considered.

Further problems in communication were observed in seeming disregard of given information. Although the addressee perceives the information from the speaker, he/she reacts neither verbally nor with any particular action. In such cases, the speaker cannot know whether the information has been perceived or not. Additional communication is required in order to confirm that the addressee has clearly perceived the information. For secure effective communication, the verbal reaction is very important. If the addressee reacts to the given information only by handling, this reaction may possibly be overlooked or not observable to the speaker. The most reliable way to confirm the reaction is with verbal feedback.

In real NPP operation, the tasks are allocated to several operators and each operator has different information sources. Communication is the only way to share the necessary information with other operators. From this point of view, good communication is always required. Overview-displays may help in sharing information and facilitating communication, co-ordination and co-operative problem solving in multi-person teams. In other words, they support the situation awareness of individuals and teams (Roth et al., 1998).

Perspectives on the Process Control Group's Results

The *Process Control Group* analyzed communication problems in nuclear power plants in regards to two aspects: event analysis from real operation and empirical simulation study. The results provide a number of insights into both language processing and the way to integrate research and regulatory requirements.

Language Processing Insights

With regard to language and communicative behaviour, the eye tracking data and the task-oriented areas of interest approach provide further proofs for observed behaviour. This approach complements the approaches developed in the other GIHRE groups, in particular the protocol analysis methods developed in the *Linguistic Factors Group* and the *Language Processing Group*. For instance, the issue about turn taking was investigated in these projects. Eye tracking data in the NPP simulator study of the *Process Control Group* clearly showed that the operator's attention does not shift if the turn taking is not successfully accomplished and the two operators speak simultaneously. Eye movement as a part of non-verbal communication is, therefore, a complementary method that reveals further insights into this issue (see further discussion in Chapter 12)

Integration of Research and Regulatory Requirements

The approach followed in the *Process Control Group* was driven by the specific constrains present in any human factors (HF) related study. An approach for overcoming such constraints is given in Figure 4.9.

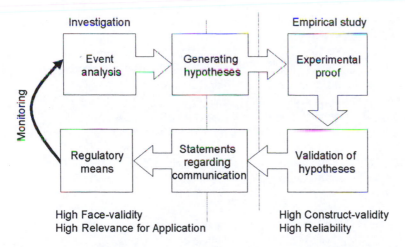

Figure 4.9   Integrating research and regulatory requirements

Any HF approach has limitations for investigating HF aspects and communication problems. Incidents show communication problems during abnormal situations but are limited in details regarding cognitive aspects. Observational field studies are lacking those abnormal situations in which communication is safety relevant, and though experimental studies can simulate abnormal events, their transferability to real operation is usually brought into question because experiments are lacking the real threats that operators may be exposed to in real accidents.

The *Process Control Group* was able to overcome the limitations of the different approaches by combining the advantages from the different approaches. As Figure 4.9 indicates, hypotheses for the experimental study were derived from incident data, which are of high relevance in the application of regulatory means. The results of the experiment provide validated and reliable statements about communication problems, their contextual conditions and the cognitive activities involved. Therefore, the approach has the advantage of including incidents to provide high face validity while experiments provide a high construct validity and reliability.

This can lead to new safety regulations more than any single method could. It also combines well with other experimental studies in GIHRE that deal with regulatory tasks. Chapter 12 describes how other experimental settings complement the findings derived from the eye tracking study and how investigations can be mutually exchanged across industries (e.g. from aviation to nuclear and vice versa). In this way, the GIHRE project's work suggests a new way of integrating HF into safety management.

Chapter 5

Linguistic Factors

Manfred Krifka, Silka Martens and Florian Schwarz

General Objectives

The general topic of this book is interaction among members of high risk teams. Linguistic communication is an important part of this interaction, and in addition, reflects many of its non-linguistic aspects. In line with this, the objective of the *Linguistic Factors Group* was to identify properties of linguistic communication that correlate with task load and performance in crews that are facing complex and potentially dangerous tasks. This project concentrated, in particular, on communication in the cockpit of commercial aircraft. The aircraft cockpit has been the classical object of study in Crew Resource Management (cf. Helmreich 1997); the current goal was to look specifically into linguistic patterns of behavior that influence the ways in which crews handle tasks, over and above the social factors investigated in CRM. A practical reason for this choice was that relevant data was available from the onset from the *Threat/ Error Group* and would later be collected by other subprojects. GIHRE members provided the expert knowledge necessary for an appropriate analysis of communication in a technical domain. Without this synergism, the work of the *Linguistic Factors Group* would not have been possible.

Communication in the cockpit has been investigated from different angles and with different methods. In a well-known study, Cushing (1994) identified properties of aviation language that caused problems, using accident reports of the National Transportation and Safety Board (NTSB) mainly based on cockpit voice recorder data, and the professional pilot magazine *Callback*. Typically, these are problems relating to ambiguity and vagueness of natural language that are aggravated under conditions in the cockpit. Linde (1988) has investigated communication behavior with respect to the asymmetric social situation in the cockpit, with a captain that has the power of command, and typically has more experience than the first officer, using NTSB accident reports. Other work on cockpit communication that concentrates on the social cline in the cockpit and works with accident reports include Orasanu & Fischer (1992) and, as a result of GIHRE, Grommes & Dietrich (2000) and Silberstein (2001). Nevile (2001) analyses communication in routine flights, and Fischer & Orasanu (1999) evaluate the judgements of pilots who were presented with a written scenario and various possible verbal reactions from a co-pilot in the scenario.

The *Linguistic Factors Group* followed authors like Linde (1988) in investigating ongoing conversation, rather than specific structural features of language. But it worked with data acquired in situations that were better controlled than real-life incidents. This called for the use of experimental data, which can be gained by observing the communication behavior of crews in flight simulators. The advantage of this method is that the level and quality of task load can be varied to satisfy the specific demands of the investigation. Of course, simulated flights are not the real thing; they cannot create the emotional pressure of situations in which the lives of passengers and of pilots themselves are at stake. But flight simulators do a very good job in mimicking reality; they are used extensively in instruction and training, and they are important instruments for professional evaluation. Severe mistakes in simulator flights may result in the revocation of pilot licenses (this did not occur in the flights observed and analyzed by this research group). Therefore, simulator flights should have the required ecological validity to be relevant for real flight situations.

The hope is that this investigation of communication in teams facing situations of high task load and potential danger will lead to at least two types of practical applications. First, certain features of linguistic communication might turn out to be diagnostics for particular types of crews or task loads. For example, there is evidence that members of well-performing crews more often refer to their crew using pronouns like *we*, and that communication density increases with high workload. While such markers may be used in the evaluation of crews, they probably should not be the targets of explicit training; a bad crew won't become better after they are instructed to use the first person plural pronoun more often. Secondly, there may be features of linguistic communication that are directly responsible for better crew performances, and such features may actually be accessible to explicit training.

Methodology

As for the theoretical framework, there were a number of choices, in particular *Speech Act Theory* and *Conversation Analysis* (see Chapter 9 on structural features of language and language use for further discussion). Conversation Analysis, as initiated by Harvey Sacks (cf. Sacks 1992, Hutchby & Wooffitt 2001), has developed ways of transcribing conversation in minute detail and of analyzing it in objective ways, without recurrence to the intentions of the participants. Phenomena like the introduction, continuation and uptake of topics of conversation, the negotiation of turn taking between participants, the methods of repairing utterances and, in general, the sequencing of contributions are crucial for the conversation analyst. Speech Act Theory, as initiated by John Austin and John Searle (cf. Searle 1969, 1975, Vanderveken 1990), started out by observing that speakers do not only state what they believe to be true when they speak, but they also perform socially relevant acts, like commands, permissions, promises, apologies, insults or even more specific acts like hiring a person or declaring an emergency. Speech acts can change the general structure of social rights and obligations, as when a teacher asks a student to read a poem or a shop owner states what customers have to pay for a pound of apples. Conversely, they can be part of a more complex communicative interaction, directly relating to preceding or subsequent speech acts, as with questions that request an answer or acknowledgements that express understanding of, or agreement with, a previous utterance. Traditionally, speech act theory is characterized by a more deductive, rather than empirical, research methodology. But there are a number of promising empirical studies, e.g. the study of class room communication by Diegritz & Fürst (1999) or the analysis of mitigation and reinforcement of Sbisa (2001), that show that versions of speech act theory can be fruitfully applied in the analysis of real communication events. Speech act theory was first developed by philosophers of language, and therefore it reasons from the intentions of speakers, which are officially off limits for the behavioral approach of conversation analysis. But arguably, insightful analysis of communication must also refer to speakers' intentions. Speech act theory often looks at utterances in isolation, but there is no reason why one could not analyze speech act sequences, the conditions under which a certain speech act can occur and the effect a speech act has on speech acts that possibly follow. In Searle's theory, speech acts are partly characterized by so-called preparatory conditions; it is easily conceivable to integrate conditions referring to the speech acts uttered before.

The *Linguistic Factors Group* primarily based its study on a refined and extended version of speech act theory. Conversation analysis certainly leads to deep insights into particular conversational interactions, and it may be very useful in illustrating good and bad communication for the instruction of pilots. But it was not obvious how such qualitative studies of particular interactions could be convincingly related to task load and crew performance in general, as bad communication occurs in well-performing crews, and good communication also occurs in poorly performing crews. Speech act theory, on the other hand, seemed to be better suited for establishing quantitative correlation between the incidence of particular speech act types with task load level and crew performance. But it was clear that the usual inventory of speech acts found in the literature had to be considerably refined, and the methods of assigning speech acts had to be objectified.

A First Application of Speech Act Theory to Cockpit Talk

The *Linguistic Factors Group* had two stages of research.[18] The first investigation was based on the transcripts of flight simulator recordings on B-727 aircraft of a study on the effect of captain personality on crew performance carried out by NASA-Ames Research Center in 1987 (see Chapter 2 and Chidester ea. (1990) for

---

[18] In the first phase, the *Linguistic Factors Group* research was carried out at the Department of Linguistics at the University of Texas at Austin, with Manfred Krifka (principal investigator) and Carrie Clarady (research assistant). A more detailed report of the first project phase of the Linguistic Factors Group is included in Krifka, Martens and Schwarz (2003).

a description). There were three pilots in each crew (captain, first officer and engineer). The transcripts of the video and audio recordings were done under the supervision of Robert L. Helmreich and J. Bryan Sexton of the *Threat/Error Group*.

The advantage of this set of data was, beyond its ready availability, that the flights followed a similar scenario of different task loads and that the crew members' performance and aviation experts independently rated the crew. The *Linguistic Factors Group* investigated five flight simulator sessions completely; the two best-rated crews and the three worst rated crews were selected, a total of about seven hours of flight time, or 6900 *thought units*. The data set analyzed here is a subset of the one that was analyzed by Sexton & Helmreich (2001), using the *Linguistic Inquiry and Word Count* (LIWC) program (see Chapter 1).

The main analytic efforts went into the classification of thought units in specific speech act categories. It soon became evident that the repertoire of speech act types provided by the literature (e.g. Searle 1975 or Vanderveken 1990) was partly too general and partly too specific for the purposes of this research. A system with 13 distinct types was developed, in particular *status reports*, which report on the current state of equipment, weather, location, etc.; *reports of action*, in which the speaker gives a report of his/her own actions; *reports of reports*, which rephrase information expressed before; *prognoses* about the likely future course of events; *diagnoses*, which are concerned with the likely cause of past events; *commands* and *permissions*, by which one crew member can directly influence the actions of others; *complies*, which verbalize actions that are performed to carry out a command; *reports of intention,* which express the intention to act in a certain way; *expressives*, which express an emotion and three types of acknowledging speech acts: simple *acknowledgments, affirmations* and *rephrases*.

This classification combines speech act types with content features (e.g. status reports, prognoses, diagnoses are all assertive speech acts that differ in their content). The last three categories, which are concerned with the proper flow of information in conversation, are often neglected in speech act theory, but they are of importance in the present context, as many turn takes belong to such regulating acts. Also, questions and answers were treated orthogonally to this classification, as they can be related to assertive speech acts like status reports or to commands. For example, *You got any problems?* was classified as a Status report / Question, and *You want me to brief with you?* as a Command / Question. A tricky problem with speech act theory is that the linguistic form often does not determine the speech act type; for example, commands can be expressed directly with an imperative (*Get the landing gear down!*), or more indirectly with a modal declarative statement (*We should get the landing gear down*) or a question (*Why don't you get the landing gear down?*). Thought units were generally classified according to the intended speech act, not the linguistic form, which involves reconstructing the intentions of speakers. This is generally avoided in the alternative theory of Conversation Analysis. Only very indirect speech acts that require inferencing (e.g. *The landing gear isn't down*) would be classified directly (here, as a status report).

In addition to speech act types, other features were recorded, in particular explicit reference to the group by expressions like *we, us, let's*, correction of previous information, evidence for misunderstanding, hesitations (insofar as they were recorded in the transcripts), hedges like *sort of, I think*; encouragement, emotional words and politeness phenomena. Also, the length of thought units, the speakers and the intended addressee were determined.

With five crews and four segments per group analyzed, it was not possible to achieve any level of statistical significance in these observations. But a number of observations could be interpreted and may be used as hypotheses for further research:

- There were more utterances per minute in the segments of high workload, and the utterances were longer, leading to a substantial difference of speech time per minute. This suggests that communication density could be used to measure particular types of workload. There was no clear relation to the performance level of crews;
- While the captain assumed the speaker role most often (typically, about 40 per cent of the time), the engineer assumed the role of speaker more often in high task load segments;
- Prognoses and diagnoses are more frequent in good crews;
- Reports of intention are more frequent in the good crews and in segments of high task load;
- More questions were answered in the good crews, suggesting a more coherent style of communication;
- Commands occurred more frequently in the poor crews and so did complies (overt linguistic verbalizations that commands are carried out);
- As for the speech act types that acknowledge or confirm another speech act, there were more simple acknowledgements in the good crews, and fewer in the segments with high task load;
- Expressive speech acts and emotion words occurred more frequently in the poor crews;
- Linguistic evidence for misunderstandings was found in one poor crew;
- Hesitations occurred slightly more frequently with the poor crews. In these crews, the incidence of both hesitations and hedges increased with high task load;
- Politeness elements occurred slightly more often in good crews. Interestingly, good crews had fewer politeness elements in segments of high task load, just the opposite of poor crews;
- As for explicit reference to the group, a potential group-building measure, Sexton & Helmreich (2001) found that reference to the group increases over a crew's life and that captains use more reference to crews than first officers or engineers;
- Encouragements could be found more frequently in the best-performing crew, and was absent in the worst performing crew.

While the first project phase led to some interesting preliminary results, it was also clear that it could be improved in a number of ways. The classification of segments as normal task load/high task load turned out to be too coarse-grained. The scenarios of the simulation flights were not constrained enough to secure comparability between the flights. The quality of the transcripts used was uneven, and, in general, lack of access to the original data was a problem, as intonational features, which might have been relevant for the speech act analysis, were lacking. Information about the flight scenario was rather limited, and there were no means for large-scale testing of interrater reliability. Additionally, it turned out that the speech act classification was not fine grained enough; quite a few intuitively important distinctions were covered by rather general categories like *status report*.

Speech Acts in Cockpit Talk: A Refined Study

In the second phase of research, the *Linguistics Factors Group* could improve on the nature of the data, its collection and the theoretical concepts used for data analysis.[19] The study used new simulator data with a much more tightly controlled scenario that was developed by Gerhard Fahnenbruck and his colleagues and carried out by Lufthansa CityLine on a CanadAir Regional Jet simulator. The scenario stressed communicative interaction; for example, different instrument failures occurred on the displays of captain and first officer, requiring constant negotiations between the pilots to find out what was going on and to keep one another updated about any changes.[20] There was direct access to audio and video data, including video data collected with frontal cameras, which made a close transcription possible since the movements of the lips could be followed and many

---

[19] This phase of research took place at the Institute for German Language and Linguistics at the Humboldt University, Berlin. Principal investigator was Manfred Krifka, with Silka Martens and Florian Schwarz as investigators.

[20] The scenario consists of three parts: first, a so-called circling approach in which the runway has to be approached with the wind from behind due to an instrumental landing system (ILS) failure on the ground. With the runway in sight, the crew has to circle around the airport in preparation for landing. The pilots have to brief and prepare for this particular type of approach. When they are about to land, another plane is blocking the runway and the crew has to fly a go around. In the second phase that begins at this point, the ILS has been repaired and a normal approach to the runway can be flown. During the approach, however, the glide slope, a part of the instrumental landing system, breaks down at 1500 feet. Constant communication about the altitude both within the crew and with the tower is necessary in order to be able to land under these conditions. After the landing, the third section starts with a take-off. Shortly after the plane is in the air, and while it is in the clouds, an instrument failure related to the artificial horizon occurs on both sides: the pitch component (which indicates whether the nose of the plane is pointing up or down) on the captain's side and the roll component (which indicates whether the wings are level) on the first officer's side display incorrect values, the failure on the captain's side being far more dangerous. This section is especially interesting from a linguistic point of view, as there is an increased need for communication in order to exchange the correct values of the defective instruments.

utterance parts that would otherwise have been unintelligible (in particular given the background noise of the simulator) could be tracked in detail.

The transcription was done following the conventions of GAT (a German acronym for 'Conversation-Analytic Transcription system') described in Selting e.a. (1998). This format comprises proposals for the general structure and layout of transcripts and for the notation of segmental, prosodic and non-verbal phenomena. Two flights were transcribed fully and six flights in three selected parallel segments. These three segments were analyzed for eight flights, for which three well-performing crews, three average crews and two poorly performing crews were selected. The crew ratings, as well as the ratings of the pilots, were done independently following LOSA and NOTECHS (cf. *Behavioral Markers Group*, Chapter 2) and were not known during this analysis.

In a number of ways, the newly collected data was not easily comparable with the data used in the first project phase. The aircraft was smaller, the crews were smaller (reflecting the elimination of flight engineers on most commercial aircraft), the scenarios were shorter and the cultural background and the language of the pilots were different (German, with many English phrases and terms). Also, it was not evident how to identify passages of low, medium or high task load; the relatively short simulation flights were typically in the range of medium to high task load, with variation in the type of task load for different crew members in different segments. For example, in the third segment, there is a high mental task load for the pilot non-flying, as she/he has to analyze a complex problem, whereas there is a high manual task load for the pilot flying in the first segment, as she/he will typically fly without the autopilot. So, the main focus concentrated on the correlation of markers of linguistic communication with the performance ratings of the crews, rather than on correlation with task load. The inventory of speech acts was also substantially revised, mainly under the influence of the study of Diegritz & Fürst (1999), which was designed to analyze communication between teachers and students in the classroom. These authors have also developed a method of identifying speech act types, *Qualitative Verlaufsanalyse*, or *qualitative progress analysis*, which rigorously requires the researcher to pay attention to a number of factors, including the preceding and following context in which a speech act is uttered. Thus, in a sense, they combine techniques of Conversation Analysis and Speech Act Theory and are inspired by other methods, such as interaction analysis.

The speech act inventory was also developed largely on Diegritz & Fürst. This inventory, called STACK for (a German acronym for *Speech act Type-inventory for the Analysis of Cockpit Communication*), is considerably more fine-grained than the one used in the first project phase; it uses about 70 distinct categories. The inventory is listed in Appendix VI, together with short descriptions and some examples. The working descriptions include many more examples and are explicit about the features that distinguish between similar speech act types. The narrow definition of speech acts types, together with the structured method to assign speech act types to utterances, raised the reliability in assigning types considerably. All segments were rated by three researchers independently and achieved a high level of consistency. The fine mesh used bears the risk that any given category has only few members in it. But if required, distinct categories can be combined later for analysis, as has been done extensively here. To illustrate, consider the following transcription of a conversation between captain and first officer in which timing and pauses are indicated together with the classification. The signs (?), (,) and (.) indicate high rising, rising and falling intonation, and (hh) indicates audible breathing.

Cpt:	*so.*	STRUCTURE
Cpt:	*wie weit sin mer?*	QUESTION (INFORM)
	'how far are we?'	
Cpt:	*flaps ham wir twenty.*	STATE
	'as for flaps, we have 20.'	
F/O:	*ja*	AGREE
	'yes'	
F/O:	*dann warten wa bis auf n intercept*	SUGGEST
	'then we wait till (we get) the intercept'	
Cpt:	*weißte wir sollten alles raussetzen,*	REJECT PROPOSAL
	gear down und flaps thirty.	
	'you know we should everything ready,	
	gear down and flaps thirty'	
Cpt:	*dann ham wa das schon*	JUSTIFY
	'then we're already done with that'	
Cpt:	*is keen problem für uns*	CLAIM
	'that's not a problem for us'	
Cpt:	*okay?*	REQUEST REPLY
F/O:	*hh hmm*	DELIBERATE
F/O:	*ich bin mir nich sicher ehrlich gesagt.*	OBJECT
	'I'm not so sure, frankly.'	
F/O:	*aber gut. versuchn wa s mal*	CONCEDE
	'but o.k, let's try it.'	

Figure 5.1 Transcription of conversation between captain and first officer

Parsing utterances into speech acts and classifying the speech act, follows certain rules called *Qualitative Progress Analysis* (Qualitative Verlaufsanalyse). Take the captain's first three utterances as an example: *so. wie weit sin mer? flaps ham wir twenty*. In a first step, the sequence is described rather informally, using all available information. Here, one observes that after initiating the utterance with the particle *so*, the captain utters a question with rising intonation. Directly following this, as the captain is looking at the instrument panel, he utters a statement with strongly rising intonation. In a second step, the sequence is partitioned into speech acts; here, there are three acts: *so / wie weit sin mer? / flaps ham wir twenty*. Now, look back at the context in which the sequence was uttered. Due to an instrument failure, the first officer had informed the captain that he could only fly in stand-by mode. The captain agreed that it would be best not to split up the tasks but to let the first officer fly alone in stand-by mode. The captain remarks that he can still help a little bit. In the next step, the three speech acts are paraphrased. *So*: 'We have made it clear how we will proceed.' *Wie weit sin mer?* 'Let us check out the current state to see how far we are in respect to the planned approach with the instrument failure.' *Flaps ham wir twenty*: 'I go ahead and check the flaps, which are twenty.' The next step concerns the so-called perlocutionary effects that the speech acts are intended to produce. The immediate intended effect is that the first officer agrees, which he indeed does, cf. the confirming *ja*. Now consider the general development present in this part of the conversation. Observe that the captain marks a thematic break by ending the previous sequence of clarification of how to proceed and goes on to tackle important parts of the problem himself. One can also observe that the captain integrates the first officer actively and in a co-operative way in the problem solving process by asking himself and the first officer, and partially answering the question himself. The assignment of speech act types (for definitions, see Chapter 9) is now rather obvious: *So* is of the type STRUCTURE, a structuring signal, meaning 'I indicate that the previous discussion is over and that I am about to start a new speech-act sequence.' *Wie weit sin mer?* is a QUESTION related to factual INFORMATION: 'I ask you and myself about the current state of events.' *Flaps ham wir twenty* is a speech act that gives information; in this case, the information could have been obtained by the addressee himself, as well as by looking at the instrument panel, which qualifies this as being speech act type POINT OUT.

The main results, at the time of this writing, are the following:

- First, good crews talked more. This was true in particular for the absolute number of words and speech acts, and to a lesser degree for words per second and for speech acts per minute. (Good crews granted themselves more time altogether in critical situations);

- In particular, first officers of well-performing crews talked more than first officers of poorly performing crews, which probably reflects a less biased situation in the cockpit;

- Captains, in general, talked more, but there was no correlation between the number of words spoken and their performance;

- Pilots flying talked less than pilots non-flying, as expected. But the pilot flying tended to talk more in the good crews investigated, which is somewhat surprising because one might think that speaking during high task load creates an extra burden that should be kept on to a minimal level (see Chapter 7);

- For the whole crew, speech acts that seek reassurance occurred more frequently in the good crews, and so did positive speech acts of agreement or negotiation, like acknowledgments and affirmations;

- Reminders that draw attention to things supposed to be already known occurred more frequently in the poor crews;

- Acts of indicating interest and affirming acts were typical for good captains. Obviously, good captains were more encouraging towards contributions from their first officers, which goes along with the fact that first officers talk more in these crews;

- Dissenting speech acts were slightly more frequent with the poorly performing captains;
- Somewhat surprisingly, the use of standard wording by the captain was clearly negatively related to performance. A possible reason is that standard wording, despite its benefits, can be used to mask communication deficiencies;
- Informative speech acts were found more often with captains that performed poorly. It is unclear how to interpret this; perhaps those captains were not sufficiently aware of the information state of their first officers;
- Good first officers uttered more claims, guesses and explications. They seemed to be more active in presenting their own thoughts and assumptions and appeared to have an easier time thinking out loud;
- Surprisingly, the good first officers uttered acknowledgments less frequently. It is unclear why this would be so.

Correlations with respect to the pilot flying and the pilot non-flying were also sought after. In only five of the eight crews were the roles maintained during the entire part of the scenario considered; in the other three cases, the ratings were adjusted as to how much time the captain and the first officer spent in either role, and by then taking the proportion to calculate the rating.

- The pilot flying of well-performing crews uttered fewer questions that asked what to do. It might be more evident for them, or the crews may maintain a better common ground in general, which would make such questions unnecessary;
- The good pilots flying made fewer proposals of how to act, which may be due to the fact that they leave this to the pilot non-flying, who can dedicate more cognitive resources to it;
- The good pilots flying uttered more interaction markers, indicating that they organize the conversation well. This might be related to the fact that they have to cope with a dual task situation and that in this situation communication is most manageable if it is well organized;
- The pilot non-flying of well-performing crews more often uttered speech acts of agreement or negotiation, like acknowledgements and affirmations. They also made more proposals and asked what they should do. Furthermore, they answered questions more frequently.

In both studies, captains talked more than other crew members. In general, acknowledgements were found in good crews in the Austin data, but in the Berlin data set there was a difference between captains and first officers: good captains uttered more affirmative responses, whereas good first officers uttered fewer acknowledgements. The correlation between the use of crew reference by words like *we* and crew performance did not show up in the Berlin data.

Outlook

The research reported here has shown that speech act theory can be used to gain useful insights into the dynamics of communication in aircraft crews and perhaps in teams in general. While the numbers of cases were too small to gain a level of statistical significance, they allow for the formation of hypotheses for future research.

Some of the results may lead to new behavioral markers for the analysis of crews. A particularly promising candidate here is the proportion of questions that are answered, which appears to be higher with good crews. Other results suggest that particular communicative skills should be developed in instruction and training. In particular, captains should encourage team member contribution, and good first officers should make more claims of their own, even if they are just good guesses. In general, members of crews should report their intentions in order to allow other crew members to participate in their thought process.

Chapter 6

Language Processing

Rainer Dietrich, Patrick Grommes and Sascha Neuper[21]

The Research Field

Language is the most efficient method of human communication. All people learned a language in the first four to five years of their lives and practiced it for hours and years on end every day, and, so, became highly trained experts in language use. Verbal communication is fast compared to the Morse code, simple in terms of additional technical equipment, extremely adaptable to different kinds of channels, media and situational conditions. Language processing is sturdy and secure. There is, on average, one error per thousand executions of a production procedure.

Communication is subject to an abundant number and variety of research activities, beginning over 2500 years ago with Panini's description of Sanskrit morphology and certainly not ending with today's functional magnetic resonance imaging of the language faculty in the brain. The investigation of communication under conditions of high risk, time pressure and task load is systematically located at the intersection of three fields of research: the social-psychological investigation of communicative interaction, the psycholinguistics of language production and understanding and the cognitive psychology of dual task performance.

Social-Psychology of Communicative Interaction

The focus of the social-psychological investigation from the language processing perspective is focused on linguistically evident features of the team members' behavior under conditions of increasing task load.

When asked about the effects of time pressure on his communicative behavior, an air traffic controller, whose exposure to high workload conditions is similar to that of pilots, spontaneously answered: 'I talk faster, a lot faster – I talk so fast that they have to slow me down because they don't understand me any more.' In addition to the accelerated rate of speech, another obvious effect of high workload is the shortening of utterances. Just a superficial look at cockpit voice recorder transcripts reveals that under conditions of stress the utterances become

[21] Contributions from Christine Janka, Katja Kühn, Maren Peters and the continuous technical support from Guido Kiecker are gratefully acknowledged.

shorter and that more reduced linguistic structures are used than under normal conditions.

In addition to this anecdotal evidence, experimental work has shown that language processing can be seriously impaired under conditions of high cognitive workload. Blackwell and Bates (1995), for example, show that normal subjects display agrammatic profiles under a dual task condition, which is a very disturbing finding, in particular with regards to the importance of communication when dealing with dangerous situations in high risk environments like the cockpit of an airplane – compare Sexton & Helmreich (1999) who show that the more the crew members communicate the better they perform.[22]

The importance of communication for efficiency and safety in aviation has been recognized for a long time. In the 1970s, several accidents occurred that were mainly related to crew co-ordination, communication and team-building factors in the cockpit, e.g. the crash of Eastern Airlines Flight 401 into the Everglades during its approach to Miami International Airport in 1972. Another key accident was the crash of United Airlines Flight 173 in Portland, Oregon in 1978. In this accident, the poor use of crew resources played a crucial role. Because of a malfunction of the landing-gear warning system, preparation for an emergency landing preoccupied the captain and, despite warnings from other crew members about the low fuel level, he delayed the landing. The airplane crashed because of total fuel exhaustion, but a contributing factor was 'the failure of the other two flight crew members either to fully comprehend the criticality of the fuel state or to successfully communicate their concern to the captain' (Kanki & Palmer (1993, p.101).

These two accidents contributed to a re-evaluation of cockpit organization. As a result, the US National Transportation Safety Board (NTSB) has increasingly paid attention to the possible impact of crew communication and crew co-ordination on accident patterns. Increased efforts have been undertaken to raise the safety level by developing the concept of Crew Resource Management (CRM) – a specific training program that focuses on interpersonal and communication skills.[23] The increased interest in language-related issues has led to a still growing volume of studies that investigate communication processes in the cockpit.[24]

Psycholinguistics of Communication

Speaking is more than the physical activity of structured expiration and movement of the vocal chords, the tongue and the lips. Speaking is, in the first place, a complex cognitive activity comprising separate, yet hierarchically structured and interconnected subsystems of information processing. The highest system is the (non-verbal) system of communication planning. In dyadic conversation, things are

---

[22] The existence of a correlation between the amount of communication and performance was first suggested by Foushee and Manos (1981) who found that better performing crews communicate more overall.

[23] For a description of CRM see Helmreich and Foushee (1993) and Chapter 2.

[24] A recent collection of relevant papers can be found in Dietrich (2003).

even more complex in that each communication partner has the additional task of switching roles between speaker and listener in an organic and socially controlled and adjusted way. Each interlocutor has, accordingly, to carry out three major linguistic activities more or less in parallel:

- Keeping track of the complex subject matter as has been developed in the preceding phases of the discourse (understanding);
- Linking his/her new contribution coherently to the point actually being treated in the flow of consciousness. This can be done by leaving it unchanged or by shifting it to a new question. In the latter case, this has to be semantically related to the previous stretch of the discourse. Here, these alternatives will be called the *maintenance* and the *shift* of the conversational flow (coherent turn taking);
- Planning his/her own contribution to the discourse and coding it by the use of linguistic means that have to be carefully chosen to convey the message to the addressee and to fit the situational parameters (speaking).

A comprehensive analysis of the situational conditions and the related forms and features of language in use is found in Clark 1996. Grommes and Dietrich 2002 have proposed an integrated model of the prerequisites and the features involved in successful coherent turn taking.

Cognitive Psychology of Dual Task Performance

Being the most important method of information interchange, verbal communication is also a highly suitable instrument for the continuous co-ordination of primary tasks executed by co-operating members of a team. Typical examples are operating on a tumor, driving a high-speed rally car from Paris to Dakar, or fighting a huge fire in a big chemical plant. Not all sorts of primary tasks are easy to combine with language processing. Decision making is a prime sample of cognitive activities that cannot always easily combine with language processing. Denis Davis, Deputy Chief Officer of the Cheshire Fire Brigade at the time of the great Ellesmore Port-fire, put it this way: 'all of these considerations [supplying information technology, risk assessment, responding to political requirements, etc.] were made in stressful situations in incident centers [...] where questions were constantly being asked which required urgent if not immediate responses' (Davis 2002, p.102).

People's ability (or inability) to process different cognitive tasks at the same time is an issue of psychological research and a question of considerable practical relevance. 'Human performance limits have played an important role in catastrophes that have occurred in aviation and other fields' (Pashler & Johnston 1998, p.155). Roughly speaking, there are two clusters of theories about human attentional capacities and limitations, the *resource* and the *time-sharing* theories.[25]

---

[25] More background and more details are presented in the introductory paragraphs of Chapter 12.

The task load capacities of different forms of question answering in dual task situations were analyzed experimentally.

Aims and Objectives, Methods, Data and Sample Results

This section starts with a short overview of the specific issues in this investigation. The methods and data part describes broadly the leading methodological principles and includes illustrations. Results are summed up in the question answering part of Chapter 12. The end of the section will provide possible conclusions about the results of this research group within the larger context of the other GIHRE research groups.

Social-Psychology of Communicative Interaction

Aims and objectives The ultimate goal of aviation-related communication research is to apply theoretical findings to the real aviation world in order to improve safety. In other words, its aim is to 'enable researchers, trainers, line pilots, government regulators, engineers, and designers to make recommendations that enhance the safe and efficient operation of aircraft' (Kanki & Palmer, 1993, p.126). This application perspective includes the aspect of developing training patterns for aviation personnel – an aspect that constitutes a fundamental objective for researchers from the psychologically oriented approach. Their studies try to crystallize those communication patterns that are associated with effective CRM principles, and they aim at transforming these findings into training programs. These studies presuppose that effective communication patterns can be trained. But they do not take the impact of stress on human ability to communicate into consideration. Up to now, it has not been clear how stress affects the ability to communicate and whether or not it impedes trained patterns. The exact character of natural limitations, which might inhibit human beings from communicating reliably under growing pressure, is not well enough known. In order to draft appropriate training programs, there is not only a need for a fuller understanding of which communication skills should be trained but also a need for more knowledge about whether they can be trained at all.

Therefore, a different perspective is taken here: linguistic performance is investigated and described under varying degrees of stress in order to find out if linguistic patterns change in relation to the amount of workload. The goal is to learn more about the effects of stress on the underlying mechanisms of communication. In order to achieve this goal, the following questions should be considered:

- How does linguistic interaction vary in relation to the level of workload? Which elements of the utterances and which mechanisms of language production persist and which are eliminated under the conditions of high workload and danger?
- What do the linguistic form and the content of samples of communicative utterances under different degrees of task load say about the crew members' performance in non-verbal domains like situational awareness, crew resource management and emotional affectedness?

Methods and data For the most part, communication research in aviation is not interested in language as such, but rather in the social dimension of communication and the psychological categories behind actual language use. Communication patterns are interpreted as indicators of social aspects of behavior, for instance, as an indicator of a person's role, focus of attention and so on. In addition to the social component, this kind of research is also related to performance. It investigates which communicative patterns contribute to effective teamwork and whether differences in crew performance are reflected by particular communication patterns. One typical example of this approach is a study conducted by Kanki, Palmer & Veinott (1991), that analyzes the links between a captain's personality, communication and team performance.[26] This direction of research is called the psychologically oriented approach.[27] Steven Cushing takes a different approach. He is interested in the actual structural properties of language itself that might lead to misunderstandings, especially in situations of high cognitive workload. Cushing (1994) analyzes language-related misunderstandings in air-ground communication that have been a crucial contributing factor in aviation accidents. This direction of research could be called the linguistically oriented approach. The present study is indebted to both approaches.

As Kanki & Palmer (1993) point out, cockpit voice recorder (CVR) data are a valuable source for communication research. Being real-time accounts of unfolding events, they are a primary resource for learning what occurs in an accident sequence, and they often reveal what went wrong during the flight. The analysis of CVR data identifies critical communication problem areas: 'the communications contained in CVR data have pointed to a wide range of CRM problems related to command authority, maintenance of vigilance, monitoring and cross-checking, briefings, planning, and crisis management in addition to assertiveness and participative management' (Kanki & Palmer 1993, p.102).

Taking this into account, authentic CVR data was used, thus providing, at the same time, a useful control of the ecological validity of simulator data used by the *Linguistic Factors Group*. From 20 authentic flight documentations, stemming for the most part from the US National Transportation Safety Board (NTSB), 14

---

[26] This study found that those captains who were characterized as having less achievement motivation in interpersonal and flying skills were also the captains who initiated communication the least and who led crews that performed least well.

[27] The most important studies that belong to this approach are described in Kanki and Palmer (1993).

examples were linguistically analyzed to identify potential stress-sensitive linguistic categories.[28] This method makes it possible to detect utterances and passages that are conspicuous in some way, e.g. because of a strange structure or because of a content that does not fit into the thematic flow. The following excerpt, which is taken from the transcript of the Birgenair accident in 1996, might serve as a first example. It illustrates communication under high workload conditions; the captain is the flying pilot:

(1)	Captain:	There is something wrong, there are some problems.
(2)	F/O:	Direct Pokeg? *[i.e.: "Should we head for the navigational fix POKEG"]*
(3)	Captain:	Okay.
(4)		There is something crazy, do you see it?
(5)	F/O:	There is something crazy there at this moment. Two hundred only is mine and decreasing, Sir. *[i.e.: refers to the speed of the aircraft]*

Figure 6.1   Example 1: Birgenair accident, 1996

This passage is linguistically marked because of its communicational dynamics: the first officer has to solve two communicative tasks. One is standardized and the other unexpected: in (1) the captain informs the F/O that a problem has just occurred. The first officer does not respond to this unexpected turn but continues in the standardized procedure, which requires that the current heading be determined (2) – that is, the F/O solves first the communicative task that corresponds to the script. It is only after the captain refers to the problem again (4) that he takes up the unexpected topic. This observation suggests that the capability to readily adjust to unexpected events might be hindered by the existence of competing standardized tasks. When faced with competing communicative demands people tend not to respond to the *unexpected* task but prefer the one that belongs to the script. To *depart* from the script requires higher processing capacity, which is particularly difficult in situations of already high cognitive workload. The potential stress-sensitive linguistic category revealed here is called responsiveness.[29]

This kind of text analysis was applied to the whole database of 14 transcripts. By looking at communicative behavior in different types of situations, it was possible to find out which aspects of communication were impaired in situations of high workload and danger.

---

[28] Krifka, Martens and Schwarz (2003) contains a detailed analysis of cockpit communication speech acts created on the basis of simulator data.

[29] There is additional evidence presented in the analysis of the verbal interaction in the nuclear power plant; compare the distinction between cognitively congruent vs. incongruent conditions of communication in Chapter 12.

The definitions of different levels of workload are given in Table 6.1. The case-by-case study yielded altogether nine linguistic categories that were affected by stress; for short definitions see Table 6.2.

Table 6.1   Levels of workload

Level of workload	Definition and typical examples
Normal low workload (N1)	Situations of normal working conditions and low cognitive workload. Typical examples are: taxi, cruise.
Normal high workload (N2)	Refers to situations that are characterized by high cognitive workload under normal working conditions, for instance take-off, approach and landing.
Danger 1 (D1)	Occurrence of an unexpected incident, e.g. the malfunction of some minor instrument. The flight behavior of the plane is not impaired, and there are no warning signals.
Danger 2 (D2)	Much more dangerous situation. The plane is difficult to control; its flight behavior is impaired, and there are warning signals.
Danger 3 (D3)	Highly critical situations. Vital systems of the airplane do not function any more and the plane is hardly controllable. The flight behavior of the plane is seriously impaired, and there are several warning signals.

Table 6.2   Social-psychological categories of communicative behavior

Behavioral category	Short definition
Information Sharing	Refers to the information flow within the crew. The category is used to indicate whether the individual crew members tell each other what they observe, think and intend to do. The category has two values [*yes*] and [*no*]
Initiation of Crew Resources	Describes the linguistic means (and their effects) that are used to organize teamwork within the crew. The category has four different values: [*activate resources*], [*react*], [*order*] and [*none*].
Receptiveness	Refers to language processing in multi-task situations. Describes how much information from different channels (crew members: cockpit crew, flight attendants; radio: controllers, other crews) is processed. The category has four values: [*broad*] = react to all incoming information, [*focused*] = concentrate on those channels that are crucial in the current situation, [*selective*] = narrowed or reduced attention, choice of channel does not function appropriately, and [*none*] = no reaction.
Responsiveness	Describes the ability to switch patterns, to adapt one's current behavior to unexpected situational changes. It aims at higher cognitive processes, namely, how new information is integrated into established conceptualizations of the situation. The values of this category are [+ *responsive*] and [- *responsive*].
Register	Refers to the social component of language use. Two values: [*formal*], [*informal*]
Coherence	Relates to the communicational dynamics. Values: [*coherent*] and [*incoherent*]. Which of the two values applies, depends on how the communicative interaction and the transition from turn to turn are organized and whether the participants follow the conventionalized rules of linguistic interaction. Criteria: • Do the participants work on a shared communicative task? • Do they answer questions directed at them by othercrew members? • Do they complete a current communicative task before opening a new turn? • Do they allow one another to finish their utterances, or do they interrupt each other?
Information Quality	A combined category describing relevance, ambiguity, adaptedness to the current situation of the individual utterances. Two values: [*well formed*] and [*not well formed*].
Emotion	Values [*calm*] and [*emphatic*]

Table 6.3   Strength of influence on different communicative behavior aspects

Category	Strength of influence
Register Responsiveness	No general significant influence. Varies between different teams.
Information Quality Information Sharing Relation to Task	Slightly influenced (more positive than negative values in the danger conditions)
Coherence Emotion Initiation of Crew Resources Receptiveness	Strongly influenced (more negative than positive values in at least one of the danger conditions)

Sample results   This section provides a short summary of the results and briefly relates them to the mechanisms of language processing and language production:

- The analyses reveal nine linguistic parameters that were impaired by high workload and danger in individual transcripts: information sharing, initiation of crew resources, receptiveness, responsiveness, relation to task, coherence, information quality, register and emotion;
- The quantitative analysis shows how often each category was impaired in the whole data set. The observed distribution of values indicates whether the category in question is systematically influenced by workload and danger.Table 6.3 summarizes the strength of influence on the individual categories as observed in this data set.

In addition to these quantitative results, hypotheses were developed concerning the effects of standardization:

- Prescribed phraseology is automatically retrieved;
- Highly standardized situational scripts can hinder the adjustment to situational changes; compare example (1) above (Figure 6.1).

With these results in mind, the following question can be considered: which mechanisms of language processing persist and which are impaired under conditions of high workload and danger?

- **Comprehension**: The strong influence of the danger-condition on the category of *receptiveness* suggests that the mechanisms of language processing are highly impaired under these conditions. This assumption is confirmed by results from the *Process Control Group*. The analysis of the relation between the focus of attention (as measured by eye movement) and the content of language planning shows that the latter is systematically detrimented in the case of simultaneous processing of incompatible operational problems.

- **Production**: The other eight categories have to be placed on a relatively high level in the production process. They belong to the conceptual stage – the level at which the so-called *preverbal message* is generated. That is, the processes that are likely to be impaired under the danger condition are the controlled conceptual processes. This result is also confirmed by data from dual task experiments, see Chapter 12. Increase of task load affects the subject's performance in question answering.

There seems to be a tendency for those categories that require a high degree of hearer-related planning, e.g. *coherence* and *initiation of crew resources*, to be more strongly impaired than categories that do not require such a high degree of hearer-related considerations, e.g. *information quality*.

The utterances, as such, are grammatically correct. There are almost no syntactic mistakes and only a few slips of the tongue. This means that, in contrast to the controlled processes, the automatic syntactic processes seem to persist under the condition of high workload and danger; this is confirmed by findings from the experimental investigations, (see Chapter 12).

Psycholinguistics of Communication

Aims and objectives Medical teams and cockpit crews often have to communicate verbally during normal operations. But communication is also of the essence and has to be managed under abnormal or threatening conditions. Since airline pilots and doctors and nurses in anesthesia, surgery and intensive care are trained to perform at a stable level when facing different degrees of time pressure, threat and danger, one would expect them to be capable of efficient verbal interaction under these conditions, too.

However, analysis of accidents and incidents in the past did not just reveal that human error or human failure are core issues in the development of adverse events, but, more precisely, it revealed that errors and failures in communication and interaction are core issues. Therefore, in addition to human factors research, a more problem-oriented communications research is needed. Communication and interaction are core issues in Crew Resource Management (CRM) training programs, which have been integrated into cockpit crew training since the 1980s. From the linguistic point of view CRM can be boiled down to two maxims: 'make all the information needed accessible to all people solving the current problem,' and 'make problem resolution a joint task.' CRM has now been proven successful. CRM trained crews perform significantly better in adverse situations than crews not trained in CRM (Helmreich and Foushee, 1993, Kanki and Palmer, 1993, for further details on CRM and its outcomes).

The structure of verbal interaction in cockpit and OR teams appears to be similar. For example, utterances become shorter with increasing workload, because redundant parts are no longer explicitly expressed, and side structure utterances that are not fully task-related are avoided. Given this background research has been initiated in order to transfer CRM-methods to the medical field (Helmreich, 2000, Helmreich and Schaefer, 1994, Howard et al., 1992). There are, however, clear differences on the functional level of verbal interaction between the two professional fields. Reduced linguistic structures lead to a decline in the efficiency of cockpit communication, whereas in OR teams there seems to be no such decline. Here, the communicative goals can still be achieved. Some sample results of research in this topic are given below. More about parallels and non-parallels between the cockpit and the OR setting is presented below, along with other results, in the chapter on determinants of effective communication, (see Chapter 11).

Methods and data The data for the analyses are taken from cockpit voice recorder transcripts of air traffic incidents available on the Flight Safety Foundation website and the website of the National Transportation Safety Board and from a series of about 30 surgical operations recorded on videotape and MiniDisc in two German hospitals. The methodology sketched in Chapter 3 was applied to this data. In the present case coherence was concentrated on as a feature of discourse that can be affected by varying degrees of task load. The purpose was to gain an idea about the general structures of linguistically successful team interaction, whereas the co-ordination study focused on specific (in) coherence patterns and their relationship to overall co-ordination behavior.

Sample results The overt linguistic data from OR and cockpit settings respectively show rather similar formal features: short utterances, ellipses and little background information. However, the similarity of the phenomena cannot be explained by one and the same underlying mechanism.

A functional analysis of the OR data reveals that the communicative interaction remains successful under conditions of high workload and multi-tasking. The data are analyzed with respect to these parameters of communication: the psycholinguistic procedures for producing coherent discourse in interaction and the social-psychological parameter of shared knowledge and common ground. It was found that maintenance and shift of the current discourse topic determine the dynamics of verbal interaction. Furthermore, the proportion of common ground shared by the interlocutors determines the amount of linguistic effort necessary for successful communication.

The results of the analysis of the cockpit communication confirm these findings. The distribution of labor among the crew members excludes, however, the possibility of visually establishing sufficient shared knowledge. An emergency situation does not offer the time conditions for verbally bridging the gaps of shared knowledge. The psycholinguistic mechanism is blocked and communication breaks down. These results do not seem to be completely in the line with the theoretical expectations of the *Threat/Error Group*. However, the explanations presented in Chapters 9 and 11 will show that the seemingly contradictory findings can be perfectly co-ordinated in a more refined model of communicative interaction.

Cognitive Psychology of Dual Task Performance

Aims and objectives   The object of investigation here is the cognitive processes during dyadic communication. Dyadic communication is typically a series of coherent speech turns taken between two people, examples of which include question and answer, assertion and commentary, etc. From a psycholinguistic viewpoint, communication is a complex cognitive task in which linguistic, as well as non-linguistic, mental systems take part. Communicating puts a strain on the working memory, among other things, and communicative performance can be affected if the cognitive system is being used simultaneously in other ways. Anyone who has ever tried to drive a car in the inner city and carry on a discussion with a passenger has experienced this. The degree to which communicative performance is affected by a competing cognitive demand is dependent on many factors: the difficulty of the communicative task itself, the relationship between the contents of the discussion and the competing task, the noise level etc. Therefore, differential disturbances of verbal reactions to different messages can tell something about the cognitive sources of impaired performance if the distinctive marks of messages are properly described. The question answering experiments investigated possible sources of performance detriments in the answering of the most frequent but semantically different question forms: *yes/no questions* and *wh-questions* under conditions of additional task load.

Yes/no-questions clearly differ from wh-questions in semantic structure (wh-questions begin with a question word, like *what*, *when* etc.). In broad terms yes/no-questions are verification tasks. In their simplest form their intention is to have an addressee judge the truth of a proposition. Therefore, the answer is either *yes* for true or *no* for false propositions. In contrast, wh-questions take an incomplete proposition and intend for an addressee to utter the element that makes a complete and true proposition. For this, yes/no and wh-questions necessarily differ in the output that is the answer to the question.

Yes/no and wh-questions are widely distributed in verbal communication. Teams in high risk environments often use questions. For example, a reanalysis of the simulator transcripts in Krifka, Martens and Schwarz (2003) showed, that 9.8 per cent of all utterances were yes/no and wh-questions. Other question forms included alternative questions, (e.g. do you want tea or coffee?) and echo questions (these are questions of the type: the speaker repeats, what he/she heard immediately before and stresses the last word. Mostly it means something like: did you say this exactly?). This question type only had a frequency of 1.2 per cent in all utterances. This means that 87.7 per cent of all questions were yes/no and wh-questions. Yes/no-questions were used more frequently (70 per cent) than wh-questions (30 per cent). Interestingly, a statistical comparison showed that the frequency of yes/no increased in high workload segments, whereas the frequency of wh-questions did not.

In regards to their different semantic structures, yes/no and wh-questions can be considered to be two different, natural communication tasks. One can deduce that the processing of these tasks differs. The question answering experiments investigated cognitive factors that enable tasks to be distinguished, especially in dual task situations. Think again of the above mentioned example: cockpit teams seem to prefer yes/no-questions in high workload situations. Is it possible to identify advantages in the answering of this question type that make it more secure or easier to answer? The leading question of this investigation can, therefore, be formulated as follows: how does question type affect answering performance in dual task situations with different levels of task load?

Methods and data Questions such as this one can be investigated experimentally in the so-called dual task-paradigm. In a dual task experiment, the subjects have to perform a primary and a secondary task simultaneously. For the purposes of this investigation perceptual-motor co-ordination tasks, which provided different levels of task-load, were used as the primary task. Subjects had to simultaneously solve question-answering tasks, which were used as secondary tasks (see Chapter 12). Voice onset latencies and number of errors were measured.

Sample results Use of a particular question type alone does not make answers faster or more accurate, but some characteristic cognitive demands that typically make yes/no-questions faster and sometimes more secure are associated with question types. Variation in the amount of knowledge and questions referred to was useful in making question types different according to error rates and answer latencies. The number of propositions participants had to learn preceding the experimental measures had a significant negative influence on answer latencies with wh-questions. Consequently, in combination with a primary task in a dual task situation, answer latencies with wh-questions suffered most in high task load situations. This indicates that answers to yes/no-questions have a temporal advantage in situations with high additional task load; explanatory hypotheses are discussed in Chapter 12. The variation of working memory load was also shown to differentiate between answers to different question types under high task load conditions: if facts had to be stored for short lengths of time, answers to yes/no-questions were more accurate in situations with high task load. This shows that question answering was generally impaired through additional task load in latency and/or accuracy for both question types. However, under the same dual task conditions, yes/no-questions are less impaired than wh-questions when cognitive demands, such as the amount of knowledge or the working memory load, associated with questions, expand.

Summary

The *Language Processing Group* investigated three facets of communication under varying conditions of task load. This was investigated using social-psychological modes of communicative behavior, psycholinguistic capability of coherent communication and the influence of independent cognitive task load on the capacity of utterance processing on memory processes. The different approaches utilize different types of data (authentic communication, reactions to different types of questions in a question answering task) and complementary types of methods (social psychological analysis of communication, discourse analysis and experiments). The major findings can be related to one another in the following respects:

- All three investigations reveal a clear impact of task load on communicative behavior;
- The components of the human communication capacity that are primarily affected under increased task load are the so-called higher cognitive processes of memory storage and/or retrieval and utterance planning;
- The parameters of the communicative setting, especially of the relative amount of shared knowledge and shared focus of attention illicit a strong influence.

Do these results shed any light on principles and guidelines for improving safety? In fact, they do. There is a list of clear recommendations given in Sexton et al. (2004). There are two illustrative examples. Combining verbal communication with attention demanding cognitive tasks affects the speaker's ability to pay attention to speaking, listening and solving the non-verbal task. Therefore, one should communicate as long as there is minimal to no cognitive load originating from simultaneous cognitive tasks that require the speaker and listener to use memory and/or working memory capacities. Second: avoid intervening in an addressee's task processing with thematically new and unrelated communicative initiatives.

Chapter 7

Task Load and the Microstructure of Cognition

Werner Sommer, Annette Hohlfeld and Jörg Sangals

Introduction

Group interaction in high risk environments can be viewed as communication under the influence of task load, such as time pressure or impending danger. The task load imposed on operators strongly depends on the number of tasks to be performed simultaneously and on the difficulty of the task(s). The basic perspective taken in the project *Task Load and the Microstructure of Cognition* – from here on referred to as *Microstructure Group* – is the view of cognitive psychology from which the human mind is perceived as an information processing device, consisting of separable but interrelated processing stages, levels or modules that are arranged in a certain order or have a particular architecture. Each of these modules deals with a specific aspect of the processing task: receiving information from sensory organs, transforming and transmitting it to subsequent stages. Classic examples are suggested modules that are specialized for parsing speech input into phonemes or for recognizing faces (Fodor, 1983). Important issues in cognitive psychology include the identification of processing stages and their mode of operation. A separate issue is the flexibility of information processing, that is, if the mode of operation or the architecture of the cognitive system changes as a function of factors such as demands on speed or accuracy, expertise or fatigue.

Approach

The *Microstructure Group* investigated both the question of whether or not the cognitive architecture and mode of operation of information processing is affected by different kinds of task load, as well as how this is the case. To this aim a strictly laboratory based approach was adopted. This made it possible to rigorously control the variables in questions and to relate findings to those of others, as well as to established theories. A disadvantage of this approach is the apparent loss of ecological validity, both in terms of the situation and the population under scrutiny. When compared to a real cockpit situation, the control room of a nuclear power plant or an intensive care unit, laboratory paradigms may appear to be wildly different, extremely impoverished and entirely lacking any emotional aspects. However, there are at least two arguments that support why laboratory studies may not be completely unrealistic situations after all. Firstly, the *Microstructure Group* made a serious effort to select paradigms that portray important aspects of applied situations. Thus, in most experiments, multiple task situations were used. The necessity for multi-tasking or processing several streams of information is a typical element of high risk situations. Consider, for example, the pilot who has to manoeuvre the airplane while communicating with his/her co-pilot or the airport tower. Consider the surgeon, performing an operation while receiving and – hopefully comprehending – messages from the anaesthetist. Secondly, many applied situations, especially those with a high degree of standardization, have a distinct laboratory flavour. Not only are many work places increasingly standardized as far as instrument panels and procedures are concerned, but this is also the case for many aspects of communication and interaction between the operators (see Chapter 3). Therefore, it is not necessarily too far-fetched to connect laboratory settings and findings and the problems ensuing from task load in applied situations. As far as the population studied is concerned, expertise may make a difference in cognitive processing, the nature of which is largely unknown. Some effects of expertise – or practice – have been addressed by the *Co-ordination Group* and in two of the *Microstructure Group* studies.

Another distinct aspect of the *Microstructure Group* research is the employment of psychophysiological markers for information processing. For many controversial issues in cognitive psychology and – increasingly – also in psycholinguistics, psychophysiological markers such as eye movements, heart rate, event-related brain potentials (ERPs) or electromyogram have proven to be very helpful (e.g. Mayer et al., 1988; Sommer et al., 1996). Psychophysiological markers can be used in different ways, e.g. in order to identify the brain systems involved in a given process, to assess global arousal or the precise timing of specific processes. In the present context, ERPs were mainly used in order to study the temporal dynamics of specific processing stages and the intensity of cognitive processes in different situations and under different types of task load. Such markers are particularly valuable when combined with behavioral observations. Performance data, such as reaction times or error rates, are only directly informative about the end products of processing, and inferences about the mediating processing stages are by necessity indirect. In contrast, ERPs allow a more direct observation of cognitive processes. Thus, it is possible to show by means of ERPs that in some conflict situations operators first activate the wrong response before making the correct response (e.g. Stürmer et al., 2002). On the basis of performance data alone this sequence of covert processes cannot be distinguished from a mere delay before the correct response is chosen.

ERPs are extracted from the continuous electroencephalogram (EEG) by averaging the EEG time-point by time-point and in synchrony to a specific type of event (e.g. a certain kind of stimulus or response) over a number of trials. This procedure isolates the characteristic wave-shape in relationship to the ERP-eliciting event by reducing (averaging out) the background EEG. Numerous components, which can be referred to as peaks and troughs, within this wave-shape can be identified that have been related to specific cognitive processing stages (cf. Mayer et al., 1988). In the present project mainly two ERP components were used, the so-called N400 and the lateralized readiness potential (LRP).

The N400 is an electrically negative-going ERP component with a maximal deflection at around 400 milliseconds elicited by spoken, written or signed words. The N400 is especially clear when the eliciting word does not fit the semantic context provided by a preceding sentence fragment or even by a single word. In this group's experimental paradigm (cf. Chapter 12) a semantic context was established by a prime word, which was always a noun. This was followed by a second noun (target) that was either synonymous to the prime, such as *physician – doctor, quarrel – dispute*, or non-synonymous, for example *physician – dispute*. The N400 is best visualized by calculating the voltage difference between the ERP to context-incongruent and -congruent words (Kutas & Van Petten, 1994).

Figure 7.1 gives an illustration of the brain response to spoken words that are either synonymous (good semantic context) or non-synonymous in meaning (no context) to a preceding spoken noun. The difference wave between these ERPs is a pure measure of the N400 component.

As described in Chapter 12, there is good evidence that the N400 can be used as an index of language comprehension. The time course of the N400 indicates the temporal dynamics of context integration – or comprehension – of a word, with onset and peak latency as convenient time markers of the beginning and maximal activity of that process, respectively. The N400 amplitude reflects the neuronal activation involved in this process. Despite the extensive work on the properties of the N400 component there have been no attempts to utilize it within the context of ergonomics.

The LRP is an electrophysiological marker of response activation at the level of the primary motor cortex. It is elicited as soon as the response hand is selected, especially when the task requires choices between left and right hand. When the task requires an immediate response to the stimulus, LRP onset indicates the time demands of perceptual and decisional processes. In contrast, the interval between LRP onset and the response, conveniently measured in response-synchronized averages, reflects the temporal demands of motor programming and response execution. Importantly, the LRP can also be measured when no immediate response is required but when the operator merely prepares for a possible response to a forthcoming signal (Leuthold et al., 1996).

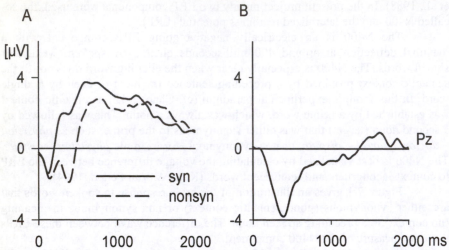

Figure 7.1   Event-related brain potential (ERPs): ERPs to spoken words at a single electrode Pz, which is located pario-centrally, i.e. just behind the vertex of the head. The abscissae show the first 2 seconds after the onset of the spoken word, whereas the ordinates show the voltage of the brain's response to those words (in microvolt). Each curve represents the grand average across 16 subjects and about forty responses per condition elicited in each subject. Panel (A) distinguishes between words that are synonymous or unrelated in meaning to a word that was presented about two seconds before (continuous vs. broken line, respectively). Evidently, there is a large difference between these ERPs, which consists of a more negative-going response to nonsynonymous words with the greatest difference around 400 ms after word onset. This is highlighted in Panel (B), which shows the difference wave between nonsynonymous and synonymous words, calculated time point by time point; this difference wave constitutes the so-called N400 component (for further explanations see text)

Until now, the LRP has mainly been used in basic research where it serves as a convenient tool for studying properties of the cognitive system and localizing the effects of experimental variables within processes that precede or follow the beginning of response activation. Only recently have there been first attempts to extend these studies to include the effects of task load (e.g. Osman et al., 2000; Sangals et al., 2002). These studies indicate that a major locus of time pressure is the motor system but that under certain conditions premotoric processes can also be affected. Figure 7.2 provides an example of the effects of time pressure on motor activation during a preparation period from Sangals et al. (2002).

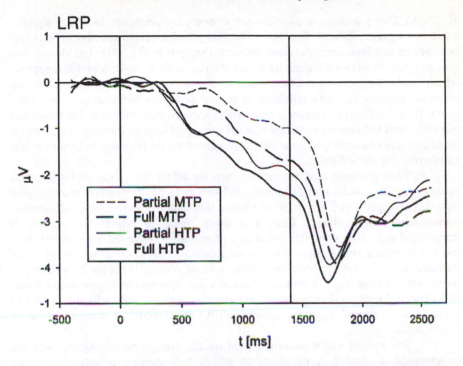

Figure 7.2 Effects of time pressure and preliminary information on preparatory brain activation as shown by the Lateralized Readiness Potential (LRP). At time t=0 (left vertical line), preliminary information about the forthcoming response was given, the so-called precue. 1400 milliseconds later (right line), a second stimulus was presented which, if needed, completed the precue information and permitted the participants to execute the prepared response. Increasing the amount of information provided by the precue (partial vs. full) and increasing time pressure (moderate (MTP) vs. high (HTP)) independently enhances the activation of the motor system already before the second stimulus, as reflected in more negative-going LRP waves

Paradigms and Main Findings

The main paradigms in which the *Microstructure Group* investigated task load were the precuing and the overlapping tasks design. In precuing, a warning stimulus is presented that conveys information about a required response to a subsequent response signal. During the fore-period, the operator prepares for the response as much as possible on the basis of the precue-information. When psychophysiological measures are used, it is possible to directly observe some of the processes taking place while the subject prepares for the response (Leuthold et al., 1996). This paradigm is of relevance to everyday situations in which signals, e.g. from a gauge, indicate that one of several possible responses may or may not be required at a later time. Previous research (Sangals et al., 2002) has shown that time pressure in such a situation increases the readiness to make a motor response, which markedly shortens reaction times to the response signal. However, if the prepared response has to be withheld, increased motor readiness causes many false starts. By extending this research, researchers showed that preparing for a speeded response does not interfere with the manual force precision of the response. Similar findings were obtained when the subject received no preliminary information but had to respond immediately.

Time pressure also appears to directly affect the mode of information processing. De Sanctis (2002) investigated the issue of information transmission between perception and action. It was found that under time pressure, information transmission might change from a discrete mode in which information is transmitted only after complete extraction of stimulus-conveyed information, to a more continuous mode. In a continuous mode partial information about some stimulus aspects may activate the motor system without necessarily eliciting a movement. Interestingly, a similar effect on the information transmission mode was observed without time pressure after practise with the task, which may in fact indicate that experts' cognitive systems differ from those of novices in rather fundamental ways.

The second major paradigm used by the *Microstructure Group* was the overlapping or dual task paradigm in which two stimuli, presented in close temporal succession have to be responded to individually. Overlapping tasks can be considered to be paradigmatic for many applied situations in which there is high task load. For example, operators in power plants have to monitor the instrument panels and be attentive and responsive to their team-partner at the same time. Two variants of this paradigm were used. In the first variant, both tasks can be considered to be non-linguistic, in the second variant, investigated in several experiments – at least one of the tasks was language-related.

In two experiments the *Microstructure Group* investigated dual task processing in non-linguistic contexts. These experiments looked at the effects of time pressure and practice, respectively, and are described in the introductory section of Chapter 12. The dual task experiments involving language processing focused on language perception under task load. Task load was manipulated by the temporal overlap with an additional task and by varying the difficulty of that task. It was found that language perception is delayed or even degraded when there is additional task load, and the impairment increased with the degree of temporal overlap and with the difficulty of decision making for the additional task. The degree of impairment of language perception depends on a number of other factors investigated in separate experiments. In short, impairment is aggravated when the message is not intentionally processed for meaning, as may be the case when the operator is intentionally focussing on the additional task. There is a general delay of message comprehension when the listener is not a native speaker of the message's language (Hohlfeld et al., in press a), as is often the case in multinational teams and for pilots from non-English speaking countries. In addition, it was observed that the interference between language perception and an additional task is more pronounced when the overlapping task requires the decoding of visual symbols (letters) as compared to when the overlapping task is purely spatial, (Hohlfeld et al., in press b) which is of relevance for the design of work places.

Perspectives and Synergies

Naturally, the issues addressed by the *Microstructure Group* could be investigated only to certain depths and other questions, such as, for example, those concerning the effects of fatigue and emotional stress, had to be ignored. Nevertheless, some of the findings from these laboratory studies may have important practical implications for the design of message displays and for the policy of language use at work places. The work done so far could, and should, be continued in several directions.

Surely, the relevance of the present findings for applied situations has a certain plausibility based on analogous findings from simulator studies, protocol analyses and real incidents. Nevertheless, a prime objective for future work should be to make the connection between laboratory-based research and real-life operator situations more stringent. Some of the questions already addressed should be followed up in more depth, and the range of theoretical issues could be broadened. How would, for example, language production and processing of complex sentences be affected by the task load manipulations used by the *Microstructure Group*? In some respects, the *Question Answering* and the *Process Control* Groups have addressed such questions and the closest co-operations have indeed been with these groups.

PART II:
Specific Issues

Chapter 8

Setting the Stage: Characteristics of Organizations, Teams and Tasks Influencing Team Processes

Gudela Grote, Robert L. Helmreich, Oliver Sträter, Ruth Häusler,
Enikö Zala-Mezö and J. Bryan Sexton

Introduction

How people perform their tasks depends on a number of factors beyond their own control, their motivation and their ability. The GIHRE project focuses on small teams performing highly critical tasks under complex and often difficult circumstances. While subsequent chapters will describe results with this focus, i.e. by looking at the interaction among team members from various angles, the present chapter deals with the organizational and task-related preconditions that serve as an influential framework for the team's performance. When interpreting the findings presented in subsequent chapters, this framework has to be kept in mind, e.g. leadership means something different in a team of two highly and similarly trained pilots than in a team that incorporates several professions and hierarchical levels such as a medical operating team.

In this chapter some crucial characteristics of the organizational settings within which teams perform, as well as some conditions set by the tasks they have to fulfill are discussed. Organizational factors affecting team performance in high risk environments will be discussed in terms of the different layers of influences in which teams are embedded. At the outermost layer there are influences such as regulatory bodies and national culture, layers more directly affecting teams are regulatory philosophies within organizations and organizational and professional cultures. The most direct influences are characteristics of the teams themselves and the task they have to perform. At the end of the chapter, the Threat and Error Management Model is presented. This model provides a framework for team processes themselves, as they will be analyzed in more detail in subsequent chapters.

When studying the empirical data presented in this and in the following chapters, it has to be kept in mind that the sources of data are very different, sometimes making comparisons difficult. Some data were obtained in work simulations (nuclear process control and aviation), while others stem from real world settings (anesthesia). Some data come from direct observation of performance, while others come from self-report or retrospective surveys. Archival data, such as those obtained from Line Operations Safety Audits (LOSA: Helmreich, Klinect & Wilhelm, 2001) or flight data recorders used to monitor normal flights (Flight Operations Quality Assurance: FOQA) provided invaluable sources of information about crew behavior. One of the strengths of the GIHRE project is the use of multiple, complementary sources of data. Convergence in results from very different sources and methodologies makes them more compelling.

Organizational Factors

Influences of Regulatory Bodies on Organization

Regulation can be described as an activity imposed on organizations by external parties in order to protect society from the potentially detrimental effects of an organization's operations (Hopkins & Hale, 2002). Regulation can be achieved in a number of different ways, with prescriptive regulation and goal-oriented legislation being two prominent and very distinct approaches. While prescriptive regulation specifies in great detail how an organization has to carry out its operations, down to the appropriate height of ladders and number of fire extinguishers, goal-oriented legislation prescribes only the goal to be achieved leaving the way in which this should be accomplished open, thereby furthering self-regulation within organizations.

The role of the regulators changes depending on which approach to regulation is chosen, as do the activities they have to perform in order to fulfill this role. From the perspective of prescriptive regulation, regulators have to draw up very specific requirements and control and enforce adherence to these requirements through detailed inspections. In contrast, goal-oriented legislation requires regulators to provide guidance as to how goals can be achieved, turning inspectors into consultants who have to find the delicate balance between advising and enforcing (Larsson, 2002).

Within the three industries studied in the GIHRE project, regulation in aviation and nuclear industries have long been very prescriptive and are gradually changing towards more goal-oriented legislation with accompanying changes in regulators' roles (cf. for the nuclear industry e.g. Reiman & Norros, 2002; for aviation in the US cf. Federal Aviation Administration, 1991). Medicine is the least regulated profession, relying most heavily on the process of peer review from professionals in the field. These peer review committees operate without formal, nationally mandated procedures or processes.

Different Regulatory Philosophies within Organizations

Organizations are formed in order to achieve certain goals through more or less complex and dynamic internal processes in more or less complex and dynamic environments. Specialized tasks performed by different subsystems in the organization have to be co-ordinated with respect to the overall goal. Co-ordination, defined as tuning interdependent work processes to promote concerted action towards a superordinate goal (Kieser & Kubicek, 1992), is needed for any activity which cannot be carried out by one person and which cannot be subdivided into independent parts (Hackman & Morris, 1975). Co-ordination is therefore a core activity in any work organization.

How co-ordination is achieved is an important characteristic of organizations that can be described in terms of different regulatory philosophies and different approaches to handling uncertainties encountered on the way to goal attainment (see Figure 8.1).

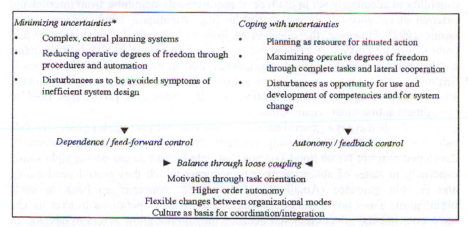

*Minimizing uncertainties**	*Coping with uncertainties*
• Complex, central planning systems	• Planning as resource for situated action
• Reducing operative degrees of freedom through procedures and automation	• Maximizing operative degrees of freedom through complete tasks and lateral cooperation
• Disturbances as to be avoided symptoms of inefficient system design	• Disturbances as opportunity for use and development of competencies and for system change

▼
Dependence / feed-forward control

▼
Autonomy / feedback control

► *Balance through loose coupling* ◄
Motivation through task orientation
Higher order autonomy
Flexible changes between organizational modes
Culture as basis for coordination/integration

* Uncertainties may stem from the system environment and/or from the transformation processes within the system.

Figure 8.1   Basic principles: organization design (adapted from Grote, 2001)

One approach is to try to co-ordinate through feed forward control that is based on minimizing uncertainties. In this case, enormous efforts are put into planning and continuous monitoring of the execution of these plans, providing minimal degrees of freedom to the people in charge of carrying out the plans and taking any deviation from plans as signs that even more planning and monitoring are necessary. Another approach, one that does not involve fighting uncertainties in an attempt to minimize them or their effect in the organization, is to enable each member of an organization to handle uncertainties locally and to allow for feedback control. From this perspective, planning is understood primarily as a resource for situated action (Suchman, 1987), not as a blueprint for centrally determined and monitored action. Local actors need to be given as many degrees of freedom as possible, achieving concerted action mainly through lateral, task-induced co-ordination. Disturbances – although momentarily annoying – are also regarded as opportunities for use and expansion of individual competencies and for organizational innovation and change.

The minimizing uncertainties approach is especially prevalent in organizations in which malfunctioning not only endangers business success but also human life and environmental integrity because production processes constitute major risks to health, safety and the environment. In these organizations not only is the chosen management style usually one of minimizing uncertainties, but external regulatory bodies also prescribe this approach. At the core of this approach to safety lies the assumption that if it is not possible to make humans redundant by automation, they are risk factors whose freedom to act has to be restricted as much as possible in order to channel their actions towards the one safe way of doing things. But it has also been argued that the minimizing uncertainty approach is less than optimal for these systems due to the system's reduced capability to adequately act in the face of requirements stemming from internal and external disturbances of normal operation (e.g. Amalberti, 1999; Perrow, 1984; Grote, 1997). However, the question of how to improve the predictability and controllability of a system while at the same time increasing its flexibility remains and has been frequently restated (e.g. Dekker, 2003a; Rasmussen, 1997; Woods & Shattuck, 2000). One way to try to achieve this is through a more systematic analysis and design of standardization, i.e. the rules and procedures used to co-ordinate action in an organization.

While there is a general understanding that rules are useful guides for safe behavior, there is also increasing concern that too many rules incrementally developed will not create good systems that help human actors do the right thing, especially in states of abnormal operation during which they would need strong and flexible guidance (Amalberti, 1999). These concerns go back to basic observations about how rules specifying exactly which operations to execute can have a detrimental effect on action because they do not allow actors to develop an underlying plan of their own, but instead further the atomization of actions and the focus on micro-difficulties (Vermersch, 1985).

Another basic problem with standardization is that, especially in non-routine situations, reliance on common standards may turn into over-reliance, impeding switches to more explicit co-ordination and accompanying switches to more complex and effortful levels of common action regulation. This problem can be exacerbated by the fact that standardization is a strong force towards shared understanding of a situation and its demands in a team, because it creates a common framework for team behavior, thus reducing the need for explicit co-ordination. As helpful as it is under most conditions, the expectation of shared goals, plans, perspectives and knowledge bases created by reference to the same set of standard operating procedures does involve the risk of not realizing the need for explicit co-ordination, e.g. in non-routine situations. In Rasmussen's terms (1997), rules should serve to clarify the boundaries of system behavior and to suggest ways of handling system states close to those boundaries.

Some authors have begun to develop typologies of rules to help in the design of rule systems that are directly tailored to the needs for guidance as well as for autonomy and control arising in different stages of action regulation (e.g. Hale & Swuste, 1998; LePlat, 1998; cf. Table 1). Some of these distinctions have already been put to practice in nuclear power plants as so-called symptom-based procedures and event-based procedures. While symptom-based procedures are designed to help the operator diagnose a plant disturbance and formulate a certain goal to achieve, event-based procedures define a way to deal with a specific disturbance and concrete actions to be performed (Shorrock & Sträter, 2004).

Table 8.1   Examples of rule types (taken from the flight operations manual of an airline)

Type of rule	Example
Rules concerning goals to be achieved	It must be clearly understood that not all combinations of cumulative operational problems (engine failure plus e.g. terrain, weather, availability of aerodromes etc.) can be covered by this policy. In such situations the solution offering the highest degree of safety should be sought.
Rules defining the way in which decisions about a course of action must be reached	In order to complete a replanning, any documented cruise systems and all means available may be used, such as flight management systems and data contained in the respective AOMs (aircraft operating manuals).
Rules defining concrete actions	Every evacuation must be carried out as quickly as possible. The passengers must be assisted to leave the aeroplane without their belongings and directed to a point at a safe distance from the airplane.

Rules analyses in different high risk settings: cockpit vs. operating room The three organizational settings studied in the GIHRE project can be differentiated in terms of the level of standardization. Operations in the cockpit and the nuclear power control room are highly standardized by means of very detailed and specific standard operating procedures covering both normal and abnormal situations. Medical operations are based on fewer and more general standards. Rules relevant in the cockpit and the operating room were analyzed by means of the categories suggested by Hale and Swuste (1998) in order to better understand those employed in the different settings and their influence on team performance (see Chapter 10).

The rules analysis for the cockpit was performed on those sections of one airline's 'General Basics Manual' and 'Aircraft Operations Manual' that were considered relevant for the simulator scenarios from which team interaction data were obtained. The 'General Basics' contain rules about navigation, routing, use of equipment, communication with air traffic control, fuel management, weather conditions, warning systems, actions in case of fire or smog, teamwork etc. The aircraft operations manual includes technical details of the aircraft and rules for the handling of the aircraft under normal and abnormal conditions, including checklists for several technical defects, like the problem in the simulator scenario used by the *Co-ordination Group* (flaps and slats jammed).

The rules analysis for the operating room was based on documents from the same hospital department in which the observation of working teams took place in the *Co-ordination Group*. One general characteristic of the rules in the hospital studied was that the rules were partly department-specific. As a consequence, those personnel that circulate between departments – anesthetist, residents, student nurses – have to work under different regulations when they work for different departments. Also, rules are often written by and for particular professional groups, i.e. anesthesia nurses are not always familiar with the rules written for residents and vice versa. Finally, the assumption in the hospital is that rules exist mainly for normal situations and should not be over-generalized. Therefore, it should always be possible to disobey a rule in this setting if someone has a good reason to do so. When interpreting the rules analysis in the medical setting, it also has to be kept in mind that there are many unwritten rules, which could not be included in the analysis. These unwritten rules are partly passed on through education and training and partly based on individually developed standards, which people use to remember and/or optimize steps of work processes. As training in the hospital is based on a systematic *learning by doing* with inexperienced team members working together with senior team members, unwritten rules are handed down informally, and often implicitly, to new members. Before a person is authorized to make a decision alone, he/she has to work and consult with superiors for a long time. At the same time, the general attitude expressed by anesthetists and nurse anesthetists is that of management by exception: let the new member work, observe whether or not everything goes well and intervene only in case of inappropriate performance.

For the rule analysis in anesthesia the following four documents were selected:

- Standard anesthesia: describes the material, equipment and activities required during standard anesthesia;
- Residents' duties: regulates work obligations and responsibilities for the residents;
- Shift organization: instructions on how to change shift, how to arrange holiday schedules, etc.;
- Instructions to fill out the anesthesia protocol: exact description of scales used in the protocol. (The protocol is a very important document, containing all crucial information about the patient and about the anesthesia process. In case of changing personnel it is a very central instrument in avoiding human failure and loss of information.)

The analysis followed the typology from Hale & Swuste (1998) and differentiated between three main types of rules: rules describing goals, rules describing processes to follow in determining the right course of action and rules describing concrete actions. Also, some characteristics related to the strictness of the rules were analyzed.

Table 8.2   Results of rule analysis according to categories from Hale & Swuste (1998)

	Aviation (n=650)	Anesthesia (n=204)
Goal rule	3%	3%
Process rule	19%	32%
Action rule	78%	65%
Advice	10%	15%
Explanation provided	29%	27%
Scope provided	47%	40%
Exception mentioned	6%	13%

The most important difference between the documents from the two professional fields is the number of process rules and action rules. Process rules seem to be quite useful in environments with a high level of uncertainty as in the operating room. They do not provide any illusion that a ready-made solution exists for every situation, while they still provide support by indicating the steps to take to define the right course of action in an unknown situation. Some other differences between the two professional fields also indicate more openness of rules in anesthesia, as rules in anesthesia are more often advice and mention exceptions more often. However, in aviation rules provide more scope. This latter finding may be related to the higher percentage of action rules whose flexibility is increased by providing some decision latitude.

From the analysis as such, it is not possible to say what a healthy proportion of the different rule types would be. The *Co-ordination Group* also collected observational data on rule violations. The four tasks that were used for the performance index for the cockpit crews were carried out properly only by four of the observed 42 teams. Overall, 63 violations were observed. However, this might also be an effect of the simulator setting, e.g. regarding the two tasks of informing cabin crew and organizing fire brigade. More serious is the violation of the very basic rule that responsibility for flying the aircraft should always be clearly assigned, which occurred in 16 teams. Of the 23 observed anaesthesia teams, ten violated rules, adding up to 11 violations overall (mainly unannounced manipulations and intubation taking too long). When interpreting this result, it is important to take into account that in the anaesthesia setting it was generally difficult to decide whether certain behaviors constituted a rule violation or a very subtle, implicit way of improving co-ordination in line with the general philosophy expressed in the hospital that rules need to be adapted to new situations or even disobeyed in certain situations.

More information concerning the overriding question of the relationship between standardization level and different forms of team co-ordination, is provided in the Leadership and Co-ordination chapter, Chapter 10.

Organizational Culture

Beyond the manifest characteristics of an organization like structures and processes, rules and regulations, the task to be performed and the people who should perform it, organizations also differ in terms of their culture. Here culture is understood as deeply rooted assumptions about human, societal and ecological categories shared by the members of an organization and their expression in values, behavior patterns and artifacts found in the organization (e.g. Schein, 1992).

In addition to being part of the organization, members of an organization are also part of a profession, a region, a country, a religion, organizational cultures and political groups etc., all of which influence the values and norms brought into the organization. In the following section, some elements of national and professional cultures that are important factors in shaping organizational culture are presented. Organizational culture as such will then be discussed from the point of view of safety culture as the core set of values, norms and basic assumptions that increase safe team performance.

National Culture

National cultures exert a profound influence on the way professionals interact and on the policies employed to deal with inevitable human error (Helmreich and Merritt, 1999; Helmreich and Sexton, 2004). Nations vary widely in the importance attached to hierarchical differences between subordinates and their leaders. In cultures high on the dimension called power distance by Hofstede (1990), juniors are extremely reluctant to question the decisions or actions of their superiors. Power distance can have a chilling effect on willingness to discuss alternatives or react quickly to emerging danger. Helmreich and Merritt (1999) identified another dimension they called rules and order in their survey of pilots from more than twenty countries in Asia, the Pacific Rim and the United States. In fact, this was the dimension showing the highest degree of variability across the population. Individuals from cultures high in rules and order endorse the view that rules should not be broken, even when it would be in the best interest of the organization. The highest scores on the rules and order concept were found in many Asian cultures while individuals from the United States scored lowest. Certainly this is a dimension of culture with strong implications for organizational behavior and with strong links to regulatory philosophies in organizations as discussed above.

Professional Culture

Professional culture exerts a strong influence on behavior in occupations that are selective and perform actions requiring special training and qualification. Helmreich and Merritt (1999) have examined the professional cultures of physicians and airline pilots and found many similarities. Both professions screen applicants rigorously and have high qualification standards. There are positive and negative components in both professional cultures. Members are proud of their professional identity and value recognition. The result is high motivation to perform well. In medicine this is reflected in a desire to provide patients with optimal care. In aviation it is seen in a commitment to the safety and efficiency of flight.

An important element of professional culture is professional ethics and standards. Airlines in many countries, notably the United States, have an independent professional standards committee. This committee, staffed by representatives of the pilots' union or association and representatives of management, deals with issues of ethics and performance. Professional standards committees usually act on information provided by fellow crew members. Issues that may bring a pilot before the committee include suspected alcohol or drug abuse, procedural non-compliance and behavioral problems, including failures in teamwork and inattention to duty, or, in the case of captains, inappropriately autocratic behavior. Committee actions can include counseling, recommendations for psychological or psychiatric assessment and treatment or, in the case of serious misbehavior, referral to management for disciplinary sanctions. Professional standards committees provide a valuable safety mechanism for aviation. Peer review committees in many hospitals are also charged with issues of competence and misbehavior, but they are often viewed by front-line personnel as punitive and are seldom used to deal with the team issues addressed in aviation.

The major advantage of the professional standards approach is that issues are handled by pilots themselves instead of solely by management. Deliberations of professional standards committees are confidential and issues are dealt with discreetly and with extreme care and respect. Pilot representatives on professional standards committees (both captains and first officers) are selected on the basis of exemplary character and professional credibility. These attributes ensure that pilots will be comfortable referring an issue to the committee and can feel sure that problems will be handled in a just and confidential manner. Unlike peer review in medicine, professional standards actions are not part of a formal disciplinary process and the process does not affect pilots' licensure. As a rule, senior management in an airline has a strong preference for handling matters at the professional standards level as a means of maintaining good relations with the pilot group.

Safety Culture

In the aftermath of the Chernobyl nuclear power plant accident, the term safety culture was coined as 'that assembly of characteristics and attitudes in organizations and individuals which establishes that, as an overriding priority, nuclear safety issues receive the attention warranted by their significance' (INSAG, 1991, p. 1). It is assumed that safety requires an organizational culture in which safe performance lies at the core of the basic assumptions and norms shared by the members of the organization.

In the nuclear industry as well as in other industries, characteristics indicating a good safety culture have been described, such as management commitment to safety, safety training and motivation, safety committees and safety rules, record keeping on accidents and close calls, sufficient inspection and communication, adequate operation and maintenance procedures, well-designed and functioning technical equipment and good house keeping (e.g. INSAG, 1991; Reason, 1993). A major problem with most existing models of safety culture is their lack of integration into general models of organization and of organizational culture. Culture is crucial as a mechanism of co-ordination and integration in an organization, and thereby can also help to solve problems related to finding the proper balance between highly standardized and flexible action as Weick (1987, p. 124) has pointed out:

> Before you can decentralize, you first have to centralize so that people are socialized to use similar decision premises and assumptions so that when they operate their own units, those decentralized operations are equivalent and co-ordinated. This is precisely what culture does. It creates a homogeneous set of assumptions and decision premises which, when they are invoked on a local and decentralized basis, preserve co-ordination and centralization. Most important, when centralization occurs via decision premises and assumptions, compliance occurs without surveillance. This is in sharp contrast to centralization by rules and regulations or centralization by standardization and hierarchy, both of which require high surveillance. Furthermore, neither rules nor standardization are well equipped to deal with emergencies for which there is no precedent.

In an attempt to bring together elements of current safety culture models and existing safety management systems, as well as more general elements of organizational culture and organizational design, Grote and Künzler (1996, 2000) have developed a socio-technical model of safety culture (see Figure 8.1), in which the following are true:

- Safety culture is embedded into more general considerations of culture, emphasizing interactions between an organization's material and immaterial reality, and
- Organizational design is related to safety, both on the material level directly affecting task orientation and self-regulation on the shop floor and on the conceptual level referring to basic beliefs about human competence and the reliability of humans and technical systems.

Two core assumptions of the socio-technical systems approach underlie the model: (1) that the technical and social subsystems of a work system need to be jointly optimized to allow for maximum efficiency in the accomplishment of the system's primary task, and (2) that a crucial criterion for joint optimization is the system's ability to control variances at their source (cf. e.g. Grote, 1997; Susman, 1976; Ulich, 1994). Linking the first assumption to safety lends support to the general tenet of safety management, i.e. the proactive resolution of conflicts between productivity and safety goals by defining the system's primary task in terms of quantity, quality and safety of production.

The second assumption leads, contrary to most industrial practice as described in the earlier section on standardization, to the argument that a high degree of self-regulation in work teams, balanced with appropriate rules to guide autonomous behavior, is beneficial to safety (Grote, 1997). This argument has two roots: (a) especially in complex systems, immediate reactions to variances and disturbances in the production process as well as anticipatory actions for their prevention necessitate the delegation of control to the lowest, i.e. shop floor, level (e.g. Perrow, 1984); (b) based on the motivation model embedded in the socio-technical approach, i.e. task orientation (Emery, 1959; Ulich, 1994), it is assumed that tasks that allow for a high degree of autonomy, task completeness and task feedback will enhance an individual's intrinsic motivation. If, as derived from the definition of the primary task, that individual's task involves safe as well as efficient action, then motivation would also be directed towards safety (e.g. studies on self-managing teams in coal mines by Trist, Susman & Brown, 1977; cf. also the review of effects of self-managing teams by Pasmore, Francis, Haldeman & Shani, 1982). However, as Perrow (1984), among others, has pointed out, tight coupling of technical systems, i.e. each component of the technical system being impacted directly by other elements without buffers or leeway, limits the possibilities for decentralized regulation of a system. Observations in so-called 'high reliability organizations' like aircraft carriers have shown that an organization's ability to switch between different degrees of centralization may be crucial (e.g. LaPorte & Consolini, 1991). The importance of cultural factors as flexible though strongly committed rules for performing these switches has already been pointed out (Weick, 1987). This also provides an important link to the issues of regulation, standardization and rules management as discussed earlier.

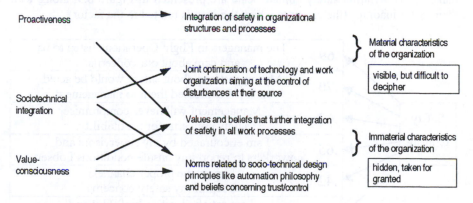

Figure 8.2 Sociotechnical model of safety culture[30]

---

[30] Reprinted with permission of Elsevier from Grote, G. and Künzler, C. (2000), 'Safety Culture and its Reflections in Job and Organizational Design: Total Safety Management', *Safety Science*, Vol. 34, p.131-150.

Safety Culture vs. Safety Climate

There is a general, but oftentimes vague, distinction between safety culture and safety climate. In psychological terms, safety culture is likened to the safety personality of an organization (stable across time and situation), whereas safety climate is more akin to a safety attitude (i.e. a snapshot of aggregate worker perceptions) of an organization (Glendon & Stanton, 2000). In their review of the arguments surrounding the use and features of safety culture and safety climate, Cox & Flin (1998) explain that safety climate is the preferred construct when psychometric questionnaires are used as the measurement instrument. Safety culture, in contrast, requires a more triangulated methodology to investigate more extensively the deeper and historically derived aspects of safety within an organization, usually via ethnographic approaches. In short, safety climate can be viewed as the surface features of safety culture, assessed through employee attitudes and perceptions at a particular point in time (Schneider & Gunnarson, 1991).

Safety climate has been related to self-reported compliance with safety regulations and procedures (Neal, Griffin & Hart, 2000). There is some evidence that various aspects of safety climate are linked to safety-related outcomes such as accidents and incidents in industrial organizations, (Zohar, 1980; Hofmann & Stetzer, 1996) construction sites (Dedobbeleer & Beland, 1991) and road maintenance jobs (Niskanen, 1994). Safety climate therefore serves as a fruitful target in the search for the determinants and components of safe performance. The research into safety attitudes conducted by the GIHRE *Threat/ Error Group* has resulted in questionnaire assessments for safety climate in medicine and aviation. Safety climate is defined as *the extent to which individuals perceive a genuine and proactive commitment to safety by their organization*. The questionnaire items that make up the aviation safety climate scale are presented in Figure 8.3, along with their factor loadings (the extent to which the item is related to the factor).

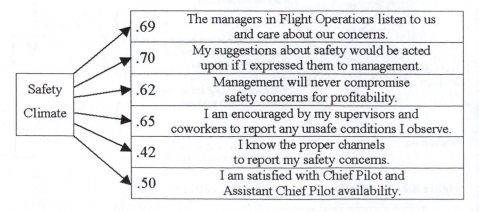

Figure 8.3   Aviation safety climate items and factor loadings

For further results, please see Chapter 1, which demonstrates the link between safety climate and outcomes in commercial aviation.

Task Characteristics and Individual Characteristics affecting Team Performance

The cultural aspects described in the previous section, as well as the recovery potentials of teams as described in the next section, are influenced by the context of team performance. Figure 8.4 illustrates the main contextual aspects of how team performance is related to task and workload. As shown in the figure, the factors discussed in the previous section regarding organizational influences have a general influence on task load and finally on workload.

The industries represented in this book (medicine, aviation and nuclear process control) vary according to their context and this makes it difficult to interpret research results achieved in one setting for the other settings. Based on the characteristics, conclusions can be drawn about:

- The similarities and differences between the specific industries investigated in GIHRE, as well as the transferability to other fields;
- The way that the basic research activities in GIHRE support research questions in applied fields;
- How the results from the applied research fields in a particular application area can be integrated into a coherent picture of cognitive issues and communication;
- How to mutually learn from experimental studies or applied studies and facilitate results from other fields (e.g. validation of results, new aspects of safety).

The reader working in a totally different industry may also have the desire to extract the relevant information for his/her own contexts. Therefore, a framework, represented in Figure 8.4 was developed to identify the commonalties between the industries involved in GIHRE, as well as to provide a framework for transferring the experiences into other fields of interest.

Workload and Task Load

Often the term workload is used as a general concept to link psychological and contextual aspects. There are many definitions of workload, including the following: the degree of internal resources required for a task; the level of demand imposed by a task; the difference between capacity required available and the presence of various stressors influencing the performance and responses.[31] Most of these definitions are related to the subjective experience of the contextual load to

---

[31] These definitions were developed and discussed within the GIHRE project, 14 October 2000.

which a human is exposed. This point of view is also applied in the GIHRE project. Workload is defined here as the subjectively experienced workload when accomplishing a certain task. It also corresponds to the terms mental workload or cognitive workload, if the load is concerning information processing rather than physical activity.

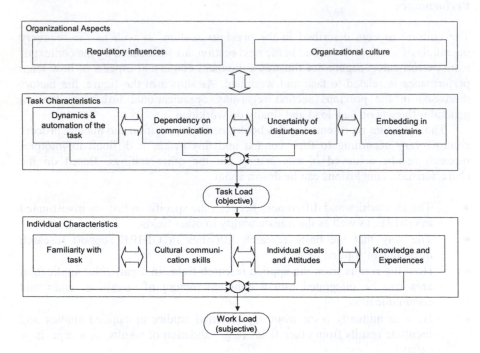

Figure 8.4   Characteristics of team performance and the influence of organizational aspects

The factors that influence workload are classified into three groups: organizational aspects, task characteristics and individual characteristics. The term task load describes an external indicator of objective load including factors like task demands or situational requirements (e.g. bad weather conditions that complicate operation). Workload is understood as the subjective experience of load in the process of coping with the conditions constituting the objective task load. In other words, the concept of task load refers to characteristics of the task, whereas workload indicates the load as a consequence for the worker performing the task. In this sense, one could say that a certain situation, like landing an aircraft with only one available engine in poor visibility conditions constitutes a high objective task load that most likely will lead to high workload for each subject performing this task. However, the actual amount of workload that will be experienced by different individuals depends on personal factors, mainly resources that are influenced by experience, skill, state of health and other personal factors.

According to the figure above, aspects of task load and workload may be distinguished as is done in the following sections.

The *Behavioral Marker Group* investigated the impact of task load on team performance. As expected, more cockpit crews show degraded team performance in high task load situations compared to moderate task load situations (detailed results are reported in Chapter 2). This confirms the importance of the contextual factor (here: *task complexity*) for team performance. Under high task load, crews subjectively experienced more workload, which was also reflected by degraded team performance, as team members' capacity to fulfil team performance aspects was reduced.

Dynamics and Automation of the Task within the System

A main contributor to task load is the dynamics of the system to be managed. Slow system responses may relieve the user for some time from operational duties and may lead to either hyper-vigilance or lack of attention, as often occurs when dealing with automated systems. Permanent engagement may lead to fatigue (resulting from a multi-hour surgery for example). Dynamics of the task could be classified into:

- Slow (hours),
- Medium (minutes) and
- High (seconds).

The dynamics of the task depend on the system's inherent characteristics and processes. Nuclear processes are comparatively slow (sometimes medium). Surgery can vary from very short procedures to multi-hour crises. Aviation challenges may occur over minutes or seconds. These are average figures for the usual range of possible disturbances. Certainly there could be slow processes in aviation as well (e.g. small leak in fuel tanks), and there could be high dynamics in nuclear process control (e.g. if the core heats up and gets close to core meltdown). The same is true for medicine: one can expect slow or high dynamics depending on the type of surgery and the nature of patient reaction.

The level of automation heavily impacts the dynamics of the task, not only with respect to monitoring and active task engagement but also with regard to the possibility of active involvement in the situation (being in the loop; e.g. Grote et al., 2000). The impact on the dynamics of the task can be as follows:

- High level of automation,
- Medium level of automation or
- Low level of automation.

Automation also changes the ability to modify the situation and hence affects task load. In the case of a disturbance to an automated system, the operator has the possibility to intervene in the failed automated system, but this usually results in high task load situations.

Nuclear power is certainly one of the most automated systems. Aviation is highly automated (flight deck), but the proportion of non-automated tasks is still relatively high (e.g. co-ordinating with air traffic control, dispatch and cabin, for example). Medicine is the least automated environment that GIHRE investigated.

The level of automation requires human engagement in system control. Human factor textbooks often state that 'humans are not good monitors.' However, human beings are certainly not good at being exclusively and permanently involved in controlling a working system. The truth is somewhere between these two. Humans are also not good at exclusively monitoring or being exclusively active in the system. Reactions depend on a balance between both types of engagement. Therefore the distinctions are as follows:

- Permanent active engagement (active task),
- Continuous change of active engagement to monitoring,
- Switching between active engagement and monitoring and
- Mainly monitoring.

Compared to aviation or process control, medicine requires active engagement. Doctors are usually engaged with few breaks. The process industry is usually biased towards monitoring. Even during plant disturbances, operators have relatively few actions to perform and then have to wait for the plant to react. Civil aviation is, compared to the other environments, perhaps the closest to being a balanced engagement, though the percentage of time devoted to monitoring is also high, in particular during long distance flights.

The change from active to passive engagement in medicine is smoother than in aviation or nuclear since medicine is much less automated and the signals to change from monitoring to active performance can generally be anticipated more easily. In nuclear process control and aviation, the jump into active involvement may be more sudden and switch-like (i.e. sudden onset of communication demands).

Dependency on Communication

The working environments depend to a different extent on verbal communication to assure safe operation. The spatial separation of persons may play a role here as well as the technology employed for interaction:

- High dependency on verbal communication,
- Medium dependency on verbal communication and
- Low dependency on verbal communication.

Nuclear power plant operations are conducted by a team of several persons inside and outside the control room. Procedures, work permission forms or checklists usually guide communication. Verbal communication is mainly used for fine-tuning the tasks. Aviation has a mix of procedural and free verbal communication (e.g. checklist for take off vs. communication with air traffic control (ATC) in an unexpected situation). Surgery is conducted by a team in close spatial relationship with eye contact, which in most cases allows each person to notice the emotional state of each partner in the working environment. However, this may change in the future with a shift to remote surgery (e.g. via Internet and robots).

This dimension shows that the different industries can learn from each other how to assure safe communication. Analyses of several incidents in nuclear plants show that the standard phraseology used in aviation may be helpful in overcoming misunderstandings associated with remote communication (i.e. communication between ATC and flight deck happens mainly in standard phraseology). Nuclear experience suggests, on the other hand, that new, automated systems in ATC may reduce the opportunity for the air traffic controller to notice whether or not a pilot is busy with additional problems in the cockpit and, therefore, unable to take requests from ATC. Medicine may consider experiences from both domains in order to cope with further automation in the operating room.

Uncertainty of Disturbances

The more complex a system is the more uncertainty may arise during an emergency. Uncertainty may also be influenced by latent weaknesses in the system. Examples are when a patient has health problems in addition to the one currently being treated or when a redundant system in aviation or nuclear process control is unavailable. Uncertainty may arise from the system itself, from the interface of the system or from the means to cope with a disturbance. All working environments investigated in GIHRE have a high level of system uncertainty. All deal with complex issues (humans flying and process control, for example) but with different levels of external uncertainties:

- Low uncertainty in external influencing factors,
- Medium uncertainty in external influencing factors and
- High uncertainty in external influencing factors.

As nuclear process control is an inherently closed system, it generally has a low uncertainty regarding external influences. Medicine has medium external threat (e.g. reliance on blood coming from outside). Aviation has the highest uncertainty from external factors due to weather, ATC, traffic and terrain influences on task execution.

The system interface (on average and in the current state of system development) may give the user a more or less precise picture of system state, thereby reducing or increasing uncertainty. The more complex and automated a system, the fuzzier the interface and its feedback to the user may become. A statement about this distinction certainly can only be made for the average.

However, it is essential for effective teamwork that one distinguishes whether the interface works as a distracter (by providing ambiguous feedback) or whether it works to support teamwork (by providing clear feedback). There are two distinctions:

- Clear feedback and
- Ambiguous feedback.

Nuclear and aviation can have quite ambiguous feedback from the interface and the operator or pilot may be forced to diagnose the status of the interface before he/she can reach conclusions about the process itself. Medicine may have a clear relation of interface information to patient-status, but this may change due to further automation and technological development of interfaces.

Contexts: Economic, Organizational and Regulatory Constraints

Beyond the task itself, the different industries are embedded in economic, organizational and regulatory contexts. Context has an impact on the task itself, especially if the task is to be performed within legal boundaries and with considerable legal consequences in the event of error. Economic constraints may have an impact on the thoroughness devoted to investigating unusual circumstances (e.g. reluctance to investigate the additional health problems of a patient, ignoring additional side effects in process control or aviation or disregarding flight-plan changes ordered by ATC). Readiness to accept economic constraints generally decreases as economic competitiveness increases. Safety therefore suffers from economic pressure. Economic pressures are usually forwarded onto the work force by management of the system. Another type of constraint may arise from the regulatory context in which the technical environment is embedded. Regulatory pressures may impact the liabilities of those doing a job.

In psychological terms, economic and regulatory constraints create additional tasks for the user, which then have to be carried out in conjunction with the main task (e.g. surgery, plant control, flying). Users are forced to balance their activities between safety and economy in any work-situation. Experimental psychology describes situations in which a task can only be performed successfully by neglecting a second one within the dual task paradigm. The basic research in GIHRE may therefore provide insights into how people balance constraints from safety and economy in critical decisions. Possible distinctions include:

- Strong influence of economic, regulatory or organizational issues on the operational task;
- Medium influence of either economic or regulatory or organizational issues on the operational task,
- Low influence of regulatory issues on the operational task.

In nuclear process control and aviation, the economic and regulatory impact is enormous. Incident investigations in nuclear process control show that peoples' adherence to procedures in critical situations is higher than in normal situations. Ironically, operators are forced to react more flexibly in such situations because procedures may no longer cover the situation at hand. This may be a result of fearing personal liability in the case that the procedure is not followed (Sträter, 2000). Medicine has less impact from regulatory issues, but the economic pressure is certainly higher than in nuclear process control because of the possibility of legal actions for malpractice, especially in the United States. Aviation can be seen as a mixture in terms of regulatory and economic constraints.

Level of Familiarity with Task

The subjectively perceived workload at a given task load is certainly influenced by the level of familiarity with the task. The more familiar a user becomes with a certain task, the less workload he/she will perceive, though the task load remains constant. Level of familiarity with a task may be structured according to Rasmussen (1986) into the following:

- Skill-based (highly routine task, which is quasi automated),
- Rule-based (combining a number of automated ways of behavior into a new pattern of behavior) and
- Knowledge-based (cognitively demanding inference processes in unpracticed or novel situations).

In medicine, an appendectomy may be more skill based than a complicated cancer operation (which would be more knowledge based). In nuclear process control, the level of familiarity can be distinguished based on the assumed disturbance. While standard disturbances (so-called design-based accidents) are well trained and fall in to the area of skill and rule based behavior, unanticipated disturbances that are not dealt with by procedures have to be assumed to be knowledge-based. Disturbances can be classified in a similar manner in aviation, as pilots have made similar distinctions between coping with scenarios for which they have received training vs. novel, untrained scenarios.

Level of Cultural Communication Skills

The cohesion of teams within the different working environments varies. Depending on the backgrounds of the team members, different communication skills may be required. Social and salary status may be an indicator of such cultural issues. Different educational backgrounds may create better or worse understanding but certainly imply additional tasks for dealing effectively with each other (e.g. people with different backgrounds have to explain what they do and what to expect). The following three categories may be distinguished:

- Team structure with same background and good implicit understanding of among team members;
- Team structure with different backgrounds but a fairly good understanding among team members;
- Team members with different backgrounds.

On the flight deck, team members usually share a common education and speak the same technical language. Understanding ATC can be assumed to be fairly simple because the communication culture is similar to that of the flight deck. Medicine has large differences in the backgrounds of team members (doctors, nurses and technicians), which may cause misunderstandings. Nuclear process control has coherent team structures in the control room but has huge differences between control-room crew and external or internal maintenance staff, especially if the maintenance issues stem from different technical areas (e.g. mechanical vs. electronic).

Individual Goals and Attitudes

Individual goals that one intends to achieve in a work situation certainly affect team performance. The *Process Control Group* investigated the impact of the current goal-state of communication partners on communication performance and found four general cases (Sträter, 2002):

- Carelessness about information on the side of the receiver (fixation on task performance of receiver leading to ignoring information from the sender);
- Wrong assumption about information received on the side of the receiver (ambiguity of the message forces the receiver to make judgments based on his/her experiences about what is meant by sender);
- Communication avoidance on the side of the sender (fixation on task performance of sender leading to communication avoidance);
- Communication breakdown, no provision of information on the side of the sender (reluctance to communicate due to being busy with other tasks, e.g. problem solving).

The presence of a common goal can have more influence on task performance than the technology with which a user is working. Conflicts in goals are known as a resource for communication problems in organizational psychology (e.g. Schuler, 1995). Therefore, an essential element of team resource management in communication is to make the goals and intentions explicit to the co-worker in order to avoid misunderstandings (e.g. VGB, 1998 or Crichton & Flin, 1999).

In addition to common goals, attitudes of team members towards the task to be performed, as well as towards the team members, play an important role in team quality (e.g., Cannon-Bowers et al., 1995). Attitudes may influence willingness to communicate although common goals exist. Roessingh and Zon (2004) investigated the influence of attitudes on teamwork and found the following attitudes to be important:

- Attitudes regarding the importance of the team for the achievement of own objectives:
    a. Belief in the importance of teamwork
    b. Belief in the continuous learning process as one of the main functions of a team
- Attitudes regarding the value of co-operation
    a. Willingness to develop team spirit, team morale and team cohesion
    b. Willingness to maintain identity of the team
- Attitudes towards team members
    a. Readiness to follow a shared team vision
    b. Mutual trust in the team members.

Attitudes about teamwork may, for instance, influence whether or not team members request help from each other (e.g. IAEA, 2001). The absence of a questioning attitude (a willingness to request additional information from each other in case of an ambiguous system status) was revealed to be an important contributor for critical events in nuclear power plants.

Team Composition: Distribution of Knowledge and Experience

Team interaction and performance are very directly influenced by the composition of the team: its size, hierarchical positions of team members, professional backgrounds and experience and familiarity among members. The teams studied in GIHRE vary substantially from very small two person and mono-professional teams in the cockpit to teams of a dozen or more people of diverse professional backgrounds and experience in intensive care units. Some teams have several hierarchical layers as in medicine; others have a clear assignment of responsibility but shared decision making, as in the cockpit. Some teams have worked together for years, as in nuclear power plants and others may only perform together once in their lives, as in cockpits.

The *Behavioral Markers Group* studied one particular aspect of team composition in aviation, the so-called cockpit authority gradient, i.e. the difference in status between captain and co-pilot that is expressed by the experience they bring to their roles. The cockpit authority gradient is seen as one causal factor of teamwork failure in incidents and accidents, when a junior crew member (lower rank and little experience) does not speak up or transfer important information to a crew member with superior status (high rank and experience) or when a senior crew member does not listen to important input from a junior. Recently, due to major reorganization in many airlines, it has become more common for co-pilots to be older and have more experience than captains, which creates a very special situation for the crew. The *Behavioral Markers Group* has investigated different patterns of crew composition in regards to number of years of experience in the position of captain and co-pilot. Four patterns of crew composition were expected to be less optimal for team performance. A first pattern of non-optimal crew composition occurs when both crew members are inexperienced in their positions as captain and first officer (low/low): both crew members are expected to be less secure in their role behavior. A second pattern entails a very new captain flying together with a highly experienced first officer (low/high); the captain possesses about the same amount of experience and hence the two might be very similar in their level of expert knowledge but not in their role status. This might lead to role insecurity from the captain or the co-pilot. A third non-optimal pattern is assumed to exist when a highly experienced captain is flying with an inexperienced first officer (high/low). In this constellation the first officer might have difficulties challenging the captain. A fourth combination consists of two highly experienced crew members (high/high). This crew composition is expected to be non-optimal, especially in non-normal situations. Both crew members have their own concept of problem management. Therefore, they need more co-ordination and, as both crew members have high role security, this can lead to more conflicts. These four distinct patterns of non-optimal crew compositions (low/low, low/high, high/low and high/high) were compared with all other crews that have other combinations of little, average and high experience in position. This comparison group is referred to as *all other crew compositions*. It was expected that crews with non-optimal composition would be lower in their team performance. The number of crews in each of the groups and their average experience are summarized in Table 8.3.

Table 8.3   Descriptives of different crew compositions

Crew composition[1]	Mean experience in position (in years)		N
	Captain	First Officer	
Low/low	0.79 (.39)[2]	0.93 (.35)	7
Low/high	1.00 (. 45)	5.67 (3.33)	6
High/low	5.92 (2.41)	0.96 (.32)	13
High/high	6.50 (2.43)	6.25 (2.75)	6
All other crew compositions	2.11 (.98)	1.62 (1.26)	14

[1] Combination of experience in position captain/first officer
[2] Standard deviation in brackets

In contrast, in the following analyses, the number of cases per group was partially reduced due to the lack of observability of certain behavioral markers used for the measurement of crew performance in some of the crews. Team performance was analyzed in three different scenarios (cf. descriptions in Chapter 2). Groups with non-optimal crew composition were compared with the comparison group (all other crew compositions) using t-tests. Table 8.4 illustrates descriptives and results for those behavioral markers with which large differences between non-optimal groups and the comparison group occurred.

Table 8.4 **Descriptives and t-tests for behavioral markers of non-optimal patterns of crew composition compared to all other crew compositions**

Scen ..	Behavioral marker	Patterns	N	Mean	SD	SE of mean	Mean diff.	t	df	Sign. (2-tailed)
1	Communica-tion environment	Low/high	5	2.6	.55	.24	-.54	-2.517	17	.022
		All other c.	14	3.14	.36	.01				
1	Briefing	High/high	6	2.33	.52	.21	-.60	-1.960	18	.053
		All other c.	14	.293	.62	.16				
1	Plans stated	High/high	6	2.5	.55	.22	-.57	-1.960	18	.066
		All other c.	14	3.07	.62	.16				
2	Assertiveness	Low/low	7	2.43	.79	.30	-.75	-2.343[++]	8.052	.047
		All other c.	11	3.18	.40	.12				
2	Communication environment	Low/low	7	2.57	.79	.30	-.71	-2.624	19	.017
		All other c.	14	3.29	.47	.13				
2	Communication environment	High/high	6	3.00	.00	.00	-.29	-2.280[++]	13.0	.040
		All other c.	14	3.29	.47	.13				
3	Briefing	Low/low	7	2.43	.79	.30	-.64	-1.988[++]	8.256	.081
		All other c.	14	3.07	.47	.13				
3	Monitoring/ Cross-check	Low/low	7	2.57	.79	.30	-.64	-2.457	19	.024
		All other c.	14	3.21	.43	.11				
3	Workload management	Low/low	6	2.50	.55	.22	-.50	-2.236[++]	5.0	.076
		All other c.	12	3.00	.00	.00				
3	Automation management	Low/high	5	3.00	.00	.00	.45	2.887[++]	10.0	.016
		All other c.	11	2.55	.52	.16				
3	Monitoring/ Cross-check	High/low	13	2.85	.38	.10	-.37	-2.375	25	.026
		All other c.	14	3.21	.43	.11				
3	Monitoring/ Cross-check	High/high	5	2.80	.45	.20	-.41	-1.845	17	.082
		All other c.	14	3.21	.43	.11				

Scen.: Scenario; All other c.: All other crew compositions; Mean diff.: Mean difference
LOSA markers are measured on a four-point scale (poor, marginal, good, outstanding)
[++] Results do not assume equal variance for both groups.

In scenario one in which crews have to manage technical failures that lead to difficulties in aircraft control, two groups with non-optimal crew composition (low/high and high/high) show some impairments of team performance. The behavioral markers concerned are communication environment, briefing and plans stated. They are all linked to establishing a team and organizing its tasks.

In scenario two, crews have to manage a technical problem that is difficult to diagnose. Two groups with non-optimal crew composition (low/low and high/high) have lower performance. The behavioral markers concerned are assertiveness and communication environment. The markers again deal with team functioning: communication and persistence in stating critical information.

In scenario three, consisting of a normal but difficult approach, three of the four groups with non-optimal crew composition (low/low, low/high and high/high) differed from the comparison group on some aspects of team performance. The group in which both captain and first officer were inexperienced (low/low) performed worse than the comparison group in briefing, monitoring/cross-check and workload management. Unexpectedly, the group with inexperienced captain but highly experienced first officer (low/high) was better in automation management than the comparison group. Obviously, the experienced first officer, who is pilot flying in this scenario, managed to fly this approach with good use of technical equipment. Monitoring/cross-check was worse in crews with highly experienced captain and inexperienced first officers (high/low), as well as in crews with highly experienced captains and first officers (high/high). In this scenario, monitoring seemed to be especially worse in most of the groups with non-optimal crew composition.

The results from the three different scenarios show that groups with non-optimal crew composition concerning position experience of crew members do have impaired team performance, especially in terms of communicating and planning work together. One reason for this could be that non-optimal team compositions may result in less role comfort. This might negatively affect communication and working together as a team. Table 8.5 gives a summary of the areas in which large differences between groups with non-optimal crew composition and the comparison group were found. As can be seen in the table, performance differences occurred for all non-optimal groups (low/low, low/high, high/low and high/high) in all three scenarios and almost always in the expected direction.

Table 8.5   Differences between non-optimal crew compositions and all other crew compositions

| Non-optimal pattern[1] | All other crew compositions | | |
	Scenario 1	Scenario 2	Scenario 3
Low/low		**Assertiveness** **Communication**	Briefing **Monitoring** WL Management
Low/high	**Communication Environment**		**Automation Mamagement**[+]
High/low			**Monitoring/Cross-Check**
High/high	Briefing Plans stated	**Communication Environment**	Monitoring/Cross-Check

[1] Four non-optimal compositions of individual experience based on years in position for captain/ first officer in crews

Behavioral markers written in bold letters show significant differences between a non-optimal crew combination and all other crew combinations.

Normal writing signifies only a trend toward a significant difference between a non-optimal crew composition and all other crew compositions.

[+] Unexpected direction of difference: a non-optimal crew composition received higher performance on respective behavioral marker

The Task Process: Achieving Team Goals and Coping with Threats and Errors in the Operating Context

Achieving goals in high risk professions not only involves primary duties, whether generating power, treating patients or flying aircraft but also involves coping simultaneously with the threats to safety posed by the operational context and the limited capabilities of human operators.

One means of depicting performance in high risk environments is in terms of the factors that can place outcomes at risk and the inevitable human errors that accompany team performance.

Background

A continuing line of research in aviation has developed a methodology called the Line Operations Safety Audit (LOSA: Helmreich, et al, 2001; Klinect, 2003) in which expert observers systematically record the behavior of flight crews during normal operations under conditions of absolute confidentiality. Central to these observations is the recording of how threats to safety (risks) in the operating environment and team errors are managed. Empirical data from this project provided the basis for development of a formal model of how threats and errors are managed, the University of Texas Threat and Error Management Model (UT-TEMM: Helmreich, Klinect). UT-TEMM can serve as a framework for the analysis of accidents and incidents in both aviation and medicine. The International Air Transport Association (IATA) uses it for classification of the global aircraft accidents and incidents while Continental Airlines employs it for the analysis of pilot reports of flight incidents. In medicine, the model also provides a framework for understanding near misses and events resulting in patient harm or death (Helmreich & Musson, 2000).

From process industry, several other error models have been developed: the generic error modeling system of Reason (1990), the model of Kanse and van der Schaaf for chemical accidents (2000), the ATHEANA model of the Nuclear Regulatory Commission for modeling errors of commission (NUREG-1624, 2000) or the Cognitive Reliability and Error Analysis Method of Hollnagel (1998). In the context of team interaction as investigated in the GIHRE project, the UT-TEMM model was seen as the most suitable, as the concepts of threat and error management can provide a coherent framework for integrating the various methodological and conceptual approaches to group performance in stressful, high risk environments. The general components of the model are described in the following section with examples from aviation and surgery.

The Threat and Error Management Model (TEMM)[32]

Threats This model defines threats as events and errors that lie outside the individual or team and require active management to ensure safety and effective performance. Threats increase the complexity of the operational environment and can be either overt or latent.

Overt threats Overt threats in aviation and medicine originate in the *system* and/or the *organization*. Overt threats in aviation include adverse weather, airport conditions and aircraft malfunctions and communication errors with external units such as company operations, dispatch, maintenance and ground errors, air traffic control errors or pressures and company operational time pressure.

Overt threats in medicine include patient condition, staff support levels and training, external errors such as improper medications or interactions among medications, misdiagnoses in the laboratory and failures of equipment such as ventilators that provide breathing support or infusion pumps that deliver controlled dosages of medication. Figure 8.5 shows overt threats present in the aviation and nuclear environment.

a) in aviation

Adverse weather	Operational time pressure
Terrain	Traffic
Airport conditions	Non-normal operations
Aircraft malfunctions	Maintenance events/errors
Automation events	Dispatch events/errors
Communications events	Ground crew events/errors

b) in nuclear

Layout of procedures	Situational conditions
Ergonomics of human machine interface	Misleading indicators
Task preparation and organization	Reliability of technical equipment
Shift between high and low vigilance	Dynamics of the process
Team structure	Latent plant conditions

Figure 8.5 Overt threats a) in aviation b) in nuclear

Latent threats Latent threats are factors not directly linked to observable threats and error that increase risk and the probability of error. Latent threats in both aviation and medicine include the inadequate supervision of personnel and/or regulatory oversight, flawed or absent procedures, scheduling and rostering practices that result in fatigue, lack of critical experience, inappropriate performance assessment practices and inadequate accident and incident investigation. Latent threats are not readily apparent before catastrophes occur but

---

[32] Empirical and conceptual research supporting the development of the model in aviation was funded by a grant from the U.S. Federal Aviation Administration, Robert Helmreich, Principal Investigator. Additional support for research in medicine has been provided by grants from the U.S. Agency for Healthcare Research and Quality, Robert Helmreich, Principal Investigator.

are the source of major risks in professions such as medicine, aviation and nuclear power generation.

Error The concept of error as a deviation from the expected or intended course of action exists in both the real world and academia. James Reason (1990, 1997) greatly changed the understanding of error by pointing out that errors often result from the alignment of a variety of latent threats and hence can be understood as system failures. Other researchers such as Dekker (2003b) go further in rejecting the idea of individual accountability for error, placing responsibility at the organizational or system level. While it is certainly true that system factors are root causes of many individual and team deviations, those who are at the sharp end of technological endeavors are not simply hapless pawns of flawed systems. Individuals and teams may willingly violate required procedures or may fail to prepare themselves for job requirements (for example, arriving at work fatigued or otherwise incapacitated). Safety requires accountability at the individual and organizational level. Classification of the types of individual and team errors that occur can provide information essential to optimizing systems and developing countermeasures against their recurrence.

Errors that are committed by teams can be placed into four broad categories. *Procedural errors* define instances when teams are trying to follow established procedures but make mistakes in task execution. In aviation an example is setting the wrong altitude in a flight management computer; in medicine omitting a step in setting up an anesthesia machine for surgery. *Communication errors* occur when information is transmitted incorrectly between team members or is misunderstood by the recipient. Examples are a co-pilot misunderstanding a captain's course order or a nurse misunderstanding a doctor's verbal instructions for medication. *Decision errors* represent a discretionary choice of action that unnecessarily increases risk. These would be reflected in a captain choosing to fly into an area of severe thunderstorms to save time or a surgeon electing to employ a high risk procedure when an equally effective, but less dangerous one is available. Finally, *intentional non-compliance errors* are instances when a crew makes a conscious decision to violate required procedures. A serious (and historically fatal) non-compliance error in aviation is the failure to complete a pre-take off checklist with the result being a stall and crash because the flaps were not extended. An equally egregious non-compliance error in medicine is a surgeon failing to scrub before beginning an operation. The most prominent error committed by teams is Chernobyl, when the overconfidence of the team in its own capabilities led to the accident (Sträter, in press).

As discussed in a previous section, there is a dramatic difference between aviation and medicine in the prevalence of mandatory procedures. Aviation has established formal procedures for almost every contingency. Fatal air crashes often result in new rules governing flight operations – a phenomenon that is called *tombstone regulation*. The widespread occurrence of intentional non-compliance with rules may be a reaction to over-proceduralization. In contrast, medicine has a dearth of formal regulatory guidance for the interpersonal behavior of personnel. For example, one major health organization in the United States began to adopt safety procedures from aviation. One of the first practices recommended to surgical teams was to conduct formal briefings before beginning an operation to make sure all team members share the same mental model of the situation and are aware of possible complications and contingency plans.[33]

Outcomes of error Three different outcomes are associated with a team error:

- The error may be inconsequential, meaning it has no effect on the outcome of the team task or the continuing processes of the team;
- It may lead to an undesired state (in aviation, an undesired aircraft state or in medicine an undesired patient state). Examples of an undesired aircraft state include improper configuration such as flaps not extended for take off or navigation on the wrong heading or at the wrong altitude. Undesired states in medicine include reactions to administration of the wrong drug or the wrong dosage of the right drug or dangerously low blood pressure caused by the slip of a surgeon's scalpel;
- The error may lead to an additional error creating an error chain.

Use of the Threat and Error Management Model (TEMM)

Figure 8.6 shows the Threat and Error Management Model (TEMM) graphically.

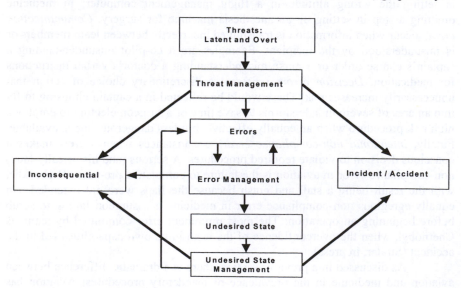

Figure 8.6   The University of Texas Threat and Error Management Model

---

[33] In collaboration with the late Hans-Gerhard Schaefer, Robert Helmreich attempted to introduce the practice of joint briefings for surgeons, anaesthesiologists, nurses and support personnel in a Swiss teaching hospital in the mid-1990s. This effort was ridiculed by many surgeons, one of whom commented that 'checklists are for the lame and the weak.'

The Threat and Error Management Model provides an over-arching framework for examining group processes in a variety of environmental conditions ranging from benign to extremely stressful. Systematically defining latent and overt threats, the response to threat as well as error and undesired states and their management can result in a better understanding of the context in which teams interact as well as the interaction processes themselves. A variety of methodological and theoretical approaches can be employed using the model to explore issues in psycholinguistics, physiological, cultural and organizational and social psychology.

Chapter 9

Structural Features
of Language and Language Use

Manfred Krifka

Introduction

While language is not only used for communication (think of thinking out loud, as in organizing one's thoughts), communication is one of the prime uses of language. And while communication is possible without language (think of gestures, signs, pictures, alarm sounds), language certainly facilitates communication and is arguably necessary for the communication of complex content. In turn, communication is essential for the co-ordination of joint actions in groups or teams.

This chapter discusses language and communication behavior in groups in high risk environments. Its purpose is to point the reader to studies that are relevant for such groups. The general way of thinking about communication developed in linguistics is important in order to appreciate the role that communication plays in co-ordination within a group and for the way in which a group copes with difficult situations. The approach of this chapter is rather eclectic, as communication has been approached from quite different angles and with different means.

The chapter first introduces the notion of common ground, which is central for the understanding of communication. It goes on to discuss human language specifics that facilitate communication. Communication is then related to the threat and error management model that is central to GIHRE. It outlines the benefits, and potential problems, of standardization in technical settings. Then a number of theoretical frameworks for the study of communication are discussed: Speech Act theory, Conversation Analysis and theories concerned with thematic coherence. Finally, some specific problems of communication under stress and high workload are discussed. In general, the emphasis is on structural features of language and language use, as contrasted to language processing, which is the main topic of Chapter 11.

Common Ground and Shared Mental Models

In order to understand the past and future behavior of others, one requires the ability to imagine how other persons perceive, think and act. Such an assumption about the minds of others is called a theory of mind. Working together in a group is facilitated if each member of the group has a theory of mind for the other members; this theory will also include the knowledge that others have a theory of one's own mind. The prime task in communication is to facilitate the establishment, maintenance and modification of such shared assumptions about one another's minds; this is the so-called *common ground* (see Clark 1996 for discussion). Communication consists, in particular, of updating the common ground, of adding information to it or modifying it in a way that is obvious to all members of the group. If such modifications are accepted, all members take it for granted that everyone knows that the modifications have became part of the common ground, and that all will, therefore, act accordingly. In this way, common ground is the basis for shared mental models that provide coherence to the actions of a group (cf. Cannon-Bowers e.a. 1993).

What types of information does one find in the common ground? Everything the participants of the group have uttered with the intention of being understood by other participants (and whether they were understood is often indicated by acknowledgements like *okay*, verbal gestures like *mm-hmm*, or non-verbal gestures like nodding). Such utterances may be factual claims, like *we have an underexcited fault light on number three*, uttered by a pilot in an aircraft cockpit. Typically, if other participants do not contradict such claims, they become part of the factual knowledge of the common ground, and henceforward are taken to be known by all participants. In turn, it is taken to be known that all participants know this. Such utterances may be questions, like *Is the fault light still on?*, or commands, like *switch essential power off of number three*, that request certain kinds of actions from other participants such as to give information that answers the question or to perform non-linguistic acts that carry out the command. The common ground does not only consist of factual knowledge that the interlocutors have agreed upon, but also includes the common goals and objectives, as well as the tasks, that the interlocutors have agreed upon in order to achieve these goals and objectives. This could be called the common agenda, but in the following discussion this is considered to be a part of a more general notion of common ground.

Two remarks are in order here. First, not all attempts to modify the common ground, or the common agenda, are successful. The other group members may not understand the attempt to modify it: they may not understand it correctly, or they may refuse the proposed modification. In the latter case, the common ground will at least contain the information that one group member has, or had, a certain belief or intention that did not become part of the common ground. Even if such contributions do not lead to a modified common agenda, they do lead to shared theories of the mental models of the members. Secondly, the common ground is also changed by actions that are not primarily intended to communicate something. If a pilot reacts to an alarm signal in a way that the co-pilot notices, the common ground will contain the information that the pilot has recognized the alarm signal and has reacted to it in a particular way. In many cases, acts of communication and other actions are tightly integrated, and the modification of common ground can only be properly understood if they are analyzed together.

In addition to the modified pieces of information in conversation, the common ground contains the huge background knowledge supposedly shared by the group by virtue of their membership in language communities, societies, professional cultures, regional affiliations and other groups. Speakers flag their allegiances with dress codes, speech style and, in more formal settings, uniforms and other identifiers. The members of the group need not have the same allegiances – consider, e.g. a surgeon and a lab technician. It suffices that they know of relevant allegiances, which leads to certain believes about the background knowledge of the other person. Reliance on background knowledge makes it possible to develop shared mental models for particular situations much more quickly, and – in the case of linguistic background knowledge – is crucial in order to be able to change the common ground: speakers assume that addressees speak the same language, and, hence, can rely on the rules of language to change the common ground. Lack of background knowledge will not only require more work in order to communicate effectively, it will also result in errors of communication especially if the lack of background knowledge is not apparent to participants.

Maintaining and extending the common ground has a purpose. This is even true for casual talk. In the cases of interest here, the purposes are to secure proper functioning of complex devices like a nuclear power plant, or to carry out complex tasks like safely flying an airplane. It is typical for such settings that not only the common ground is changing. The participants' world is changing too: problems occur and are reported; solutions are proposed and discarded or adopted. Linguists and conversation analysts have typically concentrated on discourses in stable environments, such as telling a story or constructing an argument. The dynamics of a situation itself have been largely neglected, even though this is an important factor in communication. Things happen while people are talking; these events have to be evaluated and attended to in an appropriate way, which may shift the specific goals of communication into new directions.

Language as a Tool to Manage the Common Ground

The most important device for maintaining and changing common grounds is language. The idea that language is such a device has been a very fruitful one in linguistics, and there are many important properties of language that can be understood within this perspective. One prominent formal theoretical model is *dynamic interpretation*, which defines utterances as their propensity to change common grounds (cf. Groenendijk & Stokhof 1999). The field of linguistics that investigates the use of language is called pragmatics; see Levinson (1983) for a classic overview and Levinson (2000) for a more recent treatment of more specific aspects.

One example is the use of articles such as *the* and *a*: a noun phrase with an indefinite article, *a(n)*, indicates that a new entity has been introduced into the common ground; a definite pronoun like *it* or a noun phrase with the definite article *the* usually picks up an entity that is present in the common ground because it has been introduced before or is part of the background knowledge. Example: in *we'll give you a holding pattern* the indefinite article indicates that the holding pattern is being newly introduced to the common ground; in *please change the holding pattern*, the definite article indicates a reference to a previously introduced object. In *do the standard holding pattern* (when no holding pattern has been previously mentioned), the definite article indicates that the entity referred to is part of background knowledge.

The use of definite articles is an example of a presupposition, a piece of information that is supposed to already be present in the common ground (cf. van der Sandt 1988, Beaver 1997). Some other examples of presuppositions: when a captain informs the co-pilot *I think there is one on the other side too*, the use of *one* is justified because in the situation at hand, *the ground proximity warning switch* was uttered 12 seconds earlier, hence *one* refers to the ground proximity switch. The use of *other* is justified because the captain had mentioned that he had the warning switch on his side, and the use of *too* is justified because at this point the common ground entails that there is another warning switch. The utterance *okay, we can't* makes sense in the context of the preceding utterance, which was *it says if we can identify the faulty system*; this means: *we cannot identify the faulty system (and have to work things out under this assumption)*. What these presuppositional devices have in common is that they help to integrate new information into information that already exists in the common ground. They also often allow for shorter utterances, thus overcoming a serious bottleneck of speech, its slow transmission rate (generally estimated to be of the magnitude of 10 bytes per second when counting the information inherent in phonemes, the distinctive sounds of speech).

Natural language facilitates communication in several other respects, in addition to the use of presuppositions. One important feature is heavy reliance on so-called implicatures, a concept developed by philosopher H.P. Grice. It refers to those aspects of meaning that a speaker wants the addressee to understand, even though they are not part of the literal meaning of what the speaker says. Implicatures are a pervasive phenomenon of communication, a fact that is often not recognized at all by native speakers. If a captain utters the command *Pull up!* then this is normally understood as 'pull up *now*!', not as 'pull up in 20 seconds!' If a pilot planning to divert around a thunderstorm asks *is the Southern okay?* and gets the reply, *the way around north is*, the implicature is that the southern route may not be okay. If a pilot of a three-engine plane says *we have two engines working*, what is meant is that only two, and not three, engines are working. Implicatures can be derived under the assumption that speakers follow certain rules, so-called maxims of conversation. For example, one maxim says that speakers should be as informative as possible. In the last example, the utterance *we have three engines working* would have been more informative than the utterance *we have two engines working*, and hence would have been preferred; the fact that it was not uttered gives rise to the implicature that the utterance *we have three engines working* would have expressed something false. Note, again, that reliance on implicatures allows a more efficient use of communication, a point stressed in Levinson (2000).

There are various ways in which natural language signals the relevance of a particular piece of information for the common ground. Consider the use of *but* in *but we're dragging the gear around*. It indicates that the information that the plane is flying with released landing gear is contrary to some information or goal in the common ground. An issue in the context of this utterance is whether or not the plane has enough fuel for a second approach landing; the utterances immediately following were *fifteen on the gas right now; I guess that's enough for a second approach, probably, huh?* The information that the landing gear has been released is contrary to the information that there is enough fuel for a second approach landing, as released landing gear means higher fuel consumption. There are many so-called discourse particles that direct the integration of new information into the common ground, like *well, however, actually, now, you know* or *luckily* (cf. Schiffrin 1988). Intonation can also perform similar functions, often of a very general nature (cf. Pierrehumbert & Hirschberg 1990).

Natural language can also highlight what is new or particularly important about a piece of information. Many languages, including English and German, rely mainly on intonation for this purpose; others, including Romance languages, make heavy use of syntactic reorganizations of the sentence. For example, the sentences *the left engine is WORKING* and *the LEFT engine is working* express the same information (they are true in the same circumstances), but they do so with different emphasis. The first sentence could be uttered out-of-the-blue, with no previous information that points to the fact that there is something going on with the engines. The second sentence presupposes that some engine is working, and adds, as new information, that it is the left engine. The first sentence could be an answer to a question like *what's going on?*. The second one could be an answer to a question like *which engine is working?* The identification of new parts helps the hearer to integrate information into the common ground in two ways: first, it allows for a quicker phonetic realization of the old parts (they are deaccented, pronounced faster and often elided; as in *the LEFT engine* or *the left ENGine*). Second, it suggests to the addressee that the speaker had a notion of the common ground that required a specific type of information, and thus helps to maintain a shared notion of the common ground.

Threat and Error Management in Communication

Although language is an excellent tool for the maintenance of common ground that has been shaped and sharpened by evolutionary pressures over much of the development of *homo loquens* and has proven crucial for the success of our species, errors, sometimes fatal, do occur.

The Texas Aviation Threat and Error Management Model (TEMM) identifies communication errors as one of five fundamental types of error, (see Chater 8). But communication itself can be seen from a TEMM perspective. An error in communication consists, essentially, of a failure to properly update the common ground. There are various reasons that this failure can occur: perhaps the common ground is not updated at all because a group member thinks that this is not necessary or does not feel secure enough to do so, or a group member attempts to update the common ground but does so in an inefficient or misleading way. Or the update is performed quite well, but other members fail to perceive and integrate this update in the intended way. The result is that participants end up with mental models of the situation that differ in crucial respects, which leads to misunderstandings and unco-ordinated actions.

There are a number of distinguishable threats, that is, factors that increase the likelihood of communication errors. For example, high workload distracts the attention of team members and may impede the ability to produce and understand utterances; background noise or restricted information channels, such as intercom lines, reduce the acoustic and visual information of utterances; faulty terminology may invite misunderstandings; attempts to save face, in particular in socially asymmetric crews, may induce crew members to withhold or to disregard crucial information. And there are techniques, such as improving terminology, communication technology or communication procedures, that lead to the better management of errors. They may be directed at reducing threats, or they may be directed at discovering errors as early as possible. Increasing redundancy, repeating information, utilizing explicit verbalization of presuppositions, thinking out loud or practicing vigilance for apparently incongruous communication behavior may be helpful in detecting errors at an early stage.

Reducing threats and improving management of error may sometimes be relatively straightforward – for example, by arranging consoles in such a way that allows for eye contact or by introducing a term like *roger* for acknowledgments (used to identify the letter R, for 'message received,' as in Morse code). But improvements are often either difficult to achieve, or may have detrimental side effects. For example, increasing redundancy and repetition of information, or making inherent presuppositions explicit also strains the crew members' linguistic and cognitive resources. As a case in point, the *Linguistic Factors Group* found that captains with an overall poor rating produced relatively *more* speech acts that informed or reminded the first officer of relevant states of affairs. Any one who attempts to reduce threats stemming from communication will have to walk a narrow path between the conflicting goals of ensuring sufficient redundancy on the one hand and avoiding distracting verbosity on the other. Human communication, in general, walks this narrow path, as recognized by philosopher H. P. Grice in his conversational maxim of quantity, which states: (i) Make your contribution as informative as is required (for the current purpose of the exchange), and (ii) Do not make your contribution more informative than is required.

Requirements of Terminology: Expressiveness, Economy, Standardization

One obvious important factor in efficient communication is the development of adequate terminology with which to deal with situations that may be encountered during the execution of a task. This terminology should be expressive enough to clearly distinguish classes of such situations wherever necessary, and, in particular, when misunderstandings would lead to serious consequences. It also should be economical in the sense that situation types that occur frequently or objects referred to often can be identified using shorter expressions than rarer situation types or objects that are addressed more rarely. Natural languages, by natural processes of language change, show clear evidence for this kind of optimization (Zipf's laws, for example, automobile developed into auto). The use of acronyms, such as ILS for Instrumental Landing System, is the most obvious feature of regimented technical languages for shortening frequent expressions, but there are many other abbreviated set phrases that are often not codified. For example, a surgeon might refer to the caval vein by using the term *cava*. Economy should be a principle in the design of technical languages, but one should keep in mind that economy might also result in reduced redundancy and increased ambiguity, both of which may lead to errors in communication. An expression like *flaps two*, while short, could be either a statement or a command.

The requirement that technical languages be expressive enough to distinguish relevant classes of situations means, among other things, that they can be neither ambiguous nor vague when this would have consequences for the tasks to be solved. Here, ambiguity refers to cases in which an expression can be alternatively considered true or false, such as *John saw that gasoline can explode*, a syntactically ambiguous sentence that rests on word ambiguities such as *can*, which could mean 'have the possibility to' or 'container.' In a situation in which John witnessed the explosion of a container of gasoline, this sentence could be considered true or false, depending on its reading. *Vagueness* refers to cases in which an expression can be said to be true to a certain degree; e.g. *the plane lost its fuel* may be considered true, loosely speaking, even if some fuel remained. Many degree expressions, such as *large* or *many*, and even nouns such as *crowd* or *mountain* (in contrast to *hill*) are inherently vague.

Ambiguity is a pervasive phenomenon of natural languages and technical derivatives thereof. It is rarely perceived because either the difference between available readings doesn't matter, or the common ground is such that only one of the readings makes any sense at all. In certain types of texts, like legal or diplomatic documents, ambiguity might even be welcomed. But there are many cases in which ambiguity has led to catastrophic errors. In aviation, Cushing (1994) has reported a number of hair-raising stories. Ambiguity was arguably involved in the most severe accident in commercial aviation, the collision of two airplanes at the Tenerife airport in 1977, mentioned in Chapter 11. This incident centers around the question of whether the phrase *we are now at take-off* is to be interpreted as 'we are now at the take-off point' or as a kind of progressive tense, 'we are now in the process of taking off.' There are other such word ambiguities or structural ambiguities in aviation language. Cushing mentions the verb *hold*, which in

LIVERPOOL
JOHN MOORES UNIVERSITY
AVRIL ROBARTS LRC
TEL. 0151 231 4022

aviation parlance means 'stop what you are doing right now', but in ordinary English can also mean, 'continue what you are doing right now.' Acronyms can also be a source of trouble; Cushing mentions the use of *PD* to mean 'pilot's discretion' or 'profile descent.'

There are different types of ambiguity, and only a few of them – the ambiguity of words or idiomatic phrases – can be addressed using terminology design. There is also syntactic ambiguity: *back on the power* can be read as [*back on*] [*the power*], that is, add more power, or [*back*] [*on the power*], that is, reduce the power. Furthermore, there is pronominal ambiguity, as in *A yacht ran into a ferry. It sank.* In this case it is not clear whether the yacht or the ferry sank. The likelihood that such ambiguities may occur differs with different languages. For structural reasons, English is more prone to ambiguities than German, which has a more articulate gender system. Furthermore, there is indexical ambiguity, which is caused by different possible locations of the center of reference: *the lever left of you* is ambiguous in a way that *the lever on your left* is not. The spatial arrangement of the group members, face-to-face in the operating room or side-by-side in the airplane cockpit, may lead to potential indexical ambiguity, cf. Chapter 11. Personnel may be trained to avoid these types of ambiguity when possible.

An important ambiguity type not often mentioned is phonetic ambiguity or similarity – an utterance can be understood in two ways because the phonetic realizations are equal, or similar enough, to be confounded. This is especially important when phonetic realization or recognition is affected because the speaker or the addressee has a high workload, or when the phonetic transmission is disturbed, as can be the case when intercoms are used or with the presence of background noise. As an example, Cushing reports a case in which *climb two five zero* is understood as *climb to five zero*, and another in which *cleared to eleven thousand* is understood as *he's clear at eleven thousand*. Phonetic ambiguity can sometimes be reduced, as when *three* is [tri:] instead of [θri:] in aviation, which prevents the high frequency noise of the *th*-sound [θ] that is transmitted incompletely in narrow bandwidth transmissions, or, in German, the use of *zwo* [tswo:] ('two') instead of the standard *zwei* [tswai] to distinguish it from *drei* [drai] (three). As many of these types of ambiguities can hardly be foreseen in advance, it is important to identify them in debriefings, to keep a record of them and to use this in order to gradually improve terminology and technical communication.

As for vagueness, one can generally observe that the reduction of vagueness increases the speaker's task load. If one wants to be precise, more information has to be gathered and verbalized, which is not economical. Vagueness also increases the addressee's task load, because more information has to be understood and integrated. So, it is crucial to ask whether or not the excess work of being more precise is worthwhile. In many cases, it might be sufficient to talk about a *steep ascend* instead of an *a 12 degree ascent*. One conventional way of indicating vagueness with measure terms is the use of rounded numbers; a term like *one thousand feet* generally allows for a more vague interpretation than *nine hundred sixty-five feet*. It may be necessary to indicate explicitly that the intended interpretation should be precise, such as *exactly one thousand feet* (cf. Krifka, 2002).

Common, non-technical language and rules of communication are adaptively optimized for everyday purposes, typically without explicitly stating rules or terms that are formally defined. More specialized fields need specialized languages and communication procedures that are often explicitly standardized. Technical fields differ in the amount of standardization required or expected in communication. While all technical fields have specialized and standardized terminology, they differ in the extent of standardized communication procedures (see Chapter 11). In the three areas studied by GIHRE, the level of standardized communication procedures is high in aviation, somewhat lower in the operation of nuclear power plants and relatively low in the surgical operating room. This roughly corresponds to the general standardization levels in these domains.

In aviation, the use of standardized phraseology in communication is most highly developed and is generally considered to be something that pilots should strive for. In addition, certain formal rules of communication have been established that strive to minimize misunderstandings, like acknowledgments from the addressee that a message has been properly understood, often by reading back, or paraphrasing what has been said. Also, there is a rule of *sterile cockpit* in effect if the plane is below 10,000 feet, which means that only task related communication is supposed to take place.

An operation handbook for nuclear power plant operations describes many procedures, both during normal operations and in the case of difficulties. Operators are supposed to pay attention to the essential information in a systematic way. The handbook also contains recommendations regarding verbal communication: a report should be loud and clear, so that all the attendants can understand it. The speaker must make sure that a report is understood using, for example, eye contact or verbal confirmation, and the addressee should acknowledge that procedural steps that are communicated verbally have been properly understood. Verbatim repeat backs are normally not necessary, but the use of paraphrasing is encouraged (IAEA, 1998).

Chapter 11, on determinants of effective communication, discusses the question of whether the standardization of communicational procedures is always a good thing. One problem pointed out in this chapter is that standardization may bind cognitive resources that, in an emergency, would be better devoted to something else. In the *Process Control Group*, the eye tracking data showed that working through a checklist influenced the distribution of attention: the checklist values are more frequently focused on the screen than on values not mentioned on the checklist. Grommes & Grote (2003) analyze cockpit voice recorder data from an aircraft accident caused by the loss of a propeller engine in which the pilots try to follow the single engine emergency checklist but are interrupted and distracted by ATC, which is following the standard procedure for ATC by trying to find out the position of the plane. This shows that, while the standardization of procedures and communication is generally of great importance, there may be situations in which it is necessary to step back and get a broader picture of the situation and its necessities.

Within the investigation reported in Chapter 5, poorly performing captains actually showed more instances of standard wording in exactly the same type of situation. This can be interpreted as showing that over reliance on standard wording may mask communication deficiencies.

The Role of Speech Acts in Maintaining Common Ground

Language philosophers such as Robert Stalnaker and David Lewis have developed the idea that communication can be seen as maintaining and elaborating on the common ground between the participants of a conversation. Another fruitful idea from 20th century natural language philosophy is that linguistic utterances should be seen as actions in well-defined rule-governed activities with social impact. This is the theory of speech acts as developed by John Austin (1962) and John Searle (1968) with roots in the late work of Ludwig Wittgenstein, especially in his notion of language games. The two approaches are intimately related: speech acts performed by interlocutors have the purpose of establishing, maintaining and developing the common ground.

The main insight from speech act theory is that linguistic utterances do not just express propositions that are true or false, but that they are also acts that change the social reality in which one lives. With speech acts one can ask questions, make promises, give orders, express feelings and even – if in the right position – hire and fire people, baptize them or declare them guilty of a crime. The second group consists of examples of so-called performative speech acts, acts that change aspects of social reality in a general way. The first group of speech acts mentioned change and maintain a particular aspect of social reality, the common ground. These are communicative speech acts, and they are of particular interest here.

Austin distinguished three aspects of speech acts beyond the physical act of uttering something itself, and these are still worth keeping in mind. Assume the pilot of plane *p* says, at time *t*, to ATC: w*e are low on fuel*. With this he/she says something, namely that *p* is low on fuel at *t*; this is the *locutionary act*. In saying this, the pilot informs ATC of something: that *p* is low on fuel at *t*, and asks ATC to recognize the consequences of this fact. This is called the *illocutionary act*. By saying this, the pilot has a particular intention beyond communication itself, e.g. that ATC will give preferential treatment in the landing process. The intention to bring about such an effect is the *perlocutionary act*. There is a natural connection here to the notion of common ground or common agenda: the illocutionary act changes the common ground between the participants. After the pilot's utterance, ATC knows that plane *p* is low on fuel. The pilot knows that ATC knows this, and ATC knows that the pilot knows that ATC knows. The perlocutionary act aims at something beyond communication and maintenance of common ground; it refers to certain expectations about the addressee's behavior.

Speech acts have been analyzed in a number of ways. One well-known system from Searle (1975) distinguishes five classes: (i) representatives, which commit the speaker to the truth of an expressed proposition; (ii) directives, by which the speaker tries to get the addressee to do something; (iii) commissives, which commit the speaker to some future action; (iv) expressives, which express a certain psychological state of the speaker; (v) declarations, by which a speaker in the right position can change social or institutional states. As expressives should also comprise things like apologies and congratulations, which do not necessarily have to be accompanied by the appropriate psychological states, they are called acknowledgements in other classifications, as in the classification from Bach & Harnish (1979). Rather comprehensive systems of speech act classifications have been developed, e.g. by stating lists of conditions for particular speech acts, as in Searle's work, or by developing a formal representation language for speech acts, as in Vanderveken (1990). The empirical evidence for certain speech acts has typically come from speech act verbs like *promise*, *guarantee* or *offer*, the idea being that if a language has a word for a certain linguistic action, this action must be recognized in the community that speaks the language. The possibility that language communities differ in their speech act inventory or in the context in which certain speech acts are used has also been investigated (cf. Blum-Kulka e.a. 1989, Geis 1995, Grass e.a. 1996).

While speech act theory was developed within language philosophy and was not immediately applied to the analysis of real-life communication, there have been several attempts to use it as an insightful empirical research tool, including the work cited on speech acts in different linguistic communities (see Taylor & Cameron 1987 for a critique). For example, Diegritz & Fürst (1999) developed a considerably refined catalogue of speech act categories, which was applied in order to analyze teacher-student interaction in the classroom.

The *Linguistic Factors Group* also utilizes speech acts as crucial analytic tools. This research group settled on a detailed inventory of speech acts called STACK (a German acronym for Speech act Type-inventory for the Analysis of Cockpit Communication), derived from Diegritz & Fürst (1999) for application to cockpit communication. STACK distinguishes between the following groups of speech acts: *Information, Request, Agreement/Negotiation, Dissent, Question, Expressive* and *Interaction Markers*. See Chapter 5 for a more thorough discussion, as well as a listing of the speech act categories employed by STACK. The classification of a particular speech act follows the procedure of Qualitative Progression Analysis, as outlined and described in Diegritz & Fürst (1999).

In Chapter 5, some of the results are given that were obtained by applying this technique to a set of simulation flights that followed the same scenario, in which the success of the crews was independently rated. Good crews showed proportionally more speech acts of the type MAKE SURE, and, in general, more speech acts that ensured that communication went well, like CONFIRM, ACKNOWLEDGE and REAFFIRM. Interestingly, poorly performing crews had a higher incidence of REMIND, suggesting that they had to make use of this repair strategy more often. Good captains uttered more AGREE acts, and fewer CONTRADICT acts, thus positively acknowledging and encouraging contributions from the first officer. They also structured conversation better with STRUCTURE signals. Good first officers showed more CLAIM and SUPPOSE acts, perhaps indicating a communication climate in which it is easier to speak up for the lower-ranked crew member. This can be taken to be strong evidence that the speech act classification, as outlined above and in Chapter 5, provides good tools for identifying certain general features of communication. This even points to specific communication habits that may be improved to communication training.

Speech act theory does not typically address larger structures of conversation. But such structures can, in fact, be analyzed within speech act theory, because speech acts are said to come with certain preconditions. Such preconditions can refer to the context in which a speech act is uttered, and hence to the larger structure in which it occurs. The structural dialogue analysis of Franke (1990) is especially promising. It distinguishes between initiating speech acts and reactive speech acts, such as questions and answers (or refusal to answer), assertions and agreements (or refutations), and suggestions and accepting or rejecting a suggestion. Franke discusses cases in which speech acts retract previous speech acts, revise them or re-iniate them.

From a methodological perspective, speech act theory is relatively easy to apply to spoken text and yields results that can be compared between different groups and different types of situations. However, one should be careful about applying results obtained from speech act theory directly to training. For example, if REMIND speech acts indeed occur more often in poorly performing crews, it is still not to be recommended that speakers should be taught to avoid them. A REMIND speech act might be the best thing in a given situation.

Conversation Analysis

Another approach to communication was developed under the term of Conversational Analysis (CA), which largely follows the ethnomethodological approach of Garfinkel (1967). Garfinkel investigated social reality with methods and categories that are used by the members of a culture themselves to interpret their own social actions. In this tradition, CA, as developed by Harvey Sacks, attempts to avoid premature theorizing and to avoid the definition of *ideal* types because such definitions can have only a vague and indeterminate relationship with any specific set of events. Instead, the participants' implicit methods of interpretation in social interactions should be uncovered and applied to the analysis of conversation. This focus on the formative principles of the specific subject area of investigation – be it small talk at the breakfast table or the verbal interaction of a doctor with a patient – is a guiding principle of CA. This makes the methodologies developed by CA well suited for the analysis of communicative group interaction in technical settings, as investigated by GIHRE, because CA forces the investigator to look at the specific conditions that determine group interaction. On the other hand, results obtained for one type of group cannot be easily generalized to others. Therefore, it is the methodology itself that can be transferred from one application to the next.

According to Bergmann (1991), it is important to pay attention to seemingly irrelevant details like intonation, mispronunciations, pauses, overlaps and interruptions, which must be carefully recorded in the transcript because they often turn out to be crucial for the analysis of communicative interaction. For the analysis, sequences of verbal or non-verbal utterances should be isolated and interpreted as attempts to attain the goals and resolve problems of the interaction at hand. The CA analyst can then describe these underlying goals and problems and investigate the methods that the conversation participants relied on in attaining the goals and solving problems, as well as the methods that are available to speakers in general (cf. Levinson 1983).

This detailed observation and analysis of communication also allows researchers to investigate how communication is embedded in other activities. Nevile (2002) studied how pilots' operating hand movements are integrated into the flow of communication, which provides for better overall communication. Nevile reports a sequence in the cockpit of a non-simulated flight in which the captain orders a new flight level. The first officer doesn't reply immediately but moves his left hand to the Altitude Alert Indicator (AAI) knob in a way that is visible to the captain. Turning it, he utters *okay*, with a lengthened last vowel, which indicates that he is busy following the order. He finally utters *that's set* and removes his hand ostensibly from the knob. Obviously, the visible movements contribute as much to the communication here as what is uttered.

Even though CA argues against rash theorizing across different communicative domains, there are certain features that can be observed in many if not all instances of human communication. One form of interaction investigated prominently in CA is routine sequences of actions in conversation, which are often found in communicative interactions. Sacks (1992) assumes different types of such action sequences like greeting followed by return of greeting or question followed by answer. One of these sequences, assertion – acknowledgement, is particularly important in technical settings. According to Sacks, the adjacency relationship between utterances is the most powerful device for relating utterances because of their institutionalized nature. Recall that such sequences were often neglected in speech act analysis, hence the two theories are genuinely interested in complementary aspects of communication.

Another focus of CA has been the organization of so-called *turn-taking* in conversation. In most conversations, only one person is typically talking at a time, without doubt in order to optimize understanding by reducing processing load – even though there are many exceptions and different cultural or situational preferences for enduring or prohibiting speaking in parallel. The turns, or transitions from one speaker to the next, are often smooth, without overlaps or pauses, but overlaps and pauses do sometimes occur. There are mechanisms for regulating turn taking; a speaker can select the next speaker, or an addressee can signal the wish to speak, using linguistic means such as questions or demands to speak, paralinguistic means such as falling intonation, non-verbal means or gestures like hand waving. In more formal settings, a third party can assign the right to speak. These mechanisms do not guarantee smooth turn takes, and, so, there are repair mechanisms. Often, one person will stop speaking in order to avoid overlap, even if this was not planned. From this one can deduce the relative power of the participants.

Sacks, Schlegloff & Jefferson (1978) have investigated the rules of turn-taking. According to them, turns consist of conversational units that contain so-called *transition relevant places* (TRPs) that are evident to speaker and addressee. At TRPs, the person speaking can assign the right to speak to the addressee, or the addressee can assume this right. Often, the content of the current speaker's turn indicates some preference for the content of the next speaker's turn: assertions want to be affirmed, an invitation wants to be accepted, a biased question wants to be answered in the direction of the bias.

For institutionalized settings of groups in high risk environments, turn-taking is a particularly interesting issue that has not been thoroughly investigated. The dynamics of the situation can make it necessary to override normal turn-taking rules; e.g. if a pilot becomes aware of something of immediate relevance, he/she might interrupt turns at any moment. The situational setting might make it hard to rely on the usual channels that regulate turn-takes: the background noise might be too high to capture paralinguistic features like falling intonation or creaky voice at TRPs and limited eye contact – as with pilots in the cockpit or operators in front of computer consoles – or complete lack of eye contact in radio communication might make it difficult or impossible to use facial expressions or gestures for this purpose. The *Process Control Group* found that eye contact was observed only if the participant was very unsure about the current situation or given information.

The segment of cockpit communication (from a simulated flight) introduced in Chapter 5 will be used here as an example of an analysis of the turn-taking structure. The transcript is found in Figue 9.1. By uttering the particle *so* at (36:54) the captain (Cpt) signals that he considers the previous discussion to be over. Even though there is a pause of 1.4 seconds, this does not mark a transition relevance point, because with the particle, the Cpt initiated a change of topic. The Cpt makes it clear that he is claiming the right to talk at this moment. He initiates the next turn by asking himself, as well as the First Officer (F/O), a question with slightly rising intonation (36:57). Again, this is not a TRP, even though a question normally implies a turn switch, because the question can be seen as one posed to the crew, which includes the speaker. This is supported by the fact that the Cpt does not wait for an answer from the F/O but rather gives an answer himself after a very short pause. A long pause of 2.9 seconds follows (36:58), until the F/O finally replies (37.01). This pause, in particular, stands out, as pauses after questions are generally not preferred; a good answer satisfies the informational need expressed by a question as quickly as possible.

Following this, the Cpt's question is not answered, but the F/O makes a suggestion about how to proceed, namely to wait for the intercept, i.e. for further radio communication. In (37:03) the Cpt makes a suggestion that appears to be co-operative (it is not a command) but that has a content that he assumes to be dispreferred by the F/O (notice the short delay). The reason why it is dispreferred becomes apparent, as he is suggesting exactly the opposite of what the F/O has proposed: The Cpt does not want to wait but prefers to get everything ready. He immediately gives a reason for this in order to strengthen the dispreferred suggestion. The F/O does not respond: note the pause of 1.4 s at (37:06). At (37:08), the Cpt self-assertively reaffirms his point. The question tag *okay?* makes it clear that it is now the F/O's turn, and that a confirmation is expected. The prosody of the utterance also indicates that the Cpt is requesting a confirmation and does not want to tolerate objections. Yet, there is a pause (37:09), clearly silence from the F/O, and then the F/O signals by breathing audibly and with the verbal gesture *hmm,* that he does have objections (37:10). He pauses once again (37:10) and then (37:11), after hedging and further delaying the expected reaction, finally concedes to the Cpt.

The transcript of the sequence (Figure 9.1) follows the transcription principles of Selting e.a. (1998), which encourages a rather narrow description that also includes pauses. Relevant events are numbered, and their timing and duration is specified. (This section starts 36 minutes and 54 seconds into the simulation flight, and the whole sequence lasts only 17 seconds). Pauses are indicated as follows: (.) is a short pause, (-), (--) etc. indicate increasingly longer pauses, and notations like (1.4) indicate a pause of 1.4 seconds.

36:54-54	Cpt:	so
36:55-56	Ps:	(1.4)
36:57-58	Cpt:	wie weit sin mer, (.) flaps ham wa twenty
		how far are we (.) flaps we have twenty
36:58-01	Ps:	(2.9)
37:01-02	F/O:	ja dann warten wa bis auf n intercept
		alright then we'll wait for the intercept
37:03-06	Cpt:	ah weißte wir sollten alles raussetzen (--) gear down und flaps thirty. dann ham wa das schon
		you know we should get everything ready (--) gear down and flaps thirty then we already got that
37:06-08	Ps:	(1.4)
37:08-09	Cpt:	is keen problem für uns okay?
		that's not a problem for us okay?
37:09-10	Ps:	(1.0)
37:10-10	F/O:	.hh hmm
37:10-11	Ps:	(1.0)
37:11-13	F/O:	ich bin mir nich sicher ehrlich gesacht aber gut (.) versuchn was mal
		I'm not sure to be honest but alright let's try it

Figure 9.1 Aviation transcript

The hierarchical structure in the cockpit is quite evident here. Notice that the F/O's doubts are not clearly articulated but become apparent through the abrupt sentence endings and the long pauses. At the same time, he could easily have explained the problems he sees with the Cpt's proposal. Even though it is obvious that the F/O does not agree, the Cpt does not ask why he objects. The style that one can deduce from the question in at (37:03) and the appeal to crew obligations in (6) only appears to be co-operative, but is not really so, at least not in this segment.

Group Structure and Communication

The social structure of groups explains a lot about the type of communication in crews. As detailed in Chapter 11, crews in high risk environments can be of varying nature: they can be small (two pilots in a commercial airliner and the air traffic controller), medium-sized (doctors and nurses in the operating room) or rather large (workers on a large construction site). Members of crews can be rather familiar with each other (as, typically, doctors and nurses in a hospital or operators in a power plant are), or they might be working together for the first time, as is often the case with pilots in big airlines.

Familiarity among crew members is advantageous, as members have knowledge about one another's behavior in general as well as in times of crisis. As a side effect, the frequency of communication becomes lower. But there are disadvantages to this situation: if a regular crew member has to be temporally replaced, the newcomer receives a special status. Familiarity among crew members may lead to a certain sloppiness in behavior that could possibly be avoided when crew members do not know one another well. There are linguistic markers for familiarity in many languages. Examples include the use of *sir* in English, or politeness variations in the pronoun system, as with *du / Sie* in German or *tu / Usted* in Spanish. Such markers reflect and influence the general group climate. If the members of a crew are less familiar with each other, their professional training and the company culture, in particular, have to guarantee the background knowledge in order to establish sufficient common ground. Also, the familiarity of crew members increases while working together in the crew. For example, Sexton & Helmreich (2000) report that the use of crew-referring *we* of captains in flight crews increased during the flights that they analyzed.

Crew members might have essentially the same professional background, as with pilots or power plant operators, or they might be more specialized, as in the operating room, where surgeons, anesthetists and nurses of various specializations work together. Quite typically, there is a rank difference, often correlated with age and experience (and also, gender) that obviously affects the nature of communication. The piece of conversation between captain and first officer analyzed in the previous section is by no means untypical in this respect.

The professional cline in the cockpit and its effects on communication was the subject of several studies. In the study of cockpit communication, cf. Chapter 5 and Chapter 3, it was found that the captain produced significantly more utterances than the first officer, both in the American and in the German data, and that, in turn, the first officer produced more utterances than the engineer in the American data. This may reflect differences in the task structure for captain and first officer, but, as either the captain or the first officer can fly the airplane, it can also be seen as evidence that the social position itself results in different propensities to actively engage in communication.

Perhaps more interesting than numbers of utterances are observations regarding the nature of utterances. Linde (1988) reports studies in which she investigated the effect of the status difference in aircraft. Her crucial finding was that the lower-ranked pilots expressed things in a more subdued, mitigated way when compared to the higher-ranked captain. This means that potentially crucial information might not get the attention that it deserves. A typical illustration of this point is the engineer's remark, *not very much more fuel* to the captain of a United Airlines plane near Portland in 1978, a few minutes before the engine stopped.

The reasons for this evidently have to do with politeness, a pervasive concept in human communication, as detailed in Brown & Levinson (1987). According to this study, politeness strategies have the function of saving face, when *face* refers to the self image that an individual wants to project, the self esteem that he or she wants to maintain in public. Brown & Levinson distinguish between positive face, the way in which persons want to be seen, and negative face, the claim to personal territories and rights that might be violated by the act of others. As with communication in general, saving face is a reciprocal action: people want to save face, and hence try to do this for others, by avoiding face-threatening acts, or by mitigating them if they cannot be avoided. One strategy is to use off-record communication that can be understood ambiguously, in which one meaning is not face threatening, as in *it's messy here* instead of the bald on-record command, *clean up your room*. With on-record strategies, speakers can refer to positive face by appealing to the goals of the addressee, by expressing sympathy for the speaker, by including them in a group and referring to the goals of the group, or by making promises: *wouldn't you like it better here if the room were more tidy?* or *if you clean your room, you will get ice cream.* Or they can refer to the negative face, by using apologies, hedges, or impersonalizations, like *I know you would rather play right now, but first you should clean up your room,* or *kids should clean up their room themselves.*

All face-preserving strategies (except of course not saying anything at all) result in expressions that are generally longer and more complex. This can be interpreted to mean that the speaker explicitly shows that he/she has put in greater effort in the act of communication, or has handicapped himself/herself, thus indicating the worthiness of the communicative goal that he/she wants to achieve (cf. Zahavi & Zahavi 1998). By binding cognitive resources, politeness may well be a handicap (van Rooy 2003), a luxury that should be avoided in situations of high workload that otherwise stress the cognitive resources. In the American data from the study reported in Krifka, Martens & Schwarz (2003), fewer politeness markers, like *please* and *sir* or conjunctive verb forms like *would you* were used in situations of high workload in the well performing crews, but, interestingly, more politeness markers were used in those situations in poorly performing crews.

Obviously, the power structure between the participants, as well as the familiarity between them, goes a long way in explaining which strategies can be employed: powerful participants, or participants that are familiar with one another, need not resort to face-saving strategies in the same way as less powerful or familiar participants do. By disregarding or employing such strategies, the power cline between the participants itself is reinforced.

Fischer and Orasanu (1999) have investigated mitigation in aircraft crews. In one study, male pilots (69 captains and 88 first officers) were confronted with a weather description that strongly suggested a diversion of the flight route. The subjects were asked to imagine themselves in the role of the flying pilot who apparently is not aware of the weather situation. They were presented with a number of possible verbal reactions by the non-flying pilot that varied in focus, explicitness and directness (and quite generally, in their politeness). This included direct requests, in particular commands (*turn 30 degrees right*), crew obligation statements (*I think we need to deviate right about now*), crew suggestions (*let's go around the weather*), queries with presuppositions (*which direction would you like to deviate?*), preferences (*I think it would be wise to turn left or right*) and hints (*that return at 25 miles looks mean*). It included self centered communications, like self directives (*I am going to get a clearance to deviate around these storms*) and permission seeking questions (*you want me to ask for clearance to deviate around this weather*). The result was quite predictable: more than 50 per cent of the captains preferred a direct command (as compared to less than 20 per cent of the first officers), and about 40 per cent of the first officers preferred a hint (as compared to about 10 per cent of the captains). Captains were more likely than first officers to specify the action to be taken, and permission requests were only uttered by first officers. In situations of threat, captains used even more commands, but interestingly also more hints – the latter probably to minimize face-threat to the first officer. First officers, on the other hand, increased their commands, and also their statements of crew obligations, a more indirect form.

In follow up studies, Fischer and Orasanu looked at various factors that may influence the differential behavior of captain and first officer. A replication with pilots from three European nations showed less differentiation in communication behavior, indicating that the hierarchical distance is greater for European pilots than for American pilots. A replication with female US pilots showed no significant differences to male pilots in terms of the captain / first officer differentiation, but the female pilots reacted more often with problem or goal statements to requests and with speaker-oriented communications. In yet another study, pilots were asked which type of communication addressed to them in a given situation they would consider most effective. The findings were that communications that were supported by a problem or goal statement were considered more effective. The preferred strategy was one that is neither too direct nor blunt, like commands, nor too indirect, like permission requests. Captains judged crew obligation statements, preference statements and hints from the first officer to be more effective than commands, and first officers thought that captains were more effective with crew obligation statements than with commands, queries, hints, self directives or permission requests. In high risk situations, pilots generally preferred more direct communication strategies, but, even then, crew obligation statements were preferred over commands. With highly face-threatening situations, as when embarrassing mistakes had occurred, hints were judged most effective, together with crew obligation and preference statements.

The concept of a common ground, which results in a group shared mental model was introduced in the introduction of this chapter. However, it should be stressed that effective crews also work with the principle of division of labor, which also applies to shared information. The quality of information sharing is, in a sense, curvilinear: too much of it leads to information overload for crew members, too little of it leads to incoherent actions. Of course, it is important for each crew member to know what is relevant to other crew members so that they can carry out their own actions. This calls for the definition of interfaces between the crew members. For example, in the context of the operating room, the team around the surgeon and the anesthetist form two natural subteams that are typically visually separated by a curtain. These subteams deal with separate but interdependent tasks and have to inform each other about critical events. The flow of information might be asymmetric. The surgeon should generally be shielded from information relevant to the anesthetist except when there is an emergency; on the other hand, the anesthetist should be informed about important operation details, because this is relevant for administering drugs, which is done by the anesthetist. It is often debatable how much information should be shared. For example, how much should the pilot of a rescue helicopter know about the state of a patient? One could argue that this information is only relevant for the doctor or the nurse and that it is irrelevant for the pilot because it is distracting information. On the other hand, if he knows that the patient is in a stable condition, the pilot might avoid potentially risky maneuvers that he would perhaps consider with a patient in a critical state.

A very important aspect of crew communication is briefing before crew sessions or critical situations, as well as debriefing afterwards. Briefing establishes or confirms a measure of common ground that is necessary in dealing with a critical situation; it reduces the danger of misunderstandings in the situation and makes crew members aware of options. Debriefing allows for an informed assessment of how a situation or a crew session was handled, which is crucial for the development of future better strategies. It creates opportunities for individuals from different perspectives to join together in order to establish an informed opinion. Therefore, it is crucial that the institutional setting requires, or at least strongly encourages, such briefing and debriefing sessions.

Coherence: The Objects of Talk

Monological texts, or dialogical conversations, can be smooth and tightly integrated, that is, coherent; or they can be patchy, with parts that are only loosely connected, that is, incoherent. Of course, coherent texts and conversations achieve their communicative goal more effectively than less coherent ones that lead addressees into cul de sacs and demand that much of the necessary background necessary for understanding be filled in.

Coherence can be established in different dimensions. One way to establish it is with so-called discourse referents with which the persons, objects, events and facts mentioned in a text are managed. As already mentioned, a rather elaborate system of definite and indefinite articles, demonstratives and pronouns is used in English to track discourse referents in communication. Consider the following passages from the conversation between a captain and an engineer in a simulated flight:

(28)	Eng.	We have <u>an underexcited trip light</u> on, uh, number 3.
(29)	Capt.	Uh, say it again please?
(30)	Eng.	<u>Underexcited fault light</u> on, uh, number 3.
(31)	Capt.	Why don't we go to the book and see what you can do about <u>it</u>.
(...)		
(72)	Capt.	You've just got <u>a fault light</u>, right?
(73)	Eng.	Just got <u>a fault light</u>.
(...)		
(94)	Capt.	Hey, with <u>this fault light</u>, would you switch essential power off of number 3, please, for me?
(...)		
(111)	Eng.	I think what <u>that light</u> was, was when that field relay tripped.
(113)	Eng.	That's probably what <u>it</u> was.
(114)	Eng.	Well, I just saw <u>it</u> – <u>it</u> may have been there for awhile – I just saw <u>it</u> when I pulled and reset it.

Figure 9.2   Transcript: captain and engineer

The discourse referent for an underexcited fault light is introduced in (28) with a noun phrase with an indefinite article, the typical way for introducing new discourse referents. In (30), one finds a noun phrase without any article, which is possible in certain types of texts, like headlines or reports in a military or technical setting. Note the variation in wording: *trip light* vs. the more standard *fault light*. In (31), the fault light is referred to by the pronoun *it*, which is typically used for referring to recently mentioned discourse referents. Pronouns are short and efficient, but at the risk of potential ambiguity, as in (29): *it* does not refer to the trip light, but to the utterance (28). Here the potential ambiguity does not matter because one cannot *say* a light. Another, more elaborate way of referring to discourse referents is by definite NPs like *the fault light*, which does not occur in the excerpt analyzed here. Rather, (31) shows another use of the definite article in *the book*: here, the speaker refers to some entity that is identifiable due to the speaker and hearer's background knowledge of the plane's operating handbook. Another important use of the definite article is called *bridging*: if a thunderstorm has been previously introduced, one can talk about *the clouds* because thunderstorms come with clouds. The fault light is mentioned again three minutes later, with an indefinite NP (see 72), which is rather unusual. A definite NP, *the fault light,* could have been used here, which would have led to greater coherence. About half a minute later, the discourse referent surfaces again, this time with the help of a noun phrase with a demonstrative, *this fault light*, and then *that fault light*. Demonstratives are often used in texts if the discourse referent has been introduced but has not been mentioned very recently or if the intervening part of the text was concerned with other things (as is the case here).

The introduction and maintenance of discourse referents has been studied extensively in linguistics, for example in Centering Theory (Grosz, Joshi & Weinstein 1995) and Discourse Representation Theory (Kamp & Reyle 1993).

Centering Theory, in particular, offers a number of interesting case studies relating planning strategies and discourse structure.

Coherence: Relations between Parts of Discourse

Rhetorical Structure Theory (RST) addresses another dimension of coherence, as developed by Mann & Thompson (1988). RST assumes that coherent texts are hierarchically structured, in the sense that each part stands in one of relatively few semantic relations to other parts. There are relations like background, cause, circumstance, contrast, concession, condition, elaboration, evaluation, evidence, interpretation, justification, motivation, result, preparation, purpose, restatement or summary. The text is divided into parts, which are then hierarchically structured. As an example, consider the following short text, the beginning of a scientific article:

> (0) Lactose and Lactase. (1) Lactose is milk sugar; (2) the enzyme lactase breaks it down. (3) For want of lactase most adults cannot digest milk. (4) In populations that drink milk the adults have more lactase, perhaps through natural selection.

RST assigns the following relations to the parts of this text:

> (0) is a preparation of (1)-(4), (1)-(2) is a background of (3)-(4), (1) is elaborated by (2) (3) contrasts with (4).

RST has been predominantly applied to written texts in order to work out the structure of well-constructed texts and to show the problems of bad ones. It has been applied when analyzing passages of operating manuals or textbooks. However, RST has also been used for the analysis of spontaneous spoken texts and even of conversations.

Yet another approach to coherence is concerned with the topical structure of texts and conversations. Communication is typically about something – a topic of common interest, a problem that is to be solved or an action that has to be co-ordinated. Typically these topics, problems and actions are complex and can be broken down into parts. The techniques used to break them down are, to a large degree, part of background knowledge. Individuals perceive situations as being composed of events, processes or states, and they perceive tasks as consisting of sub-tasks and persons as agents or patients. Reality is organized using spatial, temporal or causal relations. When describing situations, tasks, persons and other things, such standard decompositions of aspects of reality are used. If one reports a car accident by phone, the police expect to be filled in about the location of the accident, the cars and people involved, whether there are any injuries and if there are injuries, what kind. These pieces of information can be seen as answers to a sequence of questions that is informed by the standard ways of analyzing reality.

Coherent communication can be seen as communication that answers such sequences of questions. This view, which goes back to classical rhetorics, has been developed in quaestio theory, cf. von Stutterheim & Klein (1989) and von Stutterheim (1997). It can be fruitfully applied to communication in technical settings, as shown in the Chapter 3, cf. also Grommes & Dietrich (2000). In this work, it is assumed that utterances are (in general) answers to an underlying *quaestio*, which can be explicit or implicit. The interlocutors must recognize these quaestiones, react to them appropriately and develop new quaestiones that relate to previous ones. Grommes & Dietrich distinguish the following relations between quaestiones: in a *new* quaestio the speaker signals the perception of a new communicative task. A *shift* occurs if the speaker takes up the quaestio of the preceding utterance and constructs a related quaestio that offers additional information. In a *restoration* or *b-shift,* the speaker goes back to an earlier quaestio and constructs a quaestio related to it. Such jumps can occur because of interruptions, repairs or intervening non-linguistic events that divert the interlocutors' attention. In the case of *maintenance,* the speaker has no further information to add to the current quaestio.

As an example, consider the following transcript from an operating room. Here, a junior surgeon has to open the thorax for a lung resection. He is supposed to identify the rib at which he wants to cut into the thorax. As he sets out to count the ribs the senior surgeon interrupts him, because he had started counting with the first rib, which is nearly impossible to touch. The senior surgeon is not very co-operative with respect to the junior surgeon's quaestiones; she frequently restores her quaestio, indicated by the marker 'back.'

(97)	Junior:	eins. zwei. drei. vier. fünf. das müsste die hier sein.	new
		one two three four five this should be the one.	
(98)	Senior:	Und sie ham die erste Rippe getastet?	shift
		and you did touch the first rib?|	
(...)			
(103)	Junior:	=dann sind wer ein weniger	shift
		then it is one less	
(104)	Senior:	=ihr seid super.=	back
		you (pl.) are great	

Figure 9.3   Quaestio: surgery transcript

The quaestio in line (97) is 'where (in relation to the ribs) should we cut?' To answer this, the junior surgeon counts the ribs and suggests where to cut. The senior surgeon develops a new quaestio (98) out of this, namely, whether or not the junior surgeon started from the first rib, which is difficult to identify. This quaestio is not answered directly, but the junior surgeon's reaction in (103) shows that he understood it very well: the quaestio to (103) is something like 'what follows if the quaestio (98) is answered negatively?' In (104) S apparently shifts back to a previous point in which the quaestio was something like: 'how good are the junior surgeons?'

Back shifts, which generally indicate some sort of interruption, can occur for a number of reasons. It might be due to the inherent properties of the task at hand, or it might be caused by interruptions of a third party. The speaker might have returned to issues that were not yet finished, but some other points sidetracked the conversation. And it might also occur because the conversation participants are in conflict about should be talked about at a given point.

Incidentally, in dialogical conversation, overt questions might provide some indication for the level of coherence. In the *Linguistic Factors Group* the questions uttered in simulation flights were identified and the proportion of them that were answered were then determined. In the American data analyzed by this group, the speech acts of well-performing crews contained a slightly higher proportion of questions, and a considerably larger amount of questions was answered: about 55 per cent of the questions in poorly performing crews, and 80 per cent of the questions in well-performing crews were answered. Furthermore, fewer questions were answered by poorly performing crews during high task load, whereas the proportion stayed about the same for well-performing crews. This can be interpreted to mean that well-performing crews showed a more coherent style of conversation and managed to maintain that even in periods of high task load.

Problems of High Workload and Communication

The last observation leads to the variance of communication related to the level of experienced workload. One observes two people walking and talking. Their conversation gets more involved; they stop and start to argue with one another. Why did they stop walking? Presumably because communication is a task that uses mental energies so that speakers sometimes cannot engage in simple activities such as walking. Obviously, in periods of high workload, the strain on cognitive resources that communication poses must be considered a potential threat to the crews.

Grommes & Dietrich (2000) observe that in high workload situations, both in the airplane cockpit and in the operating room, utterances become shorter and more elliptic and that fewer utterances occur that express background information, like utterances that explain things or give a reason for an act. Obviously, the cognitive resources are strained by the tasks at hand and cannot be applied to communication. This increases the danger of errors in communication.

In the mitigation studies by Linde and Fischer and Orasanu, it was found that even the speech acts of lower-ranked crew members become less mitigated and more direct in phases of high workload. It is likely that in such periods the additional cognitive resources for face-saving measures are not available. The *Linguistic Factors Group* observed that politeness markers occur less frequently in situations of high work load, at least in good crews and that politeness is generally correlated with a greater complexity of expressions. While this leads to more face-threatening acts that might affect the global social climate within the crew, it also increases local communicative effectiveness in high workload situations. As a part of CRM training, crew members might be taught to accept a higher level of face-threatening behavior for the sake of greater communicative effectiveness. The transcript analyzed above shows that the energies that the first officer put into face-saving measures would have been better invested in making the reservations he had about the proposed procedure overt.

Conclusion

This concludes the overview of language and communicative behavior in groups in high risk environments. It was only possible to touch on some of the relevant issues here, partly due to reasons of space, partly because still so little is known in this field.

One area not dealt with here is communication in written texts. This is an enormously important field in technical communication that affects a wide range of cases, like user guides that determine how consumers operate an MPEG player, medical textbooks that are used for the training of physicians, operating handbooks for nuclear power plants or checklists that are referred to in emergency situations in the cockpit. Many aspects of this type of communication are dealt with in the field of technical writing, an important part of human factors research. For a particularly grueling study of problems with medical textbooks, cf. Baker (1999).

Hopefully readers with an interest in crew resource management have realized that communication should be a topic of central concern in their studies: good communication is crucial for good crews, and communication deficiencies reflect general deficiencies in co-operation. The aim of this chapter was to provide readers with evidence that linguistic approaches, like speech act theory, conversation analysis and theories of coherence are highly relevant for the study of communication within crews. Readers whose main focus is in linguistics have hopefully noticed that communication processes in groups in high risk environments is a subject worth studying in detail: it poses serious challenges for theoretical notions and forces researchers to considerably refine their theories. And, more importantly, it can sometimes save lives.

Chapter 10

Leadership and Co-ordination

J. Bryan Sexton, Patrick Grommes, Enikö Zala-Mezö, Gudela Grote,
Robert L. Helmreich and Ruth Häusler

Introduction

Research on leadership has taken a variety of forms in the literature, but the discussion here is limited to leadership traits, leadership situations and leadership behaviour. Presentation of GIHRE results demonstrates the manner by which leaders influence outcomes as a function of *what* they say, *how* they say it and *when* they say it. The sources of data for this chapter are primarily commercial aviation and medicine. These data were collected through the use of attitudinal surveys, interviews of front-line personnel, direct observations of behaviour in real-time team performance, high fidelity simulator studies and transcripts of cockpit voice recorders. This chapter begins with a general discussion of leadership is followed by a section on co-ordination results from the *Co-ordination Group* and ends with a section on linguistic aspects of co-ordination.

Teams at work in high risk environments are sometimes challenged to the limits of their abilities, with little guidance about how to improve performance and/or maintain acceptable levels of performance under adverse conditions. Whether flying a commercial airliner, delivering care to patients or generating power in nuclear power plants, the existence of teams revolves around some task-oriented purpose with some degree of inherent uncertainty. Chemers and Ayman (1993) explain that leadership becomes more important as uncertainty increases. Operational settings that are lacking in predictability and standardization are inherently more uncertain, and therefore more stressful/higher workload, with a stronger need for leadership.

A common feature of task-performing teams is that over time, explicit status and power differences emerge (Schneider and Goktepe, 1983). Given the relatively stable nature of the working teams under investigation by GIHRE, team members are generally not equal in status or power, and consequently, leadership becomes an even more important component of effective team performance. NASA researchers have demonstrated this through their analyses of the causes of commercial aviation accidents and incidents (Cooper, White & Lauber, 1980; Murphy, 1980), from which they concluded that *pilot error* was more likely to reflect failures in leadership and team co-ordination than deficiencies in technical, *stick and rudder* proficiency.

Leadership Verbalization

Traditional research on leadership has focused on the dynamics through which leaders and subordinates develop a relationship. Chemers (1993) explains that leaders provide subordinates with direction and support that facilitates the achievement of goals. In other words, leaders need to provide subordinates with effective coaching and an enabling structure that fosters interaction success. There is some evidence of this leadership-subordinate dynamic in the content and linguistic analyses of GIHRE projects lead by Helmreich (see Chapter 1) and Krifka (see Chapter 5).

Chapter 1 demonstrated that one out of three comments made by the best performing captains were prompting/coaching/enabling the solution of in-flight problems (problem-solving communications), relative to five to ten per cent of comments from low and middle performance captains. Overall, captains communicate more verbal information (supporting the notion of coaching) than first officers and flight engineers, and in particular, captains use the highest rates of first person plural (we, our, us) as they refer to the team in the collective, e.g., 'We should get out the checklist; Let's get ready for this approach' (Sexton and Helmreich, 2002).

Chapter 5 reported that speech acts indicating interest and affirmation were typical of good captains. Good captains were also more encouraging with respect to the contributions of their first officers. Dissenting speech acts, on the other hand, were slightly more frequent with poorly performing captains. Similar results were demonstrated by the *Co-ordination Group* (Chapter 3); in flights in which the first officer has the active role (pilot flying) in the cockpit, a positive correlation was found between team performance and the amount of positive feedback from the captain. In other words, as positive feedback increased, so did performance – a result that was mirrored in medicine through interview material from anesthesia teams. In the interviews, positive feedback during and after teamwork was described as critical for developing high functioning teams, but providing such feedback is not the norm, and unfortunately, opportunities to process and learn from experiences are overlooked or ignored. In essence, analyses of content and linguistic factors reveal patterns along which leaders and followers differ, and perhaps more importantly, they reveal a qualitative difference in performance.

Organizational Leadership

Just as the groups under investigation by GIHRE require leadership at the team level for consistently safe and effective outcomes, the organizations in which these team environments reside also require executive leadership (e.g. president, CEO, etc.). Executive leadership can impact the performance of teams by the extent to which it creates, removes or maintains barriers to performance. This is operationally reflected in the inclusion of leadership as a component of human factors training in aviation. Recent interventions designed to improve the interface between senior leaders and front line personnel in medicine have been shown to enhance relationships, bolster quality improvement efforts and positively impact the care of patients (Pronovost, Weast, et. Al, submitted; Romanoff, 2003; and Frankel & Graydon-Baker, 2003).

A high percentage of commercial airline pilots do not trust their senior management (Helmreich & Merritt, 1998). Similarly, in medical teams, local leaders such as unit directors and nursing directors are viewed much more positively than senior leaders (CEO, President, etc.) in the hospital. Interestingly, senior leaders, who generally view their front-line personnel quite positively, do not reciprocate this less than favourable view of management by front-line personnel. In a recent survey (Sexton, Helmreich et. al, under review) of 11,000 healthcare providers the following statistics were found:

- 72.1% report that staff physicians in their clinical area are doing a good job;
- 28% report that the administration of their hospital is doing a good job;
- 41% report that hospital management does not knowingly compromise the safety of patients;
- 25% report that hospital administration supports their daily efforts;
- 58% report that trainees in their discipline are adequately supervised.

Setting the Tone: Briefings

> The leader's main task, therefore, is to get a team established on a good trajectory and then to make small adjustments along the way to help members succeed, not to try to continuously manage team behaviour in real time. No leader can *make* a team perform well. But all leaders can create conditions that increase the *likelihood* that it will, Richard Hackman (2002).

Hackman (1998) notes that over time, teams develop their own norms, but effective teams have leaders who explicitly establish these norms at the beginning of the team's life. One of the most important roles of a team leader is to open channels of communication and set the tone for the environment in which team members will exchange information. The British Psychologist James Reason (1997) explains that the processing of information is critical to the effective performance of a system. He says that 'errors are essentially information-processing problems and require the provision of better information, either in the person's head or in the workplace (pg 121).' In technologically advanced and psychologically complex environments such as the operating room, intensive care unit or cockpit, there is a clear and present need for knowing the threats and possible contingencies, establishing norms and having a formal opportunity to build the team. Briefings have been demonstrated to be an effective means by which leaders can plan for contingencies, establish norms, discuss threats and build the team all at the same time.

There are two critical components of briefings: technical and interpersonal. In the technical component, it is important for the leader (be it a captain, surgical attending or NPP shift manager) to cover the technical details of what will take place, set expectations and plan for contingencies. Regarding the interpersonal component, which is often a function of how the technical component is articulated, the leader must open channels of communication, empower team members to speak up and participate and formally establish the team. In commercial aviation, it is not uncommon to hear a captain tell the crew 'I only got 3 hours of sleep last night and am feeling off today, please keep and eye on me and don't let me do anything stupid.' The phrase 'don't let me do anything stupid' goes a long way to engage team members in the process and empower them to participate.[34] The delicate balancing act of the leader in a briefing is to display competence while disavowing perfection. In commercial aviation, it is known know that briefing content is a powerful predictor of subsequent performance (Ginnett, 1987; Hines, 1998; Sexton & Helmreich, 2000).

The *Behavioral Markers Group* has demonstrated that sub-optimal briefing is a leading deficiency of simulator crews that consistently perform poorly across three simulation scenarios. Contingency planning (part of the technical component of briefing) was a predominant behavior in crews that dealt successfully with technical problems. Also, leadership and managerial skill were associated with a risk index of crew behavior across flight segments, i.e. better leadership and managerial behaviors were associated with subsequently safer behaviors and decisions.

Leadership Roles: Managing Teams and Managing Tasks

Investigations of leadership effectiveness have identified two components of success that map onto the concept of an interpersonal factor and a task orientated factor.[35] In studies across a variety of organizations in Japan (coal mines, banks, shipyards, government offices, etc.) Misumi (1985) found that the most effective leaders were high on both task and relationship maintenance behaviors. Research into leadership effectiveness has replicated the team and task components in many other countries including India (Sinha, 1981), Iran (Ayman and Chemers (1983), Brazil (Farris and Butterfield, 1972) and Taiwan (Bond and Hwang, 1986). The two-factor distinction of interpersonal effectiveness and task motivation seems to have some evidence for cross-cultural validity. To summarize these areas of research with reference to GIHRE, the concept of a task component and an

---

[34] It is interesting to note that after several hundred observations in surgical operating rooms and critical care units the authors have never heard the phrase 'don't let me do anything stupid, ' in medicine.
[35] These two attributes also form stable components of personality related positively to attainment (Helmreich, R.L., Spence, J.T., Beane, W.E., Lucker, G.W. and Matthews, K.A. (1980), 'Making it in Academic Psychology: Demographic and Personality Correlates of Attainment', *Journal of Personality and Social Psychology*, Vol. 39, pp.896-908.)

interpersonal component appears to be valid in studies of leadership effectiveness, personality research and investigations of cohesiveness.

These interpersonal and task components of success underscore what McIntyre and Salas (1995) have described in their investigations of the evolution and maturation of Naval tactical teams. They describe two distinct and simultaneous tracks along which teams develop. The first is a task work track, involving operations-related activities, and the second is a teamwork track, involving activities that serve to strengthen the quality of functional interactions, relationships, communication and co-ordination (Morgan, Glickman, Woodward, Blaiwes & Salas, 1986). Across these different areas of research, there is a consistent distinction between two factors, task motivation and the interpersonal effectiveness. Similarly, in a study of 31 behavioral marker systems across airlines, Flin and Martin (1998) noted that the interpersonal and cognitive categories comprised the two principle components of Crew Resource Management skills into which the majority of individual markers fall.[36]

Historically, the focus in evaluating pilots was on their technical skills, but recently, much of the industry has begun including crew-level assessment of performance, with an increasing focus on Crew Resource Management (non-technical) skills. In addition, past research has focused on task work, largely ignoring the critical teamwork aspect of multi-person working groups (McIntyre and Salas, 1995). In Chapter 1, a teamwork task work model of crew behavior on the flight deck is described that demonstrates the critical role of leadership as a core teamwork behavior, and similarly, the importance of briefing content as a core task work behavior. Examination of this model of crew behavior under high workload operational environments resulted in a significant increase in the relationships between behaviors and indices of error. Through a variety of methodologies and multiple disciplines, research conducted by GIHRE highlighted the critical importance of the often-overlooked interpersonal component in effective teams and the relationship to workload.

Leadership Roles and Workload

A recent retrospective analysis of air carrier accidents conducted by The National Transportation Safety Board (1994), discovered that a disproportionately high percentage of accidents (over 80 per cent) occur when the captain is the pilot flying. This seems counter-intuitive, given that the captain is normally the pilot with more flying experience and technical skills. One explanation may be that captains flying the plane during accident situations are overloaded with multi-tasking as they try to accomplish both the pilot flying and pilot in command duties simultaneously. Recent research at The University of Texas at Austin has demonstrated that in complex/high workload situations, the best performing crews have the first officer as pilot flying, which fosters an environment in which the

---

[36] Flin notes that this is not definitive per se, but rather represents the common opinion of CRM trainers and assessors around the world.

captain can assess and manage the situation while the first officer deals with aircraft handling duties. The data suggest that if a crew encounters a high workload situation when the captain is pilot flying, it may be best to cede control of the aircraft to the first officer. In medicine or NPP, the notion of leadership during high workload situations could be applied to a variety of situations in which it may be critical to have someone with the big picture in mind (relatively free from the technical task at hand). There is some historical precedent for this notion as well, from the annals of submarine battles during World War II.[37]

> One of Commander Mush Morton's unorthodox ideas, later adopted to some degree in the submarine force, was to have his executive officer make the periscope observations, while he, the skipper, ran the approach and co-ordinated the information from sound, periscope, plotting parties, and torpedo director. Thus, so ran his argument, the skipper is not apt to be distracted by watching the target's maneuvers, and can make better decisions, Submarine Commander Edward L. Beach, United States Navy (1946).

Co-ordination

Kieser and Kubicek (1992) defined co-ordination as tuning of interdependent work processes to promote concerted action towards a superordinate goal. During the last decade, an increasing number of studies have examined co-ordination in high-risk environments. A frequent limitation of these studies is that they do not include systematic variation of organizational co-ordination mechanisms and of the types of rules to which the teams must adhere. The vast majority of the studies have been carried out in aviation settings, where a high level of standardization is the rule. Given the definition of work teams (Brannick & Prince, 1997) as '...two or more people with different tasks who work together adaptively to achieve specified and shared goals'; co-ordination is one of the team's main activities. Members of teams must co-ordinate their decisions and activities by sharing information and resources to attain shared goals' (Dickinson & McIntyre, 1997). In situations in which teamwork is essential, success depends on co-ordination. (Zaccaro et al., 2001) As reported in Chapter 3 (by the *Co-ordination Group*), co-ordination is seen as the main team activity besides the individuals' own work tasks.

An important basis for good teamwork – and of good co-ordination – is a mental model of the task and situation shared by all team members (Matieu, Heffner, Goodwin, Salas, & A., 2000). In using these models, teams require less co-ordination in the form of discussion of plans or decision making, because the plan is understood and shared by the team members. In this way, team members reduce co-ordination costs by saving time and resources for task accomplishment. The organization can foster the building of shared models by providing standard

---

[37] Robert L. Helmreich served on a destroyer during the Cold War. As executive officer, his duties included conning the ship during General Quarters and underway refueling, allowing the captain to manage the strategic situation.

operating procedures and rules. Standardization in predictable situations offers a common basis, which can be used by teams as shared mental models (Stout, Cannon-Bowers, Salas & Milanovich, 1999). This is not the case, however, if teams face unanticipated situations during which they cannot rely on rules. In less predictable situations, individuals have to devote extra resources (very often communication: assigning tasks, giving orders, making decisions, etc.) to organize activities and fulfill tasks.

A core concept in many studies of team co-ordination is the distinction between explicit and implicit co-ordination (Serfaty, Entin, & Johnston, 1998), which provides a framework for the co-ordination mechanisms mentioned above. *Explicit co-ordination* means co-ordination via communication during new tasks and new situations or when a new group of people forms a working team – in other words: when teams do not possess a shared mental model about task accomplishment. Explicit co-ordination is resource intensive, but it is an inevitable form of co-ordination when shared models still have to be developed. *Implicit co-ordination* means co-ordination via anticipation: shared mental models allow team members to predict each other's needs and actions and to act on them without communication. In well-known, highly standardized situations teams *can* use this economical co-ordination form, and they are often required to use it in high workload situations when cognitive resources are better used to problem-solve than to co-ordinate. It is necessary to prepare for high workload situations with a phase of explicit co-ordination during which a shared model can be developed to reduce communication and co-ordination costs during high workload (Orasanu, 1990, Orasanu & Fisher, 1992; cited in Orasanu, 1993).

Different mechanisms can be responsible for smooth co-ordination. In addition to the explicit-implicit distinction in co-ordination, this research focused on leadership behavior and heedful interrelating. Leadership in hierarchical teams is a central factor, since there are many co-ordinating tasks assigned to this role. The leader's behavior also exemplifies team behavior, which can become a norm in teams (Zaccaro, 2001b). Leadership behavior was not the focus per se; it was studied in as much as it is one possible mechanism for co-ordination. Also, the relationship between leadership and standardization, which occasionally are competing co-ordination forms, was examined (Kerr and Jemier, 1978).

In addition to the organizational (standardization) and structural (hierarchy) characteristics of teams, the individual effort to co-ordinate successfully is also crucial. The concept representing this effort is called heedful interrelating (Weick & Roberts, 1993). A core component of this concept based on Asch's theory of group interaction is that safety operations in highly complex situations require deliberate efforts by all actors to constantly (re-) consider effects of their own actions in relation to the goals and actions of others, or in Weick and Roberts' words (1993, p. 363; see also Table 10.1 for tentative indicators of heedful/heedless interrelating):

> ...[to] construct their actions (contribute) while envisaging a social system of joint actions [represent], and interrelate that constructed action with the system that is envisaged (subordinate).

Table 10.1   Tentative indicators for heedful vs. heedless interrelating (adapted from Weick and Roberts, 1993)

Indicators for	
Heedful interrelating	Heedless interrelating
Detailed representation of others	Less detailed representation of others
Contributions shaped by anticipated responses	Contributions shaped less by anticipated responses
Broad boundaries of envisaged system	Narrow boundaries of envisaged system
Attention focus on joint situation	Attention focus on local situation
Good comprehension of the implications of unfolding events	Little comprehension of the implications of unfolding events

In this vein, results obtained by the *Co-ordination Group* will be presented, concerning patterns of co-ordination and uses of different co-ordination mechanisms in different situations. There were two independent variables in the study design (cf. Chapter 3), standardization and task load, which were studied in two different working environments: cockpit teams and anesthesia teams. By comparing the two work environments as well as different work phases within each work environment, several hypotheses concerning the effects of standardization were tested.

In the highly standardized cockpit teams, more implicit co-ordination (and less explicit co-ordination, since explicit-implicit co-ordination are mutually exclusive categories) was expected than in the less regulated working environment, i.e. medicine. As described in Chapter 8, in the national airline where data was collected, there are numerous rules for normal, abnormal and emergency situations. Here, standardization concerns even the form and content of communication. Rules describing tasks and actions serve as common knowledge among team members and help to develop shared mental models (Mathieu et al., 2000). Less leadership behavior was expected because standards can be used as substitutes (Kerr & Jermier, 1976) and can be seen as an impersonalized form of leadership: 'effective leadership might therefore be described as the ability to supply subordinates with needed guidance and good feelings which are not being supplied by other sources.' In situations in which the tasks and roles are clear team leaders should let teams work because too much direction is unnecessary and can be perceived as reduced autonomy (Zaccharo et al. 2001).

Less heedful interrelating behavior was expected because standards also can be used as substitutes for individual co-ordination behavior. Or rather: heedful interrelating can still exist in a latent form of readiness to interact and attention helping to notice if something unexpected happens but less in an observable overt behavioral form. Table 10.2 summarizes expectations considering standardization.

Table 10.2 Expectations concerning the effects of standardization in anesthesia and cockpit teams

Low standardization Medicine		High standardization Aviation
Explicit co-ordination	>	
	<	Implicit co-ordination
Leadership behavior	>	
Heedful interrelating	>	

The expectations concerning the effects of task load were based on a definition of task load using objective criteria such as increasing complexity, uncertainty and time pressure, rather than the subjectively perceived workload, which depends strongly on the individual's experience and capacity. The hypotheses concerning task load were studied within the professional fields by comparing different work phases.

Teams under high task load were expected to have less cognitive capacity to process information, so they should use more economic co-ordination techniques like implicit co-ordination and conversely, should use less explicit co-ordination. To manage high task load situations successfully, teams have to be prepared. This is done through explicit co-ordination and leadership in a preparation phase but not in the high task load phase iteself.

Heedful interrelating plays a decisive role in high task load situations, because team success depends strongly on the team members' autonomous behavior based on knowledge of their tasks and strong individual motivation and effort. Expectations considering task load are summarized in Table 10.3.

Table 10.3 Expectation: task load by comparing different work phases within anesthesia and cockpit teams

Low task load		High task load
Explicit co-ordination	>	
	<	Implicit co-ordination
Leadership behavior	>	
	<	Heedful interrelating

So far, standardization and task load have been discussed as independent factors, but in each situation they of course operate together in various combinations. When comparing Table 10.3 and 10.4, it can easily be seen that for most combinations of different levels of standardization and task load there are no consistent predictions possible. Only for the low task load/low standardization combination, do expectations of explicit co-ordination and high leadership coincide. In all other cases, one would have to assume the dominance of either task load or standardization to be able to make predictions, or one might assume new qualities of co-ordination needs in the sense of an interaction effect between standardization and task load. To date, there is no theoretical or empirical basis for such assumptions. Therefore, the focus was on the hypotheses concerning main effects of standardization and task load in the analyses.

Results of the Comparison of Cockpit and Anesthesia Teams

The *Co-ordination Group* observed and categorized interactions in cockpit and anesthesia teams. Three behavioral categories were coded: information flow, leadership behavior and heedful interrelating. (For the entire list of observation categories see Appendix V.) Information flow includes implicit and explicit co-ordination forms, which were defined as mutually exclusive. This category comprises all interactions as well as pauses in communication during the observation. When present, leadership and heedful interrelating were coded. Some categories appear in more than one group, because it was not possible to differentiate between them theoretically: explicit co-ordination can be leadership behavior and heedful interrelating at the same time when the behavior is shown in a critical situation by a team member that is not a formally assigned leader.

The *Co-ordination Group* used data from 42 cockpit teams fulfilling a task in the flight simulator, and 23 anesthesia teams inducing anesthesia in actual surgical settings. Table 10.4 summarizes the results of the observational analysis. The values in the cells show the percentages of all interactions belonging to a given observational category. The differences between the professional groups are all statistically significant, though not all in the expected directions, as indicated in the last column with a + pointing to confirmed assumptions and a - pointing to assumptions not supported by the data.

Table 10.4 Share of co-ordination forms according to frequencies

	Medicine	Aviation	Hypotheses
Explicit co-ordination	67.7%	72.3%	
Implicit co-ordination	32.3%	27.7%	-
Leadership	14.6%	8.4%	+
Heedful interrelating	9.3%	14.5%	-

As seen in Table 10.4, cockpit teams appeared to employ explicit co-ordination more frequently than anesthesia teams, which did not support the hypothesis. Anesthesia teams showed more leadership behavior than cockpit teams, as expected, but they showed less heedful interrelating than the cockpit teams. The picture is mixed making it necessary to consider other situation and task specific factors influencing team co-ordination. Some of the possible situational factors include:

- Shared visual information in the anesthesia team and different visual information in the cockpit teams is a possible reason for co-ordinating explicitly more often in the cockpit. The pilots need an intensive and overt information exchange in order to complement each other's information sources;

- Cockpit teams have to deal with an unusual flight task in the simulator, while the anesthesia teams work in routine situations in real life. Well-known task situations can serve the function of standardization, namely reducing the need for explicit co-ordination;

- There are also differences in the communication practice: cockpit teams have attended Crew Resource Management training as part of their recurrent certification process, where they had a chance to practice certain co-ordination forms and are probably more conscious about the importance of explicit co-ordination.

One way to reduce the complexity caused by the different professional settings for cockpit and anesthesia teams is to compare the same professional groups working under different conditions, i.e. making comparisons within the same professional setting.

The *Co-ordination Group* divided the work process into phases, during which the level of standardization and the task load level differed. This procedure is in line with the idea of functional leadership (this statement can be generalized to studying team co-ordination) from Zaccharo et al. (2002): '... a critical task for researchers in team leadership, then, becomes the definition and validation of the contextual influences that enhance the efficacy of some leadership actions and diminishes some others.'

Results of the Comparison of Different Work Phases within the Professional Groups

The *Co-ordination Group* used two independent variables, standardization and task load, to classify task phases. Looking first at the data from the cockpit, the task situations are depicted in Table 10.5 (for a detailed description see Chapter 3). The number of stars indicates the level of standardization and task load (low level = *, high level = ***).

Phase one is a normal take off, a routine task for pilots. The level of standardization is high and task load is low. In phase two the pilots have to diagnose and handle a problem. It is a defect they cannot repair, so they have to follow general instructions and prepare an unusual landing. The levels of standardization and task load are both rather low, since only rather open procedures exist and they have enough time for this task. Phase three is an unusual and difficult landing. Task load and standardization are both high. In Table 10.5, the results are shown as percentages of a given category relative to all observations. The differences between the phases for the different categories are all statistically significant in the direction indicated by the hypotheses concerning the effects of standardization and task load on team co-ordination (therefore the + signs in the last two lines of the table).

Table 10.5 Co-ordination patterns during different work phases based on co-ordination frequency in cockpit teams

Description of task situation			Frequency of co-ordination forms			
	Standard-ization	Task load	Explicit	Implicit	Leadership	Heedful inter-relating
Phase 1	***	*	66%	34%	2%	2%
Phase 2	*	*	81%	19%	14%	18%
Phase 3	***	***	60%	40%	3%	19%
Hypotheses - standardization			+		+	+
Hypotheses - task load			+	(+)		+

Phases one and two, during which task load is constant, are the appropriate phases to test the hypotheses concerning standardization. In the low standardization phase, more explicit co-ordination, more leadership and more heedful interrelating could be observed.

The effect of task load was controlled by the comparison of phase one and phase three, during which the level of standardization was constant and the task load varied. The amount of explicit co-ordination decreases under the high task load condition: the amount of leadership behavior does not show a relevant difference, and the amount of heedful interrelating increases. With the exception of leadership, for which a decrease under high task load was hypothesized, expectations were supported by the data. Regarding leadership, it could be assumed that standardization works as an appropriate substitute for leadership also under low task load conditions, especially when there is no anticipation of higher task load as was the case in phase one in the scenarios. The more appropriate phase for testing the assumptions about leadership, and explicit co-ordination, having to be used under low task load situations for preparing high task situations would be phase two, but in phase two standardization also differs, which makes it difficult to disentangle the different effects. The data seem to indicate, though, that leadership and explicit co-ordination are used to a particularly high degree in phase two, which is in line with the assumptions.

The same type of data from the anesthesia teams is summarized in Table 10.6. Phase one, *preparation*, is a highly regulated phase. Most of the written rules apply to this phase. Task load is relatively low, since the task is well known. Phase two, *patient falls asleep*, has fewer written rules and more task load. Phase three, *intubation*, is still well regulated and the task load is high. Phase four, *additional preparation*, has very few written rules, and the level of task load is high. Phase five, *transport of patient*, has no written rules and the task load is low. (For a detailed description of the phases see Chapter 3).

As before, the number of stars indicates the level of standardization and task load: low level = *, intermediate level= ** and high level = ***. The percentages for a given category during a given phase in relation to the sum of all observations in that phase are shown. To test the hypotheses concerning standardization and task load, different phases in which one of the independent variables is constant were compared. The standardization hypotheses were tested by comparing phases one and five, during which the difference in standardization is considerable – most of the rules concern phase one, and there are no rules at all concerning phase five – and task load is constant. This comparison is not optimal, because moderate task load instead of low task load is compared with high task load. However, these two phases were the only ones with the same level of standardization.

Table 10.6 Co-ordination patterns during different work phases based on co-ordination frequency in anesthesia teams

Description of task situation			Frequency of co-ordination forms			
	Standard -ization	Task load	Explicit	Implicit	Leadership	Heedful inter- relating
Phase 1	***	*	59%	41.%	10%	6%
Phase 2	**	**	69%	31.%	15%	9%
Phase 3	**	***	71%	29%	17%	12%
Phase 4	*	***	74%	26%	17%	10%
Phase 5	-	*	70%	30%	22%	15%
Hypotheses – standardization			+		+	+
Hypotheses – task load			-		-	+

In phase five (without written rules about the task), a higher share of explicit co-ordination, leadership behavior and heedful interrelating were observed than in phase one, which is highly regulated. These statistically significant results support the hypotheses: one can assume that standardization can substitute for explicit co-ordination, leadership behavior and heedful interrelating, allowing for a more economical way of co-ordination during teamwork. The effect of task load is not as clear: in phase three with higher task load teams show more heedful interrelating than in phase two in accordance with expectations. For all other types of co-ordination, the differences were contrary to hypotheses but were all very small and statistically non-significant. One reason for these results may be that a moderate task load phase – instead of a low task load phase – with a high task load phase.

The results support the very general hypotheses considering the two work environments only partially. Regarding explicit and implicit co-ordination, the observed difference was in the opposite direction. As noted, possible explanations are situational characteristics. Examining differences within the professional settings between work phases proved more interesting than direct comparison of aviation versus medicine. The aviation data support all hypotheses: adaptive co-ordination behavior was observed that mirrored the effect of standardization and task load. The findings for the anesthesia data were less consistent, only the effect of standardization could be demonstrated for all co-ordination forms. For task load, only the assumed relationship with heedful interrelating was supported in this working environment.

Co-ordination Patterns and Performance

The *Co-ordination Group* used a point system to judge team performance in the cockpit teams. The performance index contained ratings from flight instructors and a rating of fulfilling four compulsory tasks. The analysis in Table 10.7 shows partly significant results with the expected tendencies for leadership behavior.

Table 10.7   Correlations between team performance and share of leadership behavior in given task phases: aviation data

	Leadership Phase 1	Leadership Phase 2	Leadership Phase 3
Correlation with performance	-0.42	0.31	-0.24
Significance	p=0.03	p=0.05	p=0.12

The relationship between performance and leadership behavior is negative in phase one and phase three, during which the standardization level is high, and it is positive in phase two, when the standardization level is low. The more leadership behavior was demonstrated in the highly standardized work phases, the worse the performance. In phase two, on the other hand, the more leadership behavior was observed, the better team performance was. This supports assumptions concerning standardization serving as a substitute for personal leadership, even indicating that leadership may be detrimental when high standardization is present.

Unfortunately, correlations with the other observational categories in the aviation setting and all relationships in the medical setting were not as clear. One possible explanation is that co-ordination becomes crucial only in extremely high task load situations, when the right distribution of resources and attention really matters and cannot be compensated for by team members' individual abilities. Therefore, repeating the study with teams operating in even more challenging situations than the ones analyzed here might be a better test of the hypotheses.

Another important consideration for the future of this research is to develop more valid performance measure for anesthesia induction. Using the traditional expert rating turned out to be unsatisfactory.

Linguistic Aspects of Co-ordination

The observational psychological research reported in this chapter has dealt with a variety of co-ordination processes. Many of these processes rely on verbal communication as a medium. As communication is the most prominent medium for co-ordination processes, there have been attempts to design this medium in a way that makes it easy to use and as failsafe as possible. The outcome of these attempts are standard procedures – most extensively used in aviation – that very often not only assign and schedule tasks, but also prescribe the wording in communication and the assignment of speaker and recipient roles. Standard procedures not only co-ordinate the content of communication, but also co-ordinate the process of communication as well.

Sample analyses are presented here as an illustration of possible conflicts between the natural organization of verbal interaction and standard procedures, conflicts between concurrent tasks that influence the ordering of contributions to conversation and the adverse communicative behavior of the participants themselves. Then the general results will be summarized. The database for the linguistic analyses is a set of 14 cockpit simulator sessions that are part of the aviation database presented in Chapter 3.

Sample Analyses

In the first example (Figure 10.1), note who initiated the sequence and when. In this situation, the first officer (FO) was the pilot flying, and, in this instance, it would have been an FO duty to ask for the engine anti-ice. However, it is the pilot in command (PIC) who comes up with this topic and only then does the FO give the anti-ice order by completing the PIC's utterance. The FO acknowledges PIC's support by adding *merci* after completing the order.

14:16	PIC	new	engine anti ice;
14:17	F/O	shift	on. please. merci.
14:18	PIC	shift	is on.
14:19	F/O	maint	checked.

Figure 10.1 Supportive request[38]

In this example, the PIC acknowledges the communicative task, the so-called quaestio (For details on the quaestio model see Chapter 3 and Dietrich and Grommes, 2003), to ask for the status of the engine anti-ice, probably because the FO appears not to be aware of this required task. The FO reacts to this quaestio,

---

[38] Notes on Figure10.1 to 10.4: The number identifies the simulator session in the database, and the time stamp of the observation. Then there is an abbreviation for the speaker (PIC, F/O) followed by a code showing the relation of this utterance to the former one. The utterances themselves are transcribed according to the transcription conventions described in Chapter 9. For non-English parts of the utterances there is a translation.

LIVERPOOL JOHN MOORES UNIVERSITY
LEARNING SERVICES

and shifts it by implicitly maintaining the reference to *engine anti-ice* and adding the order '*on. please.*' Another *shift* occurs when the PIC announces that the anti-ice actually '*is on.*' The PIC contributed to co-ordination of the flight task by hinting at the FO's duties. There is evidence that this co-ordination effort was successful by the straightforward co-ordination of the linguistic actions. The utterances are coherently tied with minimal effort and completion of both the actual action and the verbal interaction is signaled by the reference-maintaining announcement '*checked.*'

In Figure 10.2, it can be seen that co-ordination of and by verbal interaction can be more complicated. The situation is as follows: the PIC has already explained to the FO why the flaps lever should be in a certain position although it is not working. However, the FO seems to be unable to understand this and keeps asking even after he first indicates understanding.

8:255	FO	shift	stimmt do das wieder nümme hä?
			then this is wrong again
8:256	PIC	shift	isch alles gsetzt jetzt ( )
			everything is set now
8:257	FO	break	mir händ doch mir händ doch/
			but we have we have/
8:258	PIC	new	landing check available
8:259	FO	shift	okay landing check three green
8:260	PIC	maint	landing all green
8:261	FO	bshift	mir sind doch gar nöd (für) flaps zero oder nöd?
			aren't we at flaps zero?

Figure 10.2 Pushing through of procedures

Finally, the PIC supposedly thinks that the topic has been discussed sufficiently and that they should continue with their task. This is the point at which he comes up with the new quaestio, which is not immediately related to the previous discussion but mentions the next task. The FO takes up this quaestio – because it is mandatory due to procedures – but takes up his former topic again in 8:261. The point here is that the PIC refrains from joint co-ordination of contributions to conversation in order to ensure the continuation of their primary tasks. He exploits standard procedures for his purposes, which demonstrates a specific feature of standards: they imitate well co-ordinated sequences of conversation, but they are not necessarily oriented towards the spontaneous dynamics of natural conversation but, instead, are oriented towards a prescribed plan of actions. Thus they might interfere with naturally developing discussions or be employed to end them in a quite authoritarian manner as in Figure 10.3.

8:15	FO	new	gear up.
8:16	silence		(30s)
8:17	PIC	shift	gear is up.
8:18	ATC	new	swiss-air six two one, contact radar one two one (once).
8:18a	PIC	maint	one [two one (once)]. swiss-air six two one.
8:19	FO	bshift	<<pp>[checked.]>

Figure 10.3 Third party interruption

Here one can see that crews not only have to co-ordinate conversation and actions in the cockpit but also information from additional channels like ATC. In cases like this, crews receive calls from ATC that are often unrelated to the ongoing action in the cockpit – here the take-off and climb procedure –but, nevertheless, require immediate action. The additional cognitive task here is to keep the mental representation of the primary discourse available as long as the interrupting structure is being processed. The code *bshift* in the transcript signals that interlocutors in such a situation take up references from the interrupted discourse in order to bridge the interrupting sequence. In Figure 10.3, the references are taken up implicitly: the FO does not mention the gear again but simply says *checked*. He can do so, because it is clear from his role as PF that he is not a participant in the ATC sequence.

In many cases – most probably in routine or low task load situations – these occurrences do not lead to complications although they increase the team's cognitive load, but there are clear examples that these interruptions can be fatal, as was the case with the Atlanta South East flight to Gulfport discussed in Chapter 11.

5:170	PIC	shift	the runway is: (-) known. display threshold, in case of go around (.) smoothly- just to check again.
5:171	FO	new	vielleicht, dann frag ich schnell (den kru)/ *maybe then I quickly ask (the kru)/*
5:172	ATC/FO		<two turns ATC and FO concerning heading>
5:173	FO	bshift	du hast gesagt no display threshold; weil es gibt da ein/ *you said no display threshold; just because there is a/*
5:174	PIC	shift	es gibt display threshold [display threshold] *there is a display threshold*
5:175	FO	maint	[ja okay] ja. *yes okay yes*

Figure 10.4 Clarification

In Figure 10.4, the FO first breaks the coherence pattern by introducing a new quaestio that he then stops immediately. This may be due to the ATC-intervention. The FO then ties his utterance in 5:173 back to the one from PIC in 5:170 by reference to the display threshold. He asks if there really is no display threshold, and, thus, prevents PIC from just continuing with his quaestio – the suggestions for problem solution. The FO's utterance, which questions the non-existence of the display threshold, is actually a request for clarification because one can read his wording *no display threshold* as a repetition of the PIC's [...] *known. display threshold*, [...]. The phonetic similarity of *no* and *known* here leads to a possible misunderstanding and the FO just wants to avoid this.

This example highlights a further aspect of linguistic co-ordination: in well-formed discourse all information should be transparent and it should be guaranteed that all information is correctly available to all participants. Here F/O employs the *bshift*-relation to show his uncertainty with respect to specific information. He accepts the possible cognitive costs of this strategy in order to avoid an information gap that might put the whole operation at risk. So his re-organization of the information flow lays the ground for the co-ordination of flight related activities.

Overall Results

In general, the crews under investigation in this study display only a few distinct structures with respect to linguistic co-ordination.[39] A specific feature that also plays a role in three of the four examples above is the code *bshift*, which hints at breaks in the linear organization of discourse. Only 139 occurrences out of 3422 total coded linguistic contributions were found. These occurrences are not distributed equally over the different flight phases.[40] There are 27 *bshifts* in the take-off phase, 76 in the problem solution phase and 36 in the approach phase. However, this finding matches with some features of the different situations.

The first phase is highly standardized, and the workload is low. There is not much need for natural ways co-ordination, because most of the co-ordination work is covered by standards. The bshifts in this phase are task related in a way similar to the intervention in Figure 10.3.

Contrary to this, in the second phase there is almost no standardization. Workload is low, too, but there is much need for communication in order to find a solution to the technical problem. So, in this phase the crews have to communicate a lot, and they have to co-ordinate their actions and their communication without the support of standards. Therefore, they have to rely on natural devices for the co-ordination of communication. This seems to work quite well, as the small number of *bshifts* indicates, but in some cases the teams have to provide additional effort in order to secure the flow of information. The reason for the additional effort can be either positive or negative. In the latter case, one team member does not properly anticipate the informational needs of the other – one might speak of a lack of heedful interrelating. In the other case *bshifts* are employed as a heedful way to tie together information over longer stretches of conversation. Typical of this phase are sequences of conversation like those in Figures 10.2 and 10.4.

---

[39] This finding is supported by research on communication in the medical operating room reported in Grommes and Dietrich (2002). There it has been argued that the human cognitive capacity of discourse production seems to be astonishingly stable even under pressure.

[40] For a description of the flight phases see this chapter and Chapter 3.

The third phase shows features of both of the other phases. It is highly standardized like the first phase, and workload is high. Additionally, there is some higher need for co-ordination because the attitude of the aircraft during this kind of approach diverges from the norm. So there are *bshifts* of all types in this phase. The relationship between these findings and standardization and heedful interrelating can be summarized as follows: a high degree of standardization leads to a decrease in the use of natural devices for the co-ordination of communication. This is not necessarily critical, but as mentioned in the discussion of Figure 10.2, standardization and natural ways of co-ordination can come into conflict and can lead to a more complicated construction of sequences of conversation. Heedful interrelating does not necessarily lead to distinct linguistic structures, but a fine-grained linguistic analysis can reveal the sources of heedful or heedless behavior (more data and discussion on these topics are provided in Grommes and Grote, 2001; Grommes, Grote, and Zala-Mezö, 2003). In conclusion, natural strategies of linguistic co-ordination are a solid basis for investigating the processes of team interaction. However, due to their more complex structure, they may increase the cognitive load of the team members. Perhaps it is reasonable to carefully support them with standardized strategies that are flexible enough to allow for quick and easy transitions between strategies. In other words, teams should be encouraged to make use of co-ordination mechanisms like leadership, explicit and implicit co-ordination and heedful interrelating, as these have demonstrated a positive influence on the outcome of team processes.

Chapter Summary

In concluding this chapter on the processes of leadership and co-ordination in teams at work in high risk environments, it is important to understand the roles of workload, uncertainty and standardization. The successful simultaneous management of teams and tasks is clearly determined by a variety of factors, some of which were analyzed in these studies, yielding applicable results. There will always be some degree of uncertainty or unpredictability in the teams under investigation here, but actively minimizing the unexpected has a positive impact on the performance of teams. Standardized practices and procedures offer an institutional or infrastructural proxy for improving the predictability of situations (perhaps even serving as a substitute for leadership in some situations), by setting expectations for behavior and reducing uncertainty. As standardization increases, the need for leadership decreases, and indeed can be superfluous and detrimental if active leadership behaviors persist in light of already clear expectations in highly standardized situations. Standard procedures also appear to impact the content and the process (linguistically) of communication, as seen through co-ordination mechanisms such as explicit co-ordination, implicit co-ordination, bshift and heedful interrelating.

Independent of the extent of standardized procedures, briefings prior to the start of team activities more specifically address the expectations for a given team and a given task, equipping the team with a plan for contingencies. In addition, there are specific things that leaders did which were associated with improved teamwork and performance, i.e. they used higher rates of problem-solving communications; they spoke more in the first person plural; they focused on managing the situation while other team members focused on the technical tasks during high workload situations, they encouraged more communication contributions from other team members, and they gave more positive feedback to other team members. These findings, as reported from this multi-disciplinary work on leadership and co-ordination processes, offer some very accessible and applicable material for industry, researchers, regulators and front-line personnel working in high risk environments.

Chapter 11

Determinants of Effective Communication

Rainer Dietrich

Introduction

Language is, without any doubt, the most complicated means of communication between organisms, and, in general, people are well advised to say nothing. However, there are situations in which the avoidance of communication can cause even more damage to life than speaking would. Working as a member of a professional team in a high risk environment can easily supply a person with both sorts of wisdom. This chapter deals with the interrelation of communication with other types of workplace activities. Workplaces differ in many respects. This was pointed out in the introduction with reference to the sample workplaces: cockpit, operating room, intensive care unit and NPP control room. There are differences in many features, including shape, function and team structure, and one would expect that these differences create different needs for communicative behaviour. Those features of a workplace that are relevant to the form, frequency, content or strategies of communication are conceptualized as the formative characteristics of a workplace. At the beginning of this chapter, some observations will be referred to that seem to imply conflicting answers to the question of whether or not one should speak. The following paragraphs are meant to disentangle the complicated determinants of the involved classes of communicative activities. The ultimate goal is to explicate some basic principles about the interaction of communication and other cognitive activities.

Whether to Speak or Not

In September 2002, the president, the chief operating officer, the chief medical officer and the chief nursing officer of the Brigham and Womens' Hospital at Boston (BWH) decided to communicate on a regular basis with frontline workers in their hospital. They simply went to different workplaces and asked questions of nurses and physicians, physician leaders and nurse managers in the unit. This communication included questions such as:

- Were you able to care for your patients this week as safely as possible? If not, why not?
- Is there anything we could do to prevent the next adverse event?
- Can you describe the unit's ability to work as a team?
- What do you think the unit could do on a regular basis to improve safety?
- Would it be feasible to discuss safety concerns, e.g. patients with same name, near misses that happened, etc. during report?
- If you make or report an error, are you concerned about personal consequences?

The answers were registered and evaluated. According to Frankel et al. (2003), changes that resulted from these WalkRounds™ after less than two years included:

- The installation of electronic doors in the cardiac intensive care unit,
- The purchase of a mechanical lift for moving obese patients without injuring staff,
- Improvement of the Web based attending physician on call system [a nurse had reported that it had taken her a long time to identify the responsible physician to look after a patient who had fallen],
- Improvement of materials, management support and logistics by the implementation of improvement projects on some patient care units;
- An increased number of IV poles and bedside tables
- and a number of additional measures that improved the patients' safety and comfort considerably; see Frankel et al. (2003: 22).

If there is anything that can be concluded from the results of the WalkRounds™, it is clearly that communication was something good for BWH's staff and their patients. However, there is also clear counter evidence. The best known and most widely studied phenomenon that provides counter evidence is driver distraction due to a language processing task. Introspection might convince us that driving a car and, at the same time, following a demanding conversation are two activities that do not go together smoothly. There is also experimental evidence that points in the same direction. Among the more recent investigations is Salvucci's (2002) experiment, which tests a model to predict driver distraction from a primarily cognitive secondary task.

The language processing task used in this experiment was developed by Daneman & Carpenter (1980). The task is comprised of two stages. In the first stage, subjects listen to five simple transitive sentences of the form 'X does Y.' After each sentence subjects have to give a statement as to whether the proposition expressed by the sentence is generally sensible. In the second stage, subjects are asked to state the last word of each sentence in the order that the sentences were presented. 'For example, for the sentences "The boy brushed his teeth" and "The train bought a newspaper", the driver would report "yes" after the first sentence, "no" after the second and then report the memorized list: "teeth", "newspaper", etc.

The sentence span task itself involves two current activities, namely judging sentence sensibility and memorizing and rehearsing final words. When combined with driving, the task puts a substantial cognitive load on drivers as they attempt to integrate the task.' (Salvucci 2002: 2). Under the dual task condition, the drivers' capacity to follow a lead vehicle was severely affected. Brake reaction times increased significantly as did the amount of lateral deviation from the centre of the lane. At the same time, the headway distance, i.e. the distance between the driver's vehicle and the lead vehicle, shrank significantly under the language processing task condition. There is convincing parallel evidence from investigations of dual task performance on the flight deck; cf. the seminal work published in Waller, Giambastita & Zellmer-Bruhn (1999).

While the BWH evidence makes a clear case for the application of verbal communication, the driver distraction phenomenon points in the opposite direction. It suggests that communicating with the driver will probably not positively affect his/her performance or the safety of the passengers.

Still, crew resource management programs unanimously recommend the use of verbal communication to the members of a cockpit crew, an operating team and to operators in a nuclear power plant (NPP) control room. They do not differentiate between normal and high workload situations. This does not seem to be rational advice considering Salvucci's and others' findings about the distraction effect of verbal communication on other cognitive activities. The question of whether or not one should speak still remains to be answered.

What Can be Done Simultaneously

According to John Searle (1968), it is possible to effortlessly smoke a cigarette, read a newspaper and scratch your head at the same time. However, parking a car at night in a tight space while explaining to the passenger where the opera tickets are is a trickier task, one that is all the more demanding when the Overture has already started.

While some sorts of activities can obviously be performed simultaneously without stress, others cannot or are costly, at the least, when executed in parallel. Communication belongs to both sorts of activities. It should and, at the same time, should not be combined with other activities. One way out of this contradiction may be found in specific features of the verbal communication activity. Robertson (1994) proposed the *Theory of Simultaneous Understanding, Answering, and Memory Interaction* (TSUNAMI). This theory aims at modelling a prototypical communicative activity, namely question answering (QA). The QA-activity is assumed to be carried out by a human information processing system comprised of two knowledge stores, four different processors and four levels of representation; see Robertson (1994; figure 1, p. 57). The model resolves the above inconsistency by assuming two different stores and the two types of processes related to them: the *semantic memory* contains the linguistic knowledge; the *episodic memory* contains episodic knowledge. When a person is asked a question, two processes are initialized: the parsing of the linguistic form and of the content of the utterance and the retrieval of answer candidates in the episodic memory. The second follows the first one closely in time. As empirically and frequently confirmed procedures, sentence understanding and matching the result with one's world knowledge, make a further assumption possible: that processing these procedures might occur differently in a dual task condition than in a single task condition. Today's theoretical and experimental linguistic and psycholinguistic knowledge provides increasing support for the opinion that purely linguistic processes are cognitively encapsulated and somewhat immune to encroachments originating in language external cognitive processes. This is not meant to imply that all sorts of external, non-verbal cognitive activities, like driving a car or dialling a number on a cell-phone, are always detrimental to the higher communication related processes, as in this case, the retrieval of answer candidates – and vice versa. Whether or not communication related processes rather than proper linguistic processes are prone to collide with additional and simultaneous cognition is a matter for empirical research.

The Role of Communication in Threat and Error Management

Communication as a measure in the context of threat and error management has an instrumental function. Its ultimate goal is minimizing threats and the risk of errors as conditions or results of the team's primary task activities. The utility of communicating depends, accordingly, on its skilful application. Communicating is not useful per se. A participant in a chess tournament has good reasons not to communicate his/her plans to the opponent before the game. This is obvious. There are also good reasons for considering the suitability of verbal communication in internal team activities as is made clear by the driver distraction effect and other evidence considered below; for a more detailed description of the functions of verbal communication among team members, the reader is referred to the chapter on language and communication, Chapter 9. A crucial point in team communication is to know its constraints and to observe them in team interaction.

The Facets of Communication

Basic characteristics Three components of communication are relevant. The most obvious, momentous and most ignored characteristic of communication is *reciprocity*. Communication is a joint activity. It occupies two parties and absorbs (part of) their mental resources. Thus, the second characteristic is that communication is not free; it requires cognitive energy; it brings about *cognitive costs*. The third component is the inevitability of its *impact*. Communication changes the states of mind of the participating interlocutors. It has an inescapable influence on their states of knowledge, the least being that they know that there has been a communication event. Reciprocity, costs and impact are natural properties of every communicative event. They are neither good nor bad. The effect can, however, be felt as alleviation or aggravation of the situation when compared to the pre-state. In addition, different interlocutors may evaluate this differently. The circumstances that determine whether or not a communicative act combined with a demanding primary task will be felicitous or will cause damage are sketched out in the next paragraph.

Relevant setting parameters   Airplane crews are not free to use their native language in international communication. Five languages are licensed according to ICAO (International Civil Aviation Organisation) regulations: English, French, Russian, Chinese and Spanish, among which English has become the most widely used inter-language worldwide. As a consequence, *language proficiency and code switching*, i.e. using a second language instead of one's mother tongue, can, of course, be considered an obstacle to fluent and routine communication; see also the experimental findings reported in Chapter 7.

When communicating in their native language, crew members sometimes have to use a precisely regulated set of expressions laid down in checklists and in manuals of Air Traffic Control (ATC) language. The extent of *standardization* is quite different for other work places such as firefighting, rescue operations or surgery. One intuitively suspects that the effect of linguistic *standardization* can prove beneficial in some conditions but embarrassing in others. Standardisation is, accordingly, a setting parameter of prime relevance for the efficiency of communication.

In the most general terms, the goal of task related communication is the change of team members' knowledge of the world. The efficiency of a communicative activity is, accordingly, determined by the accuracy of the speaker's assumption about the knowledge he/she shares with his/her addressee, in short, by the *shared knowledge*.

Everyday experience in social interactions illustrates that both the content of and the linguistic expression used in communicative activities are related to the quality of social relations between interlocutors. Imagine an oral university examination in German literature. The student is asked to give the plot of one of Gerhard Hauptmann's narratives, preferably 'Death in Venice.' The professor's error about who the author of this text is causes a delicate communication problem for the student as to how he/she should proceed: frankly tell the professor that 'Death in Venice' was written by Thomas Mann? This might embarrass the professor and probably influence his/her opinion of the student's personality. The alternative would be not to mention the error and give the plot. This might, however, create a different risk. The professor could have mistakenly mixed up 'Death in Venice' and 'Bahnwärter Thiel' and might realize this mistake later on and, thus, have a negative opinion of the student's knowledge of literature. Communication problems such as this originate in differences in social or functional role of the interlocuters. This parameter will simply be called *social relations* in this chapter.

Another feature of workplaces that determines the form and, to some extent, the content and strategy of task related verbal behaviour is the kind of communication channel. The same forms that can be appropriate linguistic means for face-to-face verbal interaction might prove unsuitable under conditions of telephone contact, i.e. without a visual channel. Typical channel conditions in the present context include:

- Visual and acoustic contact online, no media, face-to-face or side-by-side position;
- Only oral, online with media (phone, radio);
- Written and quasi-online, but strictly sequential (electronic mail, chat, etc.).

Some Principles of Communication in High Risk Environments

The Data

The following findings are based on the results of comparative analyses of communication events in four types of high risk work places: the control room of a nuclear power plant (NPP control room), a hospital's intensive care unit (ICU), an operating room and the cockpit of a commercial airliner. They are comparable in so far as, in each case, a team of specialists performs the task and verbal communication is a crucial instrument for the interchange of task related information. In addition, verbal communication plays an important role in *setting the tone* of the team's social interaction. Although there are many similarities among them, the workplaces differ in relevant features like task profiles, time structure, size of the team, amount of automation and size and type of damage in the event of fatal errors. These groups can be assumed to represent a much larger set of high risk workplaces including chemical plants (similar to nuclear power plants), rescue teams (partly similar to work done in the ICU and in the OR), large-scale construction sites (ICU and cockpit) and space missions (cockpit and, in respect to the high proportion of automation, NPP).

The data include different but complementary types of observations collected using different methods:

- Documents of authentic events (protocols of abnormal events in the NPP, transcripts of Cockpit Voice Recorder (CVR) data, audio and video tapes of actual operations);
- Scenarios in aircraft, NPP control room and integrated OR simulators);
- Surveys of large numbers of staff (ICU).

More detailed accounts of the methods and data are given in the chapters found in Part I and in most of Part II.

The Analysis

The aim of the analysis is to establish favourable and unfavourable circumstances of communication under high workload. For each of the setting parameters and for some combinations suggested by the data, it will be proved whether or not there is an association between quantity and quality of communicative measures and whether or not the effect, if any, is beneficial to the team's performance and ultimate attainment of the primary task, i.e. flying the plane to its destination, helping a patient and running the systems of an NPP, respectively.

Results

The factors will be addressed in the following order:

- Language proficiency and code switching
- Standardisation
- Communication channel
- Social relations
- Shared knowledge and focus of attention

Language proficiency and code switching[41] There is little quantitative evidence supporting the relevance of the use of the native language. The *Microstructure Group* undertook one of the first neurolinguistic experiments to test the language factor (use of native/non-native language) in the condition of additional task load; see Chapter 12. Additionally, a rich collection of anecdotal but convincing observations is presented in Cushing's (1994) *Fatal Words*. These anecdotes show that erroneous violations in the use of standard phraseology in aviation can severely affect the safety of passengers and personnel. It was this type of violation that ended in one of the gravest accidents in the history of civil aviation. Two B-747 aircraft collided on runway 12 of Tenerife Norte Los Rodeos Airport in March 1977. The two planes, PanAm flight 1736 and the KLM flight 4805, had landed in Los Rodeos because their original destination, Las Palmas, had been closed due to a bomb attack in the terminal and warnings of a possible second bomb. When Las Palmas was re-opened, the two flights could be continued, and the planes taxied to their line up positions; KLM to runway 12 and the PanAm-Jet to runway 30, which forced them to backtrack a considerable distance on runway 12 in order to reach the intersection of runway 30. When ready for take off, the KLM pilot reported to the local ATC controller: 'We are at take off', an utterance which, according to standard, means that the plane is going to roll and accelerate on the runway for take off. The crew could be confident that this was understood because Tenerife Tower had cleared them for departure ten seconds before. KLM had confirmed clearance, and the Tower had reconfirmed. Still the Tower radio controller had obviously misunderstood the KLM transmission to mean something like 'We are lined up on runway 12 and are ready for take off.' This becomes clear from the tower's response, 'O.K. Stand by for take-off. I will call you.' which was motivated by the fact that the Pan Am B-747 was rolling on this runway in the opposite direction. It is difficult to decide who exactly misunderstood what. In any case, the accident provides a strong argument for the strict use of standardized phraseology. Many more incidents and accidents have been caused by sloppy communication. In

---

[41] This paragraph is co-authored by the members of the *Linguistic Factors Group*, Manfred Krifka, Silka Martens and Florian Schwarz.

addition, the probability of procedural violations seems to be associated with high task load.

There are a number of other accidents in aviation in which non-native command of English was a contributing factor. A recent report from *Aviation Today* mentions the case of another Spanish traffic controller at Tenerife in 1980, who gave a holding pattern clearance to a Dan Air flight by saying *turn to the left* when he should have said *turns to the left*, resulting in the aircraft making a single left turn rather than making circles using left turns. The jet hit a mountain, killing 146 people. Also, written or spoken instructions for operating a plane can be a problem. In 1993, Chinese pilots flying a US-made MD-80 were baffled by an audio alarm from the plane's ground proximity warning system system: *terrain, terrain, whoop, whoop, pull up!* A cockpit recorder picked up the pilot's last words (in Chinese): *What does 'pull up' mean?* The 1990 crash of a Colombian Avianca plane at Kennedy Airport was perhaps not only caused by low English proficiency – the Spanish-speaking pilot said *we just running out of fuel*, which could be understood as *we are just running out of fuel* or *we have just run out of fuel*. Another factor at play might have been a cultural one, an effort to save face, which prevented the pilot from declaring a fuel emergency, which would have resulted in an immediate clearance to land.

Problems of code switching do not only occur with speakers of different native languages that have to rely on a common language, which might be foreign to at least one party. There is also the problem of speakers that speak different regional varieties of a language. This can result in subtle but relevant differences, e.g. Northern German has a Dutch-style progressive aspect, and Southern German has no progressive at all. This is a much-underestimated problem in English as there are considerable differences between the so-called BANA forms of English (that is, British, American, New Zealand and Australian). There are also other forms of English like Indian, Jamaican or Singaporean English, which differ, in basic grammatical devices such as the use of progressive marking. Such differences have been a major source of trouble in the past.

Even within one language, technical parlance may differ from common vernacular. Cushing (1994) argues that this difference was a crucial factor in the 1981 accident at John Wayne Orange County airport. This case involved Air California plane 336 that was cleared for landing and Air California plane 931 taxing on the ground to the take-off position. Within less than one minute, ATC instructed AC931 to *taxi into position and hold* (i.e. stay); the captain of AC336 asked ATC *Can we hold*, and his first officer, *Ask him if we can hold* (i.e. continue with landing). ATC asked AC931 *if you can just go ahead and hold* (i.e. continue to stay). The problem here is that *hold* in aviation lingo typically means 'continue with what you are doing', whereas in ordinary English it means 'stop what you are now doing.'

In aviation, international programs are underway under the auspices of the International Civil Aviation Organization (ICAO) to develop standards for English proficiency for pilots and air traffic controllers. Such programs were instated after the midair collision of a Saudi Arabian Airlines plane with a Kazakh airline plane in 1996. This was partly caused because the Kazhak airliner misunderstood ATC.

The Proficiency Requirement in Common English Study Group (PRICESG) studies ways to improve the English proficiency of foreign pilots through standardization and testing (cf. Mathews 2003). This led to an ICAO resolution that states that by 2008, both pilots and ATC personnel must show certain defined levels of English proficiency. English proficiency cannot be reduced to the terminology in the field because there can be situations that require a more general linguistic aptitude; Mathews reports a case in which a Spanish-speaking air traffic controller did not warn an English speaking flight crew about a tethered air balloon, presumably because this fell out of the standard repertoire for which the controller was trained.

Currently, international rules state that ATC communication should be in the language used by the station on the ground and that English should be available upon request. As a matter of fact, in many countries, English is the de-facto language of ATC communication. There is evidence that a mixed language environment in ATC communication poses a threat. This was cited as a problem in a recent accident at Charles de Gaulle airport involving a larger aircraft with a French-speaking pilot and a smaller one with an English-speaking pilot.

One important question is whether or not pilots should be obliged to use English, and only English, when operating a plane, and not just when communicating with air traffic control. While this might reduce code-switching problems as in the Tenerife accident, it would clearly result in an additional cognitive burden that is especially critical in phases of high workload. There is evidence that even very proficient speakers of a foreign language have a slower word recognition in the non-native language, showing that understanding, and certainly speaking, in a foreign language takes its toll on the speaker. Hence it is not generally recommended to enforce the use of a foreign language, like English, in a professional setting if the crew members all share another native language. See Chapter 12 for details.

Standardization, communication and the primary task   The extent of standardization varies considerably across workplaces and differs in the domains of communication and primary task procedures. Cockpit crew behavior is regulated by a relatively large number of constraints applying both to primary task procedures and to the content and the form of verbal information interchange. Tables 11.1 to 11.3 show examples of standard phraseology for external (Air Traffic Control) and intra-cockpit communication.

Table 11.1 Example of standardized phraseology for *clearance for departure*

Cockpit   Tempelhof ground. This is Lufthansa 040. (Information received). Request start up and ATC clearance to Hamburg.

Ground   Starting up and cleared to Hamburg Airport via Brünkendorf, Runway 23, wind 290, 5 knots, visibility 5000 in mist, clouds few at 800, scattered at 1.500, temperature 8 to 6. Contact Berlin Radar on 136.05 ....

Cockpit   Berlin Radar, This is Lufthansa 040. Ready for departure to Hamburg, runway 23 ...

Berlin   Lufthansa 040. Taxi runway 27 L and wait ...
Ground

Table 11.2 Standardized phraseology and checks : executed during take off with a B757, for instance (PF = pilot flying; PNF = pilot non-flying)

PF   EPR select
PNF   EPR; Power is set.
PF   Checked
PNF   Eighty knots
PF   Checked
PNF   One twenty
PF   Checked
PNF   V1; rotate
PF   Positive climb. Gear up.
PNF   Positive Climb. Gear is up. All three green

Table 11.3 Standardized check list: guided procedure in case of an engine-one out, (in part; air craft type: Embraer ER)

PF	We got a left engine out. Left power lever flight idle.
PNF	Left power lever flight idle.
PF	Left condition lever feather.
PNF	Feathered.
PF	Fuel shut off. ...

There is no similar standardization for the communication in the NPP control room, whereas the primary task procedures are thoroughly pre-structured in lists of yes/no-checks like in the cockpit. No explicit standardization applies to the work or to communication in OR and ICU teams, at least in most parts of Europe and in the U.S.A.

The extent of standardization seems to be related to two circumstances in a workplace: the nature of the communication channel and the proportion of automation. The medium for crew members' verbal communication is electro-acoustic (internal) and radio transmission (external). Electro-acoustic transmission works with a considerably reduced frequency band, which affects the clearness of the consonantism. Understanding may also be deteriorated by flight noise and radio communication from third parties in the air. There are no comparable channel disturbances in the NPP, in the OR or in the ICU. Standardization of communication compensates for the vulnerability of the channel with redundancy and disambiguity. In short, the standardization of phraseology for information interchange is a safety measure that minimizes the risk originating from channel disturbances. Standardization of primary task operational procedures, on the other hand, seems to be related to the relative extent of automation in a workplace. This is high in the NPP control room and the cockpit, while it is low in the OR and ICU.

The major results of this comparative analysis can be summarized as follows:

- The more vulnerable the communication channel, the more standardized the task related communication;
- The more automatically the primary task is executed, the more standardized the primary task procedures.

These are the general principles. However, the most compelling question is, whether or not standardization is really the most efficient safeguard against communicative and procedural failure in the cockpit and in the NPP. This is an empirical question, and the answer would require comparable data from teams who stick to standardization, as well as from those who do not.

Is there more than anecdotal evidence? Silberstein & Dietrich (2003; Chapt. 6.1.6 and 6.1.8) analyzed the interdependence of phraseology violations and crew performance in a number of different domains; they also used NTSB cockpit voice recorder transcripts of flight accidents and did a qualitative and quantitative analysis of the data. From 20 more recent events, 14 were sampled, coded and counted; they contained low and high task load routine segments, as well as phases under abnormal and emergency conditions. This lent the data a relatively high degree of comparability. The results that are interesting in the present context are shown in Table 11.4.

Table 11.4 The Relation of violations of ICAO phraseology and coherence in cockpit communication

Communication problem	Task load				
	Routine, low task load (Taxi, Cruise)	Routine, high task load (Approach, landing)	Abnormal: Danger 1	Abnormal: Danger 2	Abnormal: Danger 3
% violations of phraseology	25	12,5	50	50	93,75
% incoherence of discourse	0	0	50	50	100

The results indicate an almost perfect relationship between the proportion of phraseology violations and the loss of coherence. There are almost no violations during high task load routine operations, and there is a significant increase in *danger one* and *two* conditions with a maximum in *danger three* (emergency). Given the relatively strong separation of the pilot and the co-pilot's domains of attention and the resulting augmented need for information interchange, the decrease in coherence necessarily implies an increase of risk to the safety of the flight.

Another piece of evidence, from an observation by Krifka, Martens & Schwarz (2003, p. 88), confirms the interrelation of the violation of communication standards and the primary task performance stems. They linguistically analyzed the cockpit communication of five B 727 crews and matched the results with independent flight performance ratings by pilots in training. The communication units were coded, among many other categories, for *expressives* and *emotions*. Expressive and emotional utterances are not a part of the standard aviation phraseology. A considerable proportion of such utterances in the total communication of a crew signals a decrease in task related communication control. The findings of Krifka et al. show that the average proportion of expressives and emotions of poor performing crews was more than twice that of good performing crews and almost five times higher under high task load conditions.

The findings indicate that vulnerable channel conditions and highly automated primary tasks require regulation of communication. They further suggest that observation of these regulations goes hand in hand with more efficient primary task performance.

Communication channel The choice of which communicative means to utilize is largely determined by the kind or nature of the channel used to transmit the physical signals of the utterance. Team members who can see and hear each other can use deictic lexical expressions like *here, there, over there, this one,* accompanied by a gesture for reference to places, persons and objects. Sitting side-by-side, like pilots in the cockpit, does not support the use of these expressions unless the addressee turns his/her head toward the speaker. The use of deictic expressions together with a gesture in the cockpit is, therefore, explicitly regulated if mandatory. A face-to-face setting makes it possible for team members to replace verbal communication with non-verbal means such as gestures and facial expressions according to their own intuitive judgement. This is impossible in communication via telephone or radio. The simultaneity that still holds in radio communication, which makes spontaneous interruption and continuous feedback signaling possible, is excluded with email and other strictly serial and sequential interchanges that use textual or graphic representations.

Two examples will be considered: one piece of cockpit communication and the beginning of an OP. Both examples are authentic. Transcripts are found in Figures 11.1 and 11.2.

The OR setting is face-to-face although there may be a barrier between the surgeon and anesthetist during many operations. In general, members of the surgery and anesthesia teams are turned towards one another while the members of the cockpit and the NPP control room are situated side by side or behind one another. Their spatial arrangement mirrors the structuring of their working domains, which are more complementary than overlapping. The consequences of shared vs. complementary domains of attention will be considered later. The focus of this analysis will be on channel-determined means of reference and whether this forms a source of difficulties.

The only difference between the cockpit and the OR setting is the spatial orientation of the team members (towards one another) and the head set equipment. PF and PNF are side by side and have headsets, S and A are face-to-face and do not use electro-acoustic transmission.

[*A German Lufthansa Airbus 320 approaching Warsaw Okecie Airport. Tower reports windshear on approach and over the runway; German utterances are translated into English.*]

Speaker	Utterance
PNF	You are slightly above glideslope.
. . .	
PNF	About one thumb's breadth.
. . .	
PF	Please switch on the ignition
. . .	
PF	Still from the aft [*Showers and wind*]
. . .	
PF	Rain repellent, please.

Legend:

PF	Pilot flying
PNF	Pilot-non-flying
[Italics]	Comments
. . .	Irrelevant stretches of discourse

Figure 11.1 Cockpit communication: references to objects and places

[A has to open up the thorax for the purpose of a lung resection. He/she is supposed to identify the point where he/she plans to cut in. As he/she sets out to count the ribs S interrupts him. The original discourse is in German.]

Speaker	Utterance
A	One, two, three, four, five. This one here should be the one.
	[S reminds A that touching it can never identify the first rib.]
A	Then it is one less [...] Then we have to cut in here.
S	This one is the sixth rib.
A	O.K. Then here.
S	No. At this one.
A	O.K. And then in there.
S	In there.

Legend:

S	Surgeon
A	Her assistant
[Italics]	Comments
	Irrelevant stretches of discourse

. . .

Figure 11.2 OR communication: references to objects and places

A synopsis of linguistic means for object and spatial references is listed in Table 11.4.

Table 11.4 Synoptic list of referential expressions in cockpit vs. OR-discourse

Type of referents	Cockpit	OR
Objects	*ignition; rain repellent*	*this one here; this one;*
Places	*above glideslope; from the aft;*	*here; there;*

The facts are obvious: the members of the cockpit crew use full lexical descriptions for the specification of objects and places; the OR team members use situation dependent deictic expression. This difference is related to channel differences; this becomes even more obvious in radio communication between the cockpit and the tower. Reference to the speaker and, at times, to the addressee, is also done with names or full lexical descriptions: 'Tower! Good afternoon. Lufthansa 2904. Continued ILS approach.' – 'Lufthansa 2904, you are cleared to land ...'

The second question considered was, whether the side by side channel condition that is specific to the cockpit would cause communication impairment. Consider the following example (Figure 11.3).

[Embraer *Atlantic South East flight to Gulfport. Twenty minutes after take-off one of the four blades of the left propeller separates, destroys the rest of the propeller and the engine. The special handicap of the crew members is that they have no visual access to the rapidly changing situational conditions at the places of each other. Under the condition of severe time pressure the captain seems to ignore the side by side positioning and uses deictic expressions that are not appropriately processed by the copilot.*]

Speaker	Utterance
Capt	I need some help here
Co	O.K.
Capt	I need some help on this
	[*The copilot still does not have relevant knowledge about the captain's situation. So he asks him for confirmation about the state of the propeller which is, in turn, given by the captain.*]
Capt	It's feathered.
Co	O.K.
	[*This ends the sequence from the copilot's point of view, but not from the captain's perspective. He still needs help.*]
Capt	I can't hold this thing. Help me hold it.
Co	O.K.
	[*It follows a sequence of cockpit-ground communication at the end of which the crew is no longer able to manage this additional channel of communication, because the captain can no longer hold the airplane.*]
Capt	Help me, help me hold it, ...
...	[*The plane crashes half a minute after the last call of Ground Control.*]

Legend:

Capt	Captain [= *Pilot flying*]
Co	Co-Pilot
[Italics]	Comments
...	Irrelevant stretches of discourse

Figure 11.3 Example for inadequate use of deictic expressions in a high task load situation in the cockpit

This example illustrates that under time pressure and high task load the special channel conditions of the cockpit can be forgotten. The captain simply does not realize that the co-pilot cannot see what he is referring to.

Social relations, communication and the primary task Communicative interaction is a joint activity. Participants try to achieve a common goal; their behavior is constrained by social, cognitive and linguistic rules, and the activity breaks down as soon as one of the parties interrupts his/her contribution and leaves the stage. Two social aspects that influence the content and the dynamics of interaction, and, consequently, can affect the performance of professional teams are team member familiarity and the hierarchical structure of the team. The circumstances in these two fields are different in the different workplaces.

Team member familiarity is significant. The personal composition of a cockpit crew can change with every new flight and in large airlines it often does. In up to one third of flights, the captain and the first officer do not know each other on a personal basis. Familiarity between the team members at the beginning of the flight is, accordingly, zero. Members of a surgery team normally know one another, though, in very large hospitals, this is not necessarily the case. Familiarity in the OR team is also affected by the systematic rotation of assistant surgeons (residents) within a hospital. Members of an NPP control room are generally familiar with one another since they physically occupy the same workplace for years. However, they work in a shift pattern, and, therefore in alternating team constellations.

Position hierarchies are also different in the different workplaces investigated in this project. Captains and first officers differ in rank and, normally, in age and professional experience. However, their functional profiles are rather similar and each can, in principle, do the job of the other one. Pilot-flying and pilot non-flying can be interchanged and, indeed, they routinely are. Members of an OR team differ in specialization and in hierarchical ranking. There is a correlation between ranking and breadth of functionality. The holder of the higher position can, in principle, fulfil the function of the lower ones, but the opposite is not the case. The hierarchical ranking of the positions in the NPP control room shows similarities with both of the other two workplaces; it differs from both in some respects as well. Being larger than the cockpit crew, the NPP team's ranking hierarchy is more complex than that of the cockpit crew, although the team structure depends on the type of reactor and on the operational status of the system. The typical crew structure consists of the shift leader, two operators and two technicians, which is about as large as many OR teams. However, the rank structure is more similar to that of the cockpit crew as is the hierarchy in terms of functional profiles. There are more overlapping aspects between flight crews and NPP operators than between them and OR-teams. All three teams form part of more complex units and co-operate with their specialists on a regular basis. The complex units are, of course, also teams in the present sense; a typical example is an ICU-team as a part of the team that makes up the entire hospital.

It is generally acknowledged that different social structures determine the behavior of the team members differently. Similar results would be expected in these data. In addition, there is the question of how those who hold the various social positions execute their jobs. Social rules are not computer programs; they leave options for individuals, and the higher the rank, the more latitude the holder has. The following specific hypotheses will be considered in this part of the investigation:

- If the parameter of team member familiarity has any influence upon the functioning of a team, it will show up in the cockpit crew;
- High position team members will contribute more to the amount of communication than the holders of lower positions because the co-ordination task is their responsibility;
- The style of social interaction has an effect on the ultimate achievement of the team.

Hypothesis one: the role of crew member familiarity Crew member familiarity is a heuristic rather than a well-defined, theory-related social psychological concept. Aviation psychologists found that previous experience flying together is associated with performance on the flight deck (see Foushee, Lauber, Bethge & Acomb, 1986 and NTSB, 1994). A linguistic approach to quantifying crew member familiarity was taken by Sexton & Helmreich (2003) and is discussed in Chapter 1 of this book. Sexton & Helmreich tested the assumption that familiarity would also show up in the verbal behavior of the crew members. On the basis of 17 sets of cockpit simulator data from four subsequent flight segments, they found that the use of first person plural pronouns (*we, us, our, etc.*) is a function of the number of flight segments. The frequency (percentage of total words spoken) increased from two per cent in flight segment A to four per cent in flight segment D; see Sexton & Helmreich (2003, p. 64). The verbal behavior of the pilot is of particular interest in this respect, as Sexton & Helmreich report: '... the use of first person plural was positively correlated to performance and negatively correlated to the number of errors.' Interpreting the use of first person plural words as an indicator in the sense of Driskell, Salas & Johnston, they conclude that first person plural can be taken to be a valid predictor of team performance.

Hypothesis two: position and communication The following hypothesis was supported: there are more contributions from the high position holders than from the low position holders. The task profile of the head of the team contains, as a rule, the co-ordination of the team members' activities in general, the co-ordination of diagnoses in abnormal situations, in particular, decision making, the allocation of crew resources, the crew's information about the next steps to be taken, etc. The head of a team can, accordingly, be expected to speak more in both normal and abnormal situations. One can also predict qualitative phenomena. The high position holder of the team is privileged in opening and closing a turn and in interrupting the turns of others; he/she can, at last, also be expected to be the one who introduces new topics in the discourse more frequently than other team members.

The position effect can also be expected to interact with task load. The team leader's portion of the total communication activities will theoretically increase in high task load enactment of the primary task. Finally, the effect can be predicted to be enhanced in more hierarchical teams than in those with a more flat structure ordering.

Not all of these predictions can be systematically tested using comparable corpora. An examination of the hypothesis that the strength of the hierarchical ordering interacts with the position dependent distribution of communication shares among NPP, OR and cockpit data, or at least between two of the domains, would require comparable data from all three workplaces. However, there were no recordings of authentic NPP control room conversations available. There are only simulator data available, which fail to show any position related bias in frequency or duration of speaking, while cockpit data and OR data clearly do. The data from the 17 crews in the B 727 simulator study (c.f. Sexton & Helmreich 2003, p.63) show a significant position effect. The captain produces the most words in crew communication, an effect that holds for all flight segments. There is also evidence for the interaction of the position effect with task load. The difference is increased in communication during abnormal segments. Krifka, Martens & Schwarz, did a more fine-grained analysis. They calculated the discourse shares of the captain, the FO and the flight engineer on the basis of a 120-minute segment of cockpit communication and obtained the same overall results. Additionally, they were able to show that the position effect spread almost perfectly over the time segments. Grote, Zala-Mezö & Grommes (2003, p. 145) also found strong evidence supporting the interaction assumption. While there was no great position bias in the low workload phases, the captain's portion (measured in the percentage of speech time for the entire crew) is significantly larger in the high workload condition. In the end, they showed that there is no difference between poor and good crews in the position effect; see Krifka, Martens & Schwarz (2003, p. 81). This is likewise true for surgery and anesthesia (Personal communication from Patrick Grommes, a principal investigator in the *Co-ordination Group,* who also confirms that the chief surgeon interrupts more frequently than the other team members and introduces new topics into the task related discourse more frequently as well).

Hypothesis three: social relations and the ultimate achievement of the team Here the two crucial aspects of communication in high risk environments will be revisited. As previously stated, communication is a joint activity between the interlocutors that has an instrumental function. Each member of a professional team is, accordingly, bound to take part in two *games*: the primary task game and the communication game. *Bound* means that each team member has a primary task that determines his/her domain of action, limits of responsibility and relations with other team members. At the same time, he/she has to communicate, as this is essential for the performance of the primary task. Due to his/her participation in the communication game, each team member is allotted a communication role. The assignment of the primary task functions to team members is relatively stable and constant over time; the allotment of communication roles is more ad hoc, and the initiative of taking or assigning the role of the speaker or the addressee, respectively, is left to every team member within the margins set by the primary task based script.

There is, however, one circumstance in which the complexity of the interplay of communication and primary task activities varies considerably. In the primary task game, there is an additional level of socially relevant relations: the hierarchical ordering of positions. A team member, then, plays three types of roles: a functional role, a positional role and an interlocutor role. Take, for example, the cockpit once more. The functional roles are pilot and co-pilot (or pilot flying and pilot non-flying). The positions are *captain* and *first officer*. While the team members' functional roles can be exchanged and normally are each flight, positions are personally assigned to individuals. A team member's behavior as an interlocutor can, of course, be influenced by both his/her functional and his/her positional role. The captain has the right and the duty to make decisions and to make the crew carry them out. This can cause him/her to take the role of the speaker (and automatically assign to the FO the role of the listener) and to perform the speech act of giving a command. The captain could, of course, make a proposition instead of a command. He/she is not forced by any rules to make a command every time he/she wants to communicate a decision. Interestingly, this is completely different for the reverse implication. The adequacy and, technically speaking, the success of a speech act is precisely determined by norms, and these are thoroughly linked to positional hierarchies, as will be shown. Consider again the speech act of command. When a speaker feels it necessary to give a command, he/she must prove that he/she is in the position to do so (or the recipient must be aware that this is the case). A speaker who is going to give advice must also prove whether or not he/she is in a position to do so. The command position is, however, different from the adviser position. The command position is defined in terms of power: institutional power or some other sort of power (i.e. a revolver in the speaker's hand pointing to the addressee). The advisor position is defined in terms of wisdom and/or knowledge. Asking a question is a speech act that is rather neutral in terms of positions, be they ranks or others.

Remember that the distribution of knowledge in the cockpit crew is derived from the task function and not from the positional rank. The relevance of this lies in the fact that a speaker has the choice of using speech acts that account for the properties of his/her position or his/her task function. It is clear that there are situations in which the speech act consequences of the two roles coincide.

Based on these considerations, the hypothesis can be refined and formulated as follows: the performance of a team is associated with its overall speech act strategy. Functionally communicating teams will form a larger proportion of the well performing teams than position based communicating teams.

This assumption is confirmed by a number of observations of interactions in cockpit, OR and ICU settings. In the ICU setting, the following has been observed:

- First of all, position was found to form a factor that explains a significant difference in the requirements for task related information interchange and briefings on the side of the nurses vs. that of the physicians in ICUs. While nurses focused on nurse-doctor communication, doctors clearly focused on doctor-doctor communication; see Shteynberg (2002);
- Nurse turnover is negatively associated with briefing as a common practice.

The results from the cockpit simulator study by Krifka, Martens and Schwarz (2003) confirm the expectation that position is associated with the relative frequency of speaking in the cockpit. The captain speaks more than the first officer and each of the two speaks more than the flight engineer; see Krifka, Martens & Schwarz (2003, Fig. 3). However, it cannot be concluded that this is a dysfunctional influence of position on the problem related communication. It does not make a difference for the overall performance of the team; that is to say, good and bad performing teams do not differ on this point.

Still, position does influence the quality of communication and – indirectly – the team's overall performance. Consider what was said about the three different types of roles that each member of the cockpit team is assigned in communication: the functional role (pilot flying or pilot non-flying), the position role (captain, first officer) and the communicative role, the latter being defined by the type of speech acts performed by the captain. His/her communication can be predominantly determined by either his/her position (power) or function. As discussed in Chapter 5, the results of the study of Krifka et al. (2003) present an unambiguous answer to the question as to which kind of communication strategy yields better outcome:

- More prognosis and diagnosis in good teams than in poor teams;
- More reports of intention in good teams than in poor teams;
- More questions and answers in good teams than in poor teams;
- More commands in poor teams than in good teams;
- More acknowledging speech acts in good teams than in poor teams.

Shared knowledge   This section closes the chapter on determinants of effective communication. However, the following lines do not contribute a genuine answer to the question of whether or not and to what degree different workplaces encourage different communicative strategies. To the contrary, it conveys the message that there is one recommendation that applies to all types of high risk workplaces: make the team members continuously communicate their mental models of the situation.

There is convincing empirical evidence confirming this postulate both in the aviation and in the ICU data. Krifka, Martens & Schwarz (2003, p. 86) found that the frequency of prognoses and of reports of intention is associated with the quality of team performance. They also found that there is no interaction with the amount of workload. Good cockpit crews communicated prognoses and intentions more frequently than poorly performing crews, and workload was not an independent main factor for the probability of prognoses or report of intention.

While the communication of prognoses and the report of one's own planning of the next activities is a component of the team members' spontaneous interaction, there are also more institutional ways of communicating prospective task related information. A typical example is the regular briefing of team members before the beginning of an operation. The general format of briefings and their relevance to the team members' behavior is accounted for in Chapter 10. The most recent and, probably, the most extensive empirical confirmation of these statements is provided by the results of a large scale survey on safety climate and its impact on the security of more than 100 ICUs in Great Britain and in the US. The

Threat/Error Group did the study and the two immediately pertinent findings are as follows:

- The overwhelming majority of OR personnel (anethetist 100 per cent) report that briefings are important for patient safety;
- The frequency of briefing as a common practice is associated with the amount of annual nurse turnover.

As stated above, the primary function of communication for high risk workplace teams is to facilitate, improve and – to some extent – even to enable the execution of primary task activities. One important function of communication and its relevance for the quality of the team's performance originates in two fundamental prerequisites for successful team interaction: situation awareness and continuous concurrence of the team members' mental models of the situation and of its prospective development. The chance of success or failure in planning one's own next steps as part of a team's endeavor to solve a problem depends highly on knowledge of the other team member's intentions and of other situational changes to be expected. Therefore communication of intentions and of expectations concerning upcoming events can, presumably, determine the team's chance of secure primary task management. The important role of shared common ground is explicitly dealt with in Chapter 9.

Chapter 12

Task Load Effects on Language Processing: Experimental Approaches

Annette Hohlfeld, Ryoko Fukuda, Sascha Neuper, Jörg Sangals,
Werner Sommer and Oliver Sträter[42]

Introduction

Communication can be viewed as a co-ordinated sequence of language-related cognitive processes between two or more individuals. Communication in high risk environments is characterized by additional tasks of high priority that have to be performed alongside language-related processes. Thus, a pilot has to maintain control over the airplane while he/she communicates with the tower or the co-pilot. Results from the *Linguistic Factors Group* illustrate how communication may suffer when there is high task load. In such situations, the pilot flying tends to utter fewer and shorter speech acts, suggesting that he/she may not be able to participate as much in the ongoing communication, as he/she is occupied with flying. In fact, some pilots explicitly state that they are not able to fully participate in a problem solving discussion. This example confirms the intuitively plausible idea that task load may interfere with communication; it does not, however, give concrete clues about the precise reasons or mechanisms of the interference. Experimental investigations to elucidate these mechanisms are surprisingly scant. Three of the GIHRE groups have undertaken experimental investigations into the details of cognitive processing in communication under additional task load. By setting up a common strategy, the groups achieved a systematic approach for tackling communication issues from basic research to applied research. With respect to the Threat and Error Management Model outlined in Chapter 8, the research reported here deals with the effects of a number of latent threats to safety and effective performance. The focus is on types of threats that may cause communication errors.

This chapter starts with a heuristic model of a prototypical situation of communication between operators that are engaged in an additional non-communicative task. Next, approaches from cognitive psychology are described

[42]The authors are grateful to Rainer Dietrich for inspiring discussions about the problem of question answering as well as to Florian Schwarz for linking findings to insights from flight recorder analysis.

that enable investigation into and explanation of dual task processing in general. The second part of this chapter deals with the input side of language processing under task load, that is, the understanding of verbal messages. Part three deals with a more complex aspect of such situations, namely the answering of questions. The fourth part takes a further step, focusing on communication during simulated operations in the control room of a nuclear power plant (NPP).

A Heuristic Framework for Communication under Concurrent Task Load

Ordinary verbal communication requires a minimum of two individuals. A conversation is, for example, structured in a way that one operator says something to a second operator who then hopefully realizes that he/she is the addressee and understands. In this case, he/she usually (if required or appropriate) replies verbally.

According to speech act theory, speaking is rule-based acting (Searle, 1969). People normally pursue a purpose when they talk. As anyone knows, most of the time we think about what we want to say before we say it out loud. Apart from this, what we think in order to give a reply to our communication partner should be related to the heard message; otherwise, the communication becomes incoherent and unsuccessful (Sperber and Wilson, 1995). In other words, once a conversation has started, both partners steadily switch their roles from addressees to speakers in referring their thoughts to the message they have received and reacting with a new one in reply until the conversation stops.

Additionally, many well-known situations in everyday life are typically more complex. Communication is often embedded in other activities, which may or may not be the main topic of the conversation. For example, a cycling couple often communicates. Children draw pictures and talk to their parents, who are cooking a meal. The cockpit personnel flies an airplane and communicates. In the following chapter, the people participating in a communicative act will be referred to as operators, since the focus of this chapter is real life working places. When this is not the case, the reference is to situations with established expressions/terms for the people involved.

In Figure 12.1 below, both operators are involved in non-communicative activities. These activities can consist of overt or covert actions of all kinds. Now, for some reason, e.g. due to an information deficit, operator A needs to talk to operator B. The cognitive processes that are involved from that point up until he/she articulates the intended message can be described as the speech production system (Levelt, 1989). Operator B, as the addressee, understands the message in a process called speech comprehension (e.g. Harley, 2001), which starts with hearing. Once operator B understands, the message is a cognitive task. This task may instruct operator B to do something else besides or in favour of what he/she was doing before. Often operator B will reply to A by using his speech production system because this is part of the task. Operator A, who is the addressee in turn, will go through the process of speech comprehension in understanding the message. Now A has a cognitive task to absolve. At each point in the communication process the ongoing actions of the operators influence communication and communication influences the ongoing actions.

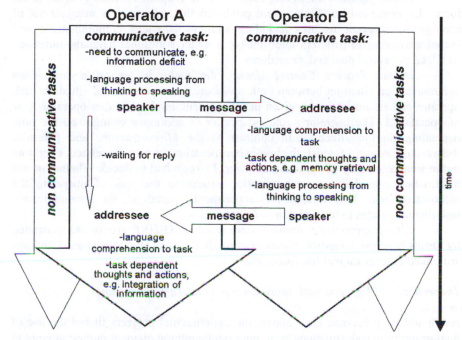

Figure 12.1 The heuristic model

The model shows a single communication turn including two exchanges of information (= messages). In real communication, information is repeatedly exchanged among several operators. Therefore, the heuristic model develops continuously in a vertical direction (Figure 12.1) as time progresses. Throughout the whole process, the role of each operator changes steadily. If operator A has requested certain information from operator B, operator A is, at first, the speaker, and operator B is the addressee. If operator B gives the answer to operator A's request, operator B becomes the speaker and operator A the addressee. Although the role of the two operators has already changed, operator A is still the information requester and operator B is the information provider. With the proper answer from operator B, this communication phase is finished and afterwards a new communication turn is started, if needed.

The heuristic model refers to situations in which operators communicate verbally and do things in parallel. It has to be understood as an open system in the way that it points out, but does not specify, the interacting parameters. The model serves as a common framework for the research questions addressed in the GIHRE groups *Microstructure, Question Answering,* and *Process Control.* The *Microstructure Group* focused on language perception when an operator was the addressee (see operator B in the heuristic model) in a communicative situation while also processing stimuli that were unrelated to the verbal message.

In the *Question Answering* section of the chapter, operator B again is the focus. Experimental conditions were produced that adhere to a minimal set of ecologically relevant features including auditory language comprehension and verbal answering of different question types under additional language-unrelated task load in several dual task procedures.

In *the Process Control Group*, the focus is set on a continuous communication situation between both operators, because in a real situation each operator can assume the roles given in the heuristic model of either operator A or of operator B. The operator's role as speaker or addressee changes all the time depending on the situation. In contrast to the *Microstructure* and *Question Answering Groups*, in which the two experimental tasks were unrelated, operators in the simulator study of the *Process Control Group* had to decide whether or not information provided by communication relates to the task of operating the technical system. Therefore, in this experimental paradigm, the communicative task directly relates to the non-communicative task.

Where appropriate, findings from the three GIHRE groups are illustrated by results from the *Linguistic Factors Group*. In this way laboratory-based findings are linked to relevant real life situations.

Theoretical and Experimental Approaches to Dual Task Processing

As should have become clear above, the experimental projects shared the use of dual or multiple task situations as an important common element in their attempt to model a crucial characteristic of operator situations under high task load. In the following section, the major theoretical viewpoints and the associated experimental paradigms are introduced that are relevant for the GIHRE groups involved in this chapter.

Scientific approaches to understanding multiple task performance have been led by two distinct types of theoretical concepts: a) resource sharing, that is, the reciprocal relationship between the performance in two concurrent tasks and b) time sharing, or the delay of processing in one task due to the occupation of exclusive processing structures by another task.

Resource sharing   Inspired by information theory, psychologists like Donald Broadbent (1958) tried to explain the constraints of human information processing by assuming a single communication channel with limited processing capacity. However, evidence for parallel processing soon led to the abandonment of this idea in favour of an explanation in terms of resource limitations. Early resource concepts (e.g. Kahneman, 1973), proposed a general limited pool of unitary processing resources that had to be shared between the tasks at hand. Again, this model had to be revised because the observed task interference appeared to depend on the type or modality of the involved tasks. Therefore, multiple resources were proposed, claiming separate resource pools for different task modalities, processing stages or types of information (Wickens, 1984; Navon and Gopher, 1979). Since resources are thought to be allocated from limited resource pools, improvement of one task may be associated with performance decrements in a concurrent second task, if (and only if) they draw on the same resource pool. Thus, multiple task performance should primarily depend on the resource overlap of the involved tasks, and, in addition, on the dynamic allocation of the available resources (Gopher, 1986).

The most elaborate experimental approach to resource sharing combines a discrete primary task (such as a choice response or a memory task) with a more continuous secondary task, which often consists of a visuo-manual tracking procedure (cf. Heuer, 1991, for a review). Resource tradeoffs are experimentally evoked either by manipulation of task difficulty or by means of priority instructions. Whereas early reports supported the view that tracking only interferes with manual primary tasks (McLeod, 1977), Jäncke (1994) showed that verbal rehearsal and speaking also disturbs tracking performance. In addition, he found speaking to disturb rightward movements in particular, possibly indicating neural overlap of left-hemispheric brain structures. Jäncke did, however, not analyze the reciprocal impairment of the language processes due to the manual task. Thus, despite the evidence for cross-talk between overlapping language-related and manual tasks, the degree of language impairment in such situations appears to be largely unknown.

The multiple resource approach has been criticized primarily because of its lack of theoretical constraints. Thus, the model could easily be adapted to account for any given pattern of interference. Therefore, the need for empirically derived constraints appears to be eminent and might be accomplished by means of psychophysiological correlates of resource allocation (cf. Kok, 1997, for a review). For example, event related brain potentials (ERPs) are thought to reflect the quantitative and precise temporal aspects of information processing as well as the transient energy expenditure of the brain (Kok, 1997). Thus, Hoffman et al. (1985) used the amplitude of the P300 component to demonstrate the flexible and graded allocation of shared resources between two concurrent tasks as a function of task priority. Others demonstrated a reduction of the P300 amplitude to a secondary task when the difficulty of the primary task was increased (Israel et al., 1980, Kramer et al., 1983). Importantly, resource sharing as indicated by P300 reciprocity appeared to diminish with dual task practice (Kramer et al., 1987, Strayer and Kramer, 1990), possibly indicating an increasing ability for multi-tasking with increasing expertise.

Discrete dual tasks and bottleneck-based models (time-sharing) An alternative account for dual task costs, in terms of processing bottlenecks, was first proposed by Welford (1951) and was elaborated upon in recent models (e.g. Pashler, 1994). This account is more specific than the aforementioned resource-based view, because it ascribes dual task interference to limitations of certain processing stages. Welford, for example, suggested that the delay in reaction time (RT) to a stimulus that immediately follows another stimulus occurs because there is only a single processing channel. While this channel is occupied with *task one*, the processing of other tasks is halted. This delay in reaction time for *task two* processing has also been termed psychological refractory period (PRP) effect. Experimental designs are often termed psychological refractory period paradigms when two stimuli are presented at relatively short stimulus onset asynchronies (SOA) that require separate responses. Modern accounts suggest that the single channel bottleneck at the heart of the psychological refractory period effect does not concern all processing stages. This is illustrated in Figure 12.2 for the case of relatively short SOA between the stimuli. While *stimulus one* is processed without halt, *stimulus two* processing stops when it requires the occupied single channel (slack period) and continues when the single channel becomes available. The slack period increases RT for *task two*, especially at short SOAs, causing the typical negative psychological refractory period slope depicted in the right panel of Figure 12.2.

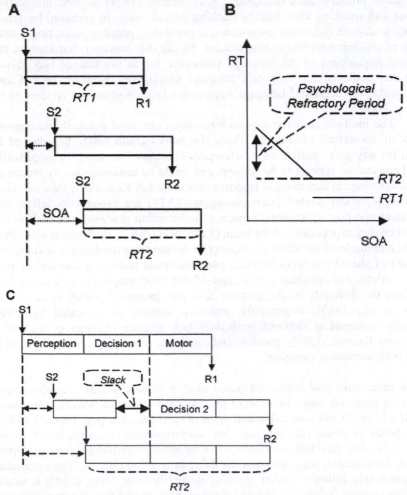

Figure 12.2 Basic design for overlapping tasks. See text for explanation

As Figure 12.2 illustrates, stimuli S1 and S2 require two independent responses, R1 and R2. The stimulus onset asynchrony (SOA) between S1 and S2 is varied across several levels and the reaction times for both responses (RT1 and RT2) are recorded. Figure B represents a typical pattern of findings from this paradigm. While RT1 is often unaffected by SOA, RT2 is longest at short SOAs and decreases as SOA increases. The delay of RT2 at short SOAs is termed psychological refractory period (PRP). Figure C represents a theoretical model for PRP effects. There is a central bottleneck during the processing of S2, consisting, e.g. of a decision to be made. Processing of S2 can proceed parallel with S1 processing until the bottleneck stage during which processing comes to a halt is reached. The ensuing slack period increases RT2 as an inverse function of SOA.

Recent developments The controversy between resource sharing and time-sharing models cannot currently be resolved. Thus, Navon and Miller (2002) have shown that typical results from psychological refractory period experiments can also be explained by resource sharing. Accordingly, recent attempts to explain dual task conflicts incorporate both time and resource sharing views. For example, Meyer and Kieras (1997) assumed executive processes such as task priority management to account for asymmetric interference effects in the psychological refractory period paradigm. Here, the relative processing priority of the involved tasks changes over time, e.g. as a function of task demands. Meyer and Kieras (1997) suggested that dual task interference might be a kind of task artifact due to a participant's strategies or lack of practice. In some cases it has indeed been shown that extensive practice can eliminate dual task costs (e.g. Schumacher et al., 2001). However, even if one accepts these reports as demonstrating perfect time-sharing, they can hardly be considered to be of practical relevance because they require very specific and extensive training.

Another recent integrative perspective on dual task interference is the so-called process-oriented approach, which also postulates bottlenecks but does not associate them with certain unitary processing stages (Dylan and Farmer, 2001). Rather, it is assumed that similar types of processing (like tracking or sequencing) might lead to dual task interference even if they occur at different processing stages. The practicability of the process-oriented approach and its implications for ergonomics have been discussed by Sträter and Bubb (2003). Low (2003) used the approach for developing a subjective workload measure.

While both the *Question Answering* and the *Process Control Groups* primarily hold resource-sharing views (see the following section), they utilize different experimental paradigms, involving mainly continuous primary tasks (*Question Answering Group*) and a simulated complex system (*Process Control Group*). The *Microstructure Group* follows the tradition of the time-sharing approach, using discrete dual task trials.

Probing the central bottleneck: effects of time pressure and practice on dual task performance To provide a solid foundation for testing communication under dual task, the *Microstructure Group* first assessed task load effects on the central bottleneck in sensory-motor tasks. Therefore, two ERP experiments on the locus of dual task limitations were conducted, with time pressure on the second task and dual task practice, respectively (Sangals, et al.,under revision; Sangals, et al., in preparation).

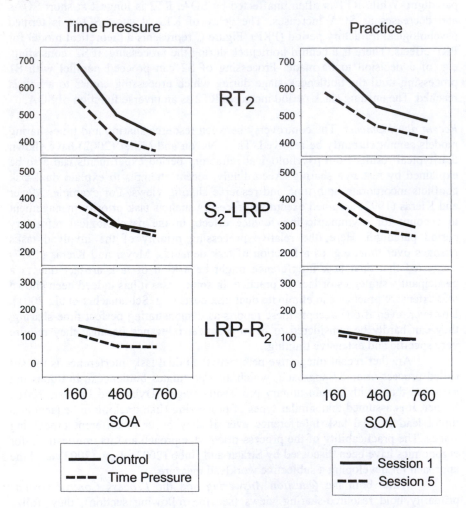

Figure 12.3 Synopsis of results of time pressure experiment (left) and practice experiment (right). Dashed lines: means from time pressure conditions after 4 sessions of practice. Solid lines: control conditions without time pressure and practice, respectively. Top panels: RT of second response; middle panels: S2-LRP onset intervals (pre-motor times); bottom panels: LRP-R2 onset intervals (motor times)

Of particular interest in the two experiments was whether the bottleneck would prevail under time pressure and after practice as would be predicted by time-sharing models (Pashler, 1994) or whether it would yield because the bottleneck is an artefact of the subjects' strategy, as proposed by Meyer and Kieras (1997). In both studies, the dual tasks consisted of left and right foot responses to high or low tones and left and right index finger responses to written letters presented between 160 to 760 ms after the tones.

Both time pressure on the second task and five one-hour practice sessions appeared to diminish the psychological refractory period (see top panels of Figure 12.3). However, there was no evidence of genuine time-sharing of decision processes. The Lateralized Readiness Potential revealed that the effects of time pressure and practice, although overtly similar, were actually due to different covert mechanisms. Time pressure primarily shortened the duration of late, motoric processing stages without eliminating the bottleneck (cf. left bottom panel of Figure 12.3). In contrast, practice shortened the time demands for pre-motoric processes (right middle panel of Figure 12.3). In neither study was there evidence for subjects making decisions simultaneously, neither under time pressure nor after five hours of praxis did subjects appear to make simultaneous response decisions about the two tasks at hand.

The initial experiments clearly confirmed the robustness of the central bottleneck for the given experimental paradigm. This was true despite the countermeasures that were incorporated: time pressure and five hours of practice. These findings not only provide a firm basis for the experiments discussed in the chapter, but also show that dual task interference is persistent against both practice and strategic variables such as time pressure. The practical implications of these findings are discussed at the end of this chapter.

The Microstructure of Language Perception

On the basis of the non-linguistic studies described above, the *Microstructure Group* carried out a series of experiments to show the effect of an additional task on an elementary aspect of communication, language perception. In these experiments, the psychological refractory period procedure was modified to include a language task alongside an additional task (see Figure 12.4). Again, the additional task required foot responses to visual stimuli, which had to be processed with priority. The language task demanded hand responses to spoken German nouns. The access to meaning was assessed by recording an event-related brain potential (ERP), the so-called N400 component (cf. Chapter 7).

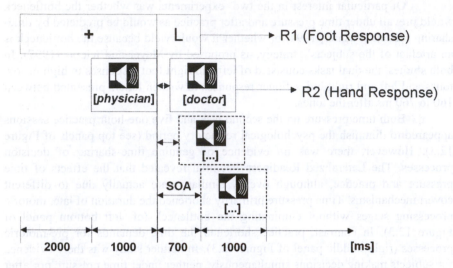

Figure 12.4 Chronometric description of an experimental trial

N400 was elicited by the second of two spoken words (target) when it was semantically unrelated to the first word, the prime. The target word required either decisions about its synonymy with the prime or about its acoustic properties (higher or lower pitch than the prime). Target words were presented at one of three possible intervals after the prime. A letter was presented as the stimulus for the additional task at a fixed interval after the prime and before the target word was presented. Task load was manipulated in two ways. First, the degree of overlap between the additional task and the language task was manipulated by varying the time between the onset of the letter and the second word (stimulus onset asynchrony – SOA). Second, the compatibility of stimulus to response mapping in the additional task was manipulated. The visual stimulus, which was either the letter R or L, had to be answered with right and left foot responses when the mappings were compatible (compatible condition). In the incompatible condition, R had to be responded to with the left foot and L with the right foot.

Language Perception while Performing Additional Tasks

The first objective was to explore whether or not language perception is affected by an additional task of varying difficulty. The second objective was to determine, whether or not such effects depend on the explicitness of processing the message's semantic content. One can imagine that in high task load situations, as in the cockpit, attention is shifted from the verbal message processing to aircraft handling. The question was whether or not it is likely that under these circumstances messages are processed on a shallow level, which leads to stronger task load effects than in the case of explicit processing. In order to answer this question, two experiments were conducted in which language stimuli processing was combined with an additional task. The first of these experiments required explicit semantic judgments of the language stimuli, thereby guaranteeing that verbal stimuli were processed for meaning. The second experiment required judgments about the acoustic properties of the nouns. Please note that this task did not make it necessary to extract meaning from the verbal input.

Processing for meaning When subjects had to give incompatible foot responses in the additional task, i.e. respond with the left foot to the letter R, language perception in the language task was slowed. As depicted in Figure 12.5 A, this is indicated by a delay in the N400 component (peak latency), particularly when the temporal overlap between the tasks was high (SOA 100).

However, when the mean amplitude for all three SOAs within a set time range was compared, no effects on the total amplitude of the N400 component over the whole recording epoch were observed. These results suggest that limitations in the availability of central processing stages postpone semantic integration, but do not necessarily compromise it. This is supported by reaction times and error rates. Although there is an increase in reaction times in the incompatible condition, there is no increase in error rates. This implies that in the incompatible dual task condition, subjects eventually perceive the nouns and give correct responses. The experimental effects on N400 activity indicate that concurrent task load genuinely affects the integration of a verbal message into the semantic context and not merely its conversion into a motoric response (cf. Hohlfeld et al., in press b; experiment 2). In this experiment, task load affected the timing of performance, but not its accuracy. However, one can easily imagine that in more demanding situations such as real life operational environments, work under time pressure or work with complex verbal messages, language perception might be seriously taxed as delays accumulate.

Processing for acoustic properties Figure 12.5 B depicts the N400 component, super-imposed for the compatible and incompatible conditions. The difference waves for these conditions are similar at the long SOA (no task overlap) but diverge at the intermediate and short SOAs (medium and high overlap). The difference wave, indicating semantic integration, is essentially zero in the incompatible condition at SOA 100. Although the brain activation that signals semantic integration is merely delayed rather than diminished when meaning is explicitly processed (see Figure 12.5 A), the activity is greatly reduced when the message is processed on a shallow level (judgement of acoustic properties, see Figure 12.5 B). In fact, N400 is abolished when overlap and difficulty are combined. This finding implies that when a message is not explicitly processed for meaning but rather at a more shallow level, its meaning may be accessible to the system only when task load is relatively low (low overlap as in the case of SOA 700 and compatible stimulus-response mappings). This is confirmed by results from single task experiments that applied identical stimulation but only required responses to acoustic or semantic properties of the nouns. In both of these experiments an N400 was found. However, the component was considerably smaller when the target noun had to be processed for acoustic properties.

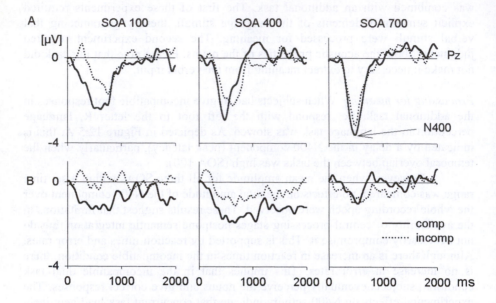

Figure 12.5 Difference waves between event-related potentials elicited by non-synonymous and synonymous target words (N400 component). This figure shows the difference waves in two dual task experiments as a function of stimulus onset asynchrony (SOA) with a letter (L or R) that had to be responded to with compatible or incompatible (comp vs. incomp) left and right pedal presses. Panels A and B show the N400 component when words had to be judged for meaning (synonymity) and for acoustic properties (voice pitch), respectively. When nouns were judged for meaning, task load delayed the N400 component (see panel A, SOA 100 incompatible). N400 was abolished when nouns had to be processed for acoustic properties under task load (see panel B, SOA 100 incompatible). The abscissae show the first 2 seconds after the onset of the spoken target word. The ordinates show the voltage of the brain's response to those words (in microvolt)

High concurrent task load appears to prevent the extraction of semantic information from a message. As mentioned above, complex situations might lead to instances in which verbal messages are processed on a shallow level. Under conditions of normal task load, e.g. under routine flight conditions, shallow processing can be sufficient for retrieving the meaning of a verbal message. However, as exemplified in this experiment, high task load in even moderately complex scenarios can reduce the retrieval of meaning to a minimum when verbal input is not explicitly processed. Therefore, it may be important to take countermeasures that prevent processing from becoming too shallow. This can be done by requiring acknowledgements of verbal information (see also section Collaborative Problem Solving).

Second Language Perception

A potentially critical aspect in many operator teams is that communication does not take place in the native language. Although team members are proficient in the second language when formal tests are applied, evidence suggests that under stress, there is a tendency to return to the native language and that mistakes in processing the second language may increase (Cushing, 1994). Therefore, it is conceivable that language perception in second language speakers may be more susceptible to task load than in native speakers. This question was addressed in a further experiment. The design of the experiment is identical to that of the semantic judgement experiment reported above (cf. *Processing for Meaning*). However, the subjects' native language was Russian. Their German was acquired after puberty and to a high degree of competency.

In this experiment, an N400 component was observed that was globally delayed when compared to first language speakers. Moreover, that the duration of semantic processing in second language speakers was longer than in first language speakers, was indicated by a wider spread of the N400 component over time. Importantly, the global delay of language perception in second language speakers was further increased by temporal overlap with an additional task. Error rates imply that semantic processing in ones' second language is even more susceptible to task load than in the first language. In a dual task context, second language speakers make more errors in a language perception task than native language speakers, particularly when there is a high degree of overlap between tasks (cf. Hohlfeld et al., in press a). These results are even more revealing when taking into account that in an offline multiple choice test, which assessed second language speakers' understanding of the presented German nouns, they performed relatively well. They had 91 per cent correct responses. Native speakers achieved 98 per cent.

Mechanisms of Interference

To obtain a better understanding of the causes of interference between overlapping tasks on language perception, a further experiment was set up to investigate the effect of different types of stimuli in the additional task. The previous experiments used letters as stimuli in the additional task, which certainly require a degree of language processing as well. Therefore, the hypothesis was that language perception might be less affected when the demands on language processing in the additional task are reduced. To minimize the amount of language processing, spatial positions of simple squares were chosen as one type of stimuli. In addition, the language-related type of stimuli (the letters L and R), which were used in the previous experiments, were also applied here. Task load was manipulated by the factors SOA (100 and 700 ms) and compatibility as described above. Letters were presented in the center of the computer screen, and the squares appeared to the right or left of a central fixation point. When trials were compatible, foot responses had to be given on the side on which the square appeared. Incompatible trials demanded foot responses opposite the presentation side. The language task required a semantic judgement of nouns, i.e. the nouns had to be processed for meaning.

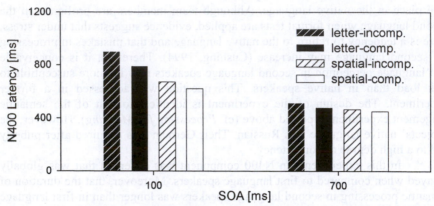

Figure 12.6 Latency of N400 maximum as a function of SOA: depending on whether the additional task stimulus was a letter (language-related) or a spatial location of a small square (spatial), as well as of the compatibility of response assignment to this stimulus (comp. vs. incomp.). Due to task overlap the peak latency of the N400 is more strongly delayed when letters had to be processed in an additional task than when squares had to be processed

The type of stimulus in the additional task had large effects on the time course of language perception. As reflected in the N400 component (Figure 12.6), the point in time when semantic integration is maximal is postponed in the case of language-related stimuli (letters) in comparison to spatial stimuli, particularly when tasks highly overlap (SOA 100). For both types of stimuli, the manipulation of compatibility affects N400 latency, i.e. semantic integration. These effects are supported by reaction times. Judgement of nouns' synonymity took more time when letters had to be processed in the additional task than when spatial stimuli had to be processed. This also applies to the effect of stimulus-response compatibility: incompatible stimulus-response assignments led to a higher increase in reaction times in the case of letters than in the case of spatial objects (cf. Hohlfeld et al., in press b; Experiment 3).. These findings imply that task interference increases when both tasks involve processing language-related items. This is consequential for the design of many work places in which operators are often confronted with overlapping acoustic and visual verbal input (for further implications see Conclusions).

Summary

The experiments requiring either semantic or acoustic property judgements, as well as the second language experiment, show that overlapping tasks interfere with neural processes that reflect language understanding at the level of integrating words into a semantic context (N400). These effects are aggravated when temporal overlap is high and when the additional task involves a difficult stimulus-response assignment. Effects are even more pronounced and show up as increased error rates when the language stimuli belong to a second language rather than to the native language. Furthermore, interference is stronger when the additional task also requires processing of verbal input. Together these findings indicate that very simple forms of language processing – the integration of single words into a semantic context – can be affected by additional task load and that these effects depend on a number of specific factors.

Relations between Question Semantics and Question Answering

The previous section focused on task load effects on the perceptual processing of speech. This section focuses on task load effects on complex ordinary communication tasks, namely, on answering yes/no- and wh-questions (for a short explanation of yes/no- and wh-questions see Chapter 6). A sample of six cockpit crew communication recordings from a flight simulator showed that nearly ten per cent of all utterances were yes/no and wh-questions (cf. Chapters 6 and 11). Interestingly, yes/no-questions were used more frequently than wh-questions in high workload segments. This shows that question utterances appear with a high frequency in team communication and that the frequency of question types varies with workload. It might be that answers to yes/no-questions are easier to give. The course of language processing, from comprehension to utterance, will be examined in the context of the different question types and then compared in order to address processing differences between them. Information processing models of question answering are mainly concerned with the temporal organization of the cognitive processes underlying question answering. Parallel processing models like TSUNAMI (Robertson, 1994) assume that the processing of cognitive stages occurs simultaneously. Serial stage models like VAIL (Singer, 1985) assume that the stages are processed in rapid succession one after another.

The suggested models agree that question answering is a complex cognitive activity, starting with *question parsing*, moving on to *matching question type and knowledge, retrieval of an answer* and finally to *output-generation*. Both models also support the idea that all of the mentioned processes are embedded in and interact with information retrieval from short and long term memory. However, while *parsing* and *output generation* depend primarily on implicit syntactic rules of language use and mechanisms of lexical access, *matching question type and knowledge* and *answer retrieval* depend additionally on episodic-knowledge and fact-knowledge, which can be stored for short, as well as for long, periods of time and can then be forgotten. This difference is important and has to be taken into account when analysing the sources of question answering impairments under additional task load. Different question types have different question-semantics, *parsing* and *output generation* necessarily vary with question semantics (Singer, 1986 alb). Therefore, a specific question semantic leads to a specific language processing in order to properly answer a question. Obviously, questions of the same type (the same question-semantic) can also vary, e.g. in syntax, but this question is not of interest in this context. For other more knowledge-based mechanisms like *matching question type and knowledge* and *retrieval of an answer* it is more difficult to formulate the relations to specific question semantics. Although these mechanisms seem to be associated with question semantics, they may have broad commonalities with general cognitive functions like memory and decision making. In the following section, manipulations of the amount of discourse knowledge, additional task load and working memory load will be applied to two semantically different question types in order to investigate relations between question semantics and the processing of answers.

Simple Question Answering

As a first step, a methodology was developed and tested in order to distinguish between language processing mechanisms, which are directly and necessarily related to question semantics, and mechanisms, which are not. It was important to find a simple form that could be acoustically applied in a dual task setting.

Yes/no- and wh-questions marked the question type and referred to common discourse knowledge. Yes/no-questions were verification tasks. Subjects heard a proposition. Then they had to judge with *yes*, if it was true or with *no*, if it was false, according to the given discourse knowledge. Wh-questions were completion tasks. Incomplete propositions had to be completed as true propositions from the discourse knowledge. For example: if the discourse knowledge consisted of the following propositions: *A is B* and *C is D*, a yes/no-question had the form: *A = B?*, *A = D?*, and a wh-question: *what is B?*. This form made it possible to apply yes/no- and wh-questions acoustically within a comparable time frame for informative elements that constituted the questions within the same time frame. Independent of this, the amount of discourse knowledge could be varied. This consisted of a minimum of two propositions in order to establish questions that could be answered with *no* and to make false answers possible. Note that such simple questions are still reasonable.

Two small single task experiments ((E-1a) and (E-1b)) were conducted in order to directly compare answer latencies to yes/no- and wh-questions. In E-1a, the answer latencies of yes/no- and wh-questions about discourse knowledge of two propositions were measured. In E-1b the discourse knowledge consisted of four propositions. All yes/no-questions and wh-questions that can be combined within the given knowledge structure were asked. The following hypotheses were tested:

- Under comparable conditions, processing times for answers to yes/no- and wh-questions will not differ substantially when the number of possible alternative answers is equal for yes/no- and wh- questions (E-1a);
- If the number of possible alternative answers is not equal (E-1b), it means that there are more possible answers to wh-questions; answers to yes/no-questions will be given faster;
- Subjects will answer faster with practice, but the effect of different numbers of answer alternatives will not disappear.

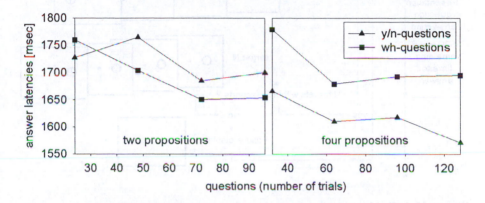

Figure 12.7 Experiments E-1a (left panel) and E-1b (right panel): latency differences between yes/no- and wh-answers are not significant when questions are about two propositions (left). Yes/no-answers are significantly faster than wh-answers when questions are about four propositions (right). Subjects get faster with practice (left and right), but answer latency differences remain persistent

As Figure 12.7 shows, all hypotheses were confirmed. This means that answer latencies are sensitive to the amount of knowledge one has to take into account. According to the above-mentioned models of question answering, processing time differences can be expected when different question-semantics (*parsing* and *output generation*) appear in combination with discourse knowledge of more than two propositions (*matching of question type and knowledge* and *output generation*).

Question Answering under Additional Task Load

The basic idea of the next experiment (experiment two) was to test directly whether or not semantically different questions, presented acoustically, can be impaired in different ways under conditions of additional task load. The question-answering task presented above was combined with the so-called *Hit-target task*. This is a self-paced perceptual motor co-ordination task (see Figure 12.8).

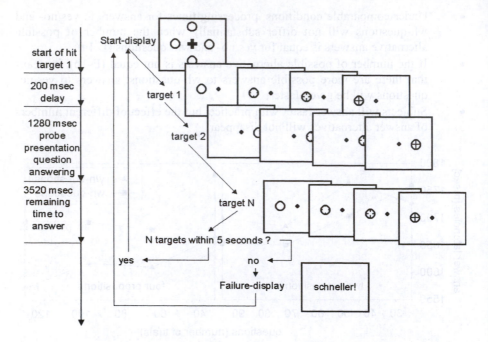

Figure 12.8 The *hit-target task*: on the left side, the temporal order of events in a dual task is described. Question probe presentation starts 200 msec after the hit target task. The right side illustrates the discrete steps of one hit-target trial. Further descriptions can be found in the text

This experiment begins with a display showing four round targets around a central cross that indicates the starting position of a cursor. Then three of the four targets disappear. Subjects have to move a cursor with a mouse to the target and click with the left mouse button. Immediately following this, the next target appears at another position, and the cursor jumps back to the central cross. This step is repeated until a subject hits a certain number of targets or exceeds the time allotted for completing the task, five seconds. If a subject does not hit all targets, feedback appears on the screen: 'faster!' Thin bars grow in discrete steps from the target circle's borders to its center, indicating a time budget for each single hit of the whole task. Difficulty is varied with target size. In hard hit-target trials, smaller and more distant targets have to be hit. The number of targets a subject has to hit within one trial differs according to a basic individual performance level in order to reach comparable difficulty levels for each subject. Because inter-individual performance varies dramatically, this procedure is used in order to align difficulty levels with individual performance. As a result, the hard task was never performed perfectly, and the easy task was always performed perfectly. Easy tasks, hard tasks and single task trials appeared in random order to lessen the effects of monotony.

Question answering tasks in the experiment require hearing and speaking. The perceptual-motor tasks require subjects to use their eyes (vision) and hands. Question answering is completely embedded in the perceptual-motor tasks. The perceptual-motor task starts first and ends last. The perceptual-motor task does not involve any semantic processing, which means that the only feature that both tasks share is that they both have to be performed within a certain time frame, which is a typical high task load condition. The structure of the dual task situation focuses on subjects' time sharing abilities: conflicts between the tasks occur when subjects cannot establish proper switching modes because deciding about two things at exactly the same time appears to be impossible without further training (as outlined in the *theoretical and experimental approaches* part of this chapter). The assumption was that the probability of conflicts between question answering task and perceptual motor task would rise with temporal decision density in the perceptual motor task.

Decision density was manipulated with the difficulty of the perceptual motor task: subjects had to hit a fixed number of targets in a fixed time interval with a mouse cursor. In the easy condition these targets were big and were quickly hit; in the harder condition they were small, and correction movements were often necessary in order to place the mouse cursor. Therefore, subjects needed more time to hit a target in the hard condition. This should diminish the time a subject needs to answer questions between the single steps of the perceptual motor task. Time-sharing difficulties should, therefore, delay reaction times in one or both tasks. It was recently shown (Ferreira and Pashler, 2002; Rohrer and Pashler, 2003) that some of the processes, which were identified above as influencing answer latency and characterised by the terms *answer retrieval* and *output generation*, need to be processed during a central decision stage. They are, therefore, subject to time-sharing difficulties in dual task situations.

The two factors described above, question type and amount of discourse knowledge, are involved in question answering and were tested again in order to circumscribe the source of possible task load effects. The first aim was to replicate the results from experiments E-1a and E-1b in a *within subject design*. These factors were combined with easy and hard hit-target tasks. Subjects also had to absolve all tasks separately, in order to make single and dual task performance comparable.

The following hypotheses were tested:

- First, the statement from the first experiments can be confirmed, namely that differences in answer latencies occur as a combination of question type and a discourse knowledge of more than two propositions;
- Second, additional task load delays answer latencies;
- Third, higher decision density in the perceptual motor task further delays answer latencies.

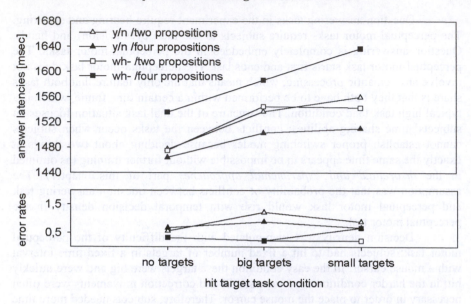

Figure 12.9 Experiment 2: answer latencies (above) show that the presence of additional tasks delays both question types under both discourse knowledge conditions. However, with wh-questions only about four propositions were further delayed in the difficult hit-target task. Mean error rates [%] (below) show no effects

As shown in the upper panel of Figure 12.9, the answer latencies pattern, described in E-1a and 1b, was observed in experiment two, as well. Yes/no-answer latencies are faster than wh-answer latencies, when the amount of discourse knowledge exceeds two propositions. This general pattern remains the same in both dual task conditions. This confirms the first hypothesis. Additional task load delays answer latencies in a general way. This confirms the second hypothesis. The more difficult task with small targets did further delay answer latencies. This is a partial confirmation of hypothesis three. This is mainly caused by wh-questions about four propositions. This means that the only condition that was substantially disturbed in the hard hit-target task was the one with the longest answer latency in the single task condition, too. The lower panel of Figure 12.9 shows no differential effects and very low error rates in all conditions. It is noteworthy that the hit target task performance was the same in single and dual task conditions. Neither single hit latencies nor overall performance differed substantially.

The following conclusions were drawn: correct answering of questions about well-known facts is remarkably robust within the context of additional and unrelated task load. Dual task situations generally have a negative impact on the time that is necessary to answer a question (compare with language perception results). The manipulation of decision density in an additional unrelated task prolongs the answer latencies of wh-answers more than of yes/no-answers when the discourse knowledge consists of more than two propositions.

Question Answering under Varying Working Memory Load and Additional Task Load

Working memory load varies independently from the semantically related language processing differences according to question type. For example, the question, 'at what height do we fly?' can either be asked immediately after the addressee has looked at the altimeter in order to determine the height or after he/she has received a large number of flight parameters in rapid succession, potentially resulting in forgetting the exact altitude. Note that language processing is the same in both cases but that the working memory load is much higher in the second case. Answers to yes/no-questions could have an additional advantage over wh-questions under conditions of high working memory load when a qualitatively different retrieval process is associated with each question type. Such a difference has been described as recognition vs. cued recall. Recognition has been shown to have advantages over cued recall (Bower, 2000, Broadbent, 1991). Evidence for dual task impairments of memory retrieval is inconsistent and a direct comparison between recognition and cued recall dual tasks has never been made (Rohrer and Pashler, 2003). Within yes/no- and wh-questions, pure recognition vs. cued recall may occur and interact with a given working memory load. Wh-questions always ask for elements that make a true proposition and, therefore, have a constant narrow focus, although, yes/no-question verification tasks can differ in focus. Sometimes, as in experiments 1a, 1b and 2, they ask for the truth of a given proposition and have a narrow focus comparable to wh-questions (given: *A is B* and *C is D, is C B?* vs. *what is B?*). At other times, as in the following experiment (E-3), they ask for the existence of a given proposition and have a wider focus than wh- questions (given: *A is B* and *C is D* in a world where *E is F* may exist: 'is *E is F* given?' vs. *what is B*). This kind of yes/no may occur in the cockpit, because communication partners may want to know whether or not something has possibly occurred. First, this classical recognition task (Sternberg, 1969) will be compared to the cued-recall case of wh-questions under varying working memory and task load in E-3. Afterwards a control experiment (E-4) will show that the effect of E-3 is a focus effect.

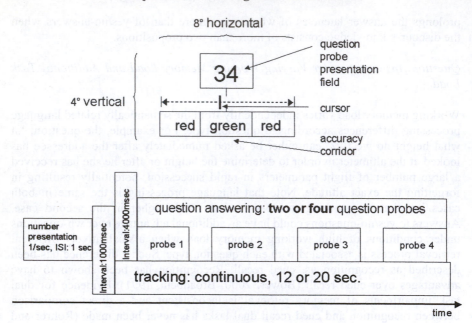

Figure 12.10 Visual display (above) and temporal order of events (below) in E-3 and E-4. The different tracking difficulties, monitoring (M), low accuracy compensation (CL) and high accuracy compensation (CH) were established with cursor behavior manipulations and accuracy corridor manipulations

This time, the additional perceptual motor task time is a one-dimensional unstable compensatory tracking task. In the monitoring condition (M), subjects have to hold the position of an unstable cursor that tends to deviate randomly to the left or right side of a center position on the screen. The cursor accelerates with increasing distance from the center (positive feedback). Moving a joystick in the opposite direction must compensate for deviations of the cursor. Subjects must avoid cursor deviations beyond a certain accuracy corridor or else a beep tone sounds as a signal to improve performance. The borderlines of the accuracy corridor are visually represented as a green bar around the center position and red bars beyond. The low accuracy compensation condition (CL) differs from the monitoring condition in that the cursor movement is additionally disturbed by a complex sine wave signal. Subjects must constantly compensate for the acceleration of the cursor and for the disturbance signal. Permanent correction movements are necessary in order to hold the cursor within the allowed accuracy corridor. The high accuracy compensation condition (CH) is the same as the low accuracy compensation condition, but the accuracy corridor is narrower. All difficulty conditions were performed in blocks. Subjects were instructed to give higher priority to performing the tracking task.

In experiment three (E-3), broad focused yes/no-questions and the established wh-questions are compared. Memory load is varied by asking questions about two or four two-digit numbers, which change in every trial. They are presented immediately before the additional task begins. Two tracking task conditions, M and CL are applied. The numbers, which have to be stored, as well as the question probes, are presented visually (see Figure 12.10).

Answer latencies show a statistically significant effect for question type and working memory load, as well as an interaction between these factors, indicating a general advantage for yes/no under lower and higher working memory load (see Figure 12.11 left panel). This was not impaired by additional task difficulty. The non-decisive character of the tracking task may explain the lack of additional task difficulty effects on answer latencies. Although the tracking task difficulty had no impact on answer latencies, it interacted significantly with the question type according to error rates of question answering. A possible interpretation of this is that knowledge that has to be stored in working memory that degrades faster under conditions of additional task load. The accelerated decay through additional task load raises error frequency for the more detailed information retrieval process associated with wh-questions, namely with cued recall (Neuper, 2003).

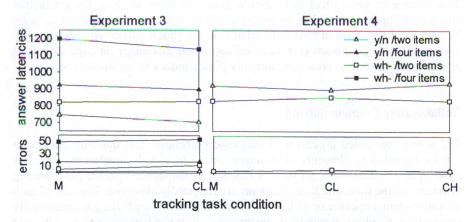

Figure 12.11 **Results from E-3 and E-4. Mean answer latencies from E-3 are in the left upper panel. Correspondingly, the right side of the figure shows experiment four (E-4) results. Additional task difficulty has no effect on answer latency. Additional task difficulty interacts with the question type in error rates when yes/no-questions have a broad focus (left, below) but not when they have a narrow focus (right, below)**

To show that the differences in error rates are related to the broad focus of yes/no-questions, a replication of E-3 with a memory set size of two was carried out. Yes/no questions had a narrow focus as in experiments 1a, 1b and 2. A third tracking task, with a stricter accuracy criterion (CH), was introduced. Results from experiment four (E-4) are shown in Figure 12.11 in the right panel.

The small manipulation in yes/no was enough to eradicate differences in error rates between question types. Time latencies for wh-answers had small advantages over yes/no, similar to those reported in experiment 1a when questions were about discourse knowledge of two propositions. From experiment three (E-3) and four (E-4) together, it can be concluded that under conditions of additional task load and high working memory demands, pure recognition (as present in broad-focused yes/no-questions in E-3) is the more reliable information retrieval process. Pure recognition can be associated with yes/no questions but not with wh-questions. This is a characteristic and important difference between the question types.

Summary

The reported evidence supports the view that differences in answering yes/no and wh-questions are caused by interactions of question semantics with the amount of discourse knowledge, additional task load and working memory demands. The existence of conditions that diminish yes/no advantages or even give a disadvantage to yes/no had to be demonstrated in order to show the interactive character of these factors. Yes/no-answers will be less disturbed than wh-answers by additional task load in terms of verbal reaction times. When working memory load is present, yes/no-answers have an additional advantage in high task load conditions according to error rates but only if they induce recognition processes.

Collaborative Problem Solving

The above-mentioned processes of language perception and question answering can be regarded as elements of communication. In a real situation in a nuclear power plant control room, airplane or hospital, communication takes place among operators all the time, and these elements are repeatedly observed. The role of each operator – either speaker or addressee – and the issue at hand changes dynamically from phase to phase throughout the process. A typical phase begins with one question from operator A and ends with the proper answer to the question by operator B (similar to Figure 12.1). If it is not sufficiently answered, operator A asks operator B for further clarification. Instead of the answer that operator A expects, operator B may provide other information, an acknowledgement, a suggestion or a question. In such cases, the context of communication changes and operator B's reaction will probably change depending on his/her thoughts. The decision making process is influenced by his/her knowledge and experiences, the contextual and situational information he/she perceives, etc.

Such a change in the decision process can be observed in incident analyses (Sträter, 2003). It can be clearly identified that communication issues arise if one of the operators is busy with complex cognitive decision making tasks (cf. Chapter 4 for details). For more details and experimental proof of this observation, the relationship between operator B's reaction to the information given by operator A and his/her thinking process was analyzed using eye tracking. The reason for this is that 'human eyes voluntarily and involuntarily fixate on those elements of an object which carry or may carry essential and useful information' (Yarbus, 1967). In other words, eye tracking makes it possible to trace the shift of a subject's attention.

The verbal reaction itself can be described in terms of speech act analysis (also cf. Chapter 11, Language and Communicative Behavior). The relationship between speech act analysis and the control task in the technical system is a key aspect in understanding how the research described in this chapter leads to valuable insights for risk assessment in real life settings. In the case of a request for information from operator A, as in the example above, operator B will provide the answer if possible. In the case of a request for action, e.g. a command or a suggestion, operator B's primary reaction may be carrying out the requested action, and giving an explicit verbal confirmation or acknowledgement of having done so.

In the following section, the open communication process is explained based predominantly on results from the eye tracking study done in the Nuclear Power Plant (NPP) simulator by the *Process Control Group*. In the NPP simulator, the two operator's communication behaviour and one operator's eye movement were analyzed while they were dealing with a transient loss of feed water supply. The relevant issues regarding the speech act analysis of the protocol data from flight simulation (*Linguistic Factors Group*) will be related.

The experiments reported in the previous sections about language perception and question answering were performed in well-defined, standardized, experimental settings. This setting makes it possible to control the reliability and validity of the experiment. However, real life settings are usually much more complex. Therefore such standardized experimental settings are lacking real life, or face, validity. The experimental setting in the NPP simulator study establishes a link between basic research and real life settings. In this way, the three experiments create a triad that links the basic research and the applied research together to create a new approach to risk evaluation.

Eye Tracking and Language Processing

The eye tracking data provide a look into the cognitive process, which is the basis for human behaviour. Therefore, the eye tracking method is applied to a variety of situations, from the reading process to information processing in driving.

Eye movement in speech perception should be mentioned. When a speaker is observed, the observer fixates on the eyes or the mouth of the speaker. (eyes: 45 – 70 per cent of each trial, mouth: 35 – 55 per cent of each trial). As the acoustic noise level increases, the mouth is more frequently fixated and the duration of fixation increases (Vatikiotis-Bateson et al., 1998). This result suggests that acoustic information and visual information are mutually used for speech perception in face- to- face communication.

Following spoken instructions, the task is carried out. The sequence of speech (spoken instructions) perception can also be traced using eye tracking.

Tanenhaus et al. (1995) assigned tasks that involved the moving of certain pictures on the display using a computer mouse and revealed that verbal instruction is processed incrementally: eye movements to objects are made immediately after hearing relevant words in the instruction. For instance, if the instruction says 'touch the starred yellow square', the gaze point moves to the target square an average of 250 ms after the end of the word that uniquely specifies the target with respect to the visual alternatives. If only one of the squares was starred, the gaze fixates on the target square after hearing 'starred.' If there were two starred yellow squares, the gaze fixates on the target square after hearing 'square.' With more complex instructions, individuals made informative sequences of eye movements that were closely time-locked to words in the instruction that were relevant to establishing reference. In this way, the study clearly showed the link between the co-ordination of eye movement and language processing.

Tanenhaus's study et al. (1995) also revealed that ambiguity of instruction delays the initiation of eye movements directed to the information relevant for the given instruction. Spivey et al. (2002) investigated this issue in more detail and revealed that the visual context supports the interpretation of ambiguous instruction. For instance, the instruction 'put the apple on the towel in the box' can be interpreted as either 'the apple should be put on the towel' (this is the preferred interpretation) or 'the apple is already on the towel and should be put in the box' (less preferred interpretation). If the given visual context consists of an apple on a towel, a pencil, an empty towel, and a box, listeners initially assumed that 'in the box' was introducing the goal. This is indicated by frequent fixations on the empty towel. On the contrary, if the given visual context consists of one apple on a towel accompanied by another set of one or more apples, listeners clearly used the phrase 'on the towel' to disambiguate which apple was intended.

A further study by Allopenna et al. (1998) reveals that speech input is continuously mapped onto potential lexical representations as it unfolds over time. Rhyme information is also applied for the mapping of speech input onto potential choices. Dahan et al. (2001) showed that the frequency of the applied word affects the earliest moments of lexical access. This result ruled out models in which frequency effects in spoken word recognition are primarily due to decision biases that apply after lexical activation is complete.

The above-mentioned studies show that visual information perception and speech perception are closely related and are influenced by factors such as context and environmental conditions. However, it is only valid in a condition in which the subject follows the given instruction immediately. In quasi-real situations, namely in a simulation study, operators can decide more independently, whether or not and when they react to the given information, because they sometimes have to accomplish other additional tasks. Furthermore, it is also possible that the addressee reacts differently than the speaker expects. The extent to which the co-ordination between eye movement and language processing observed in quasi-real situations supports and validates the results from the research projects accomplished in the standardized experimental settings is of great interest from the basic research perspective. Support for basic research for this study is of high importance from the applied point of view, because regulatory statements regarding communication then have a valid and reliable basis.

Influence of Congruency of Given Information

Eye movement differs depending on whether problem solving is performed well or not. In excellent problem solving, eye movements are systematic, whereas, in the case of poor problem solving unnecessary eye movements (eye movements to areas other than the ones needed for problem solving) are often observed (Takeda, 1993; Fukuda, 2003). This fact was the basis for the design of the study in the NPP simulation.

In the NPP simulator study, two operators must solve a given transient with lack of feed water supply. A transient is a power plant disturbance that has the potential to lead to core damage, i.e. the melting of the fuel elements contained in the reactor pressure vessel. The subjects performed as reactor operators (operator A) and were assisted by a turbine operator (operator B was performed by an experimenter). The communication behaviour of operator A was examined in detail. The transient, the user interface and the procedures were designed in such a way that certain communication tasks could be allocated to both operators. The communication tasks were designed as being either congruent or incongruent with the necessary control tasks on the technical system (also cf. Chapter 4).

In the experiment, some communication problems were observed, such as delayed or no reaction from operator A to a request from operator B. The analysis of both operators' utterances, operator A's eye tracking data showing the transition of attention, and operator A's behaviour revealed that whether the information given by the speaker matches with the current attention of the addressee or not is one of the main reasons for observed communication problems. So, the main hypothesis was confirmed: congruency of information provided by communication is an important factor in the communication problems and errors. A detailed explanation follows.

If the information provided by the speaker is congruent with the task at hand or the attention of the addressee at that moment, the given information is incorporated into the decision process without problems. The addressee showed no confusion in such cases and, if necessary, reacted to the given information immediately with corresponding handling or verbal expression. The gaze point shows no salient change in these cases; in most of the cases it stays at the current position and does not move. Because the question matches with the operator's current attention track, he/she requires no rethinking of the situation and, therefore, no search for new information (i.e. eye movements). In this case, the operator can answer immediately.

If the information given by the speaker is incongruent with the current task or attention of the addressee, the addressee is in a dual task situation involving decision making, shift of attention and prioritization. In such an incongruent situation, operator A decides based on the information given by operator B but this information does not fit operator A's task to control the system. Control tasks are prescribed in the NPP setting as procedural steps. In this situation, operator A has to start working on the procedure required in order to address the new problem that has been pointed out by operator B.

One example of a reaction from operator A to a request from operator B is shown in Figure 12.12. In this case, operator B asks for the current reactor pressure vessel (RPV) level. At that moment, operator A gazes at the measure table (gaze order one and two in Figure 12.12 right panel). Therefore, operator A's question is incongruent with operator A's focus. In this case, immediately after hearing operator B's reminder about the request, he/she moves the gaze point to the value of the RPV level (gaze order three and four in Figure 12.12 left panel). After being reminded, operator A's verbal reaction is relatively fast. In the fastest cases, the gaze point shifts to the relevant information approximately 200 ms after onset/offset of the key word in the given information and the response is given in 800 ms.

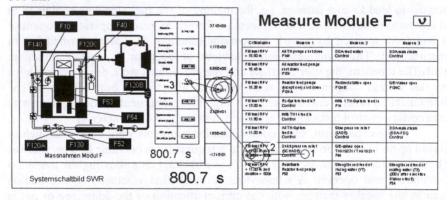

Figure 12.12 Transition of gaze point in the case of subject's immediate reaction: operator B asks for the current RPV level. The subject (operator A) regards the measure table on the right screen at that moment (gaze order one). Immediately after hearing operator B's request, the subject looks at the value of the RPV level (gaze order three and four, indicated by squares). Each circle corresponds to one fixation, and its diameter indicates the fixation duration

In some cases, the addresses' reaction is delayed. In most cases, the fixation on the relevant information itself is delayed and further reaction occurs rather quickly. This delayed shift of the attention from the former task to the new task is possibly caused by resource limitations. In order to deal with the new task, the former task needs to be finished first. Similar effects were observed in the *Microstructure Group*, which showed a delay of the N400 due to task overlap. This effect becomes greater with increased temporal overlap between two tasks. Also, the *Question Answering Group* found that an unspecific additional task load increases answering latencies. The *Process Control Group* also found this effect, which was observed in the laboratory setting.

In some other cases, the gaze point moves to the relevant information immediately after hearing operator B's utterance. However, the reaction is made with delay. Before the reaction occurs, the gaze moves to other elements on the screen. The analysis of further protocol data from operator A in an interview after the experiment made clear that difficulties with the interpretation of information, the integration of the given information or the planning of the corresponding handling caused the above mentioned delay in reaction. Thus, more time and eye movements are required in order to find the solution.

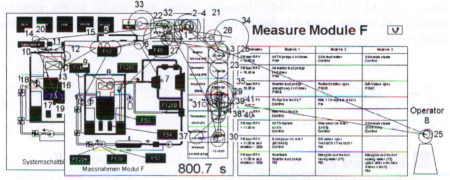

Figure 12.13 Transition of gaze point in the case of disregard of given information. The subject first continued to work on the task at hand and asked operator B, whether or not the TH14 pump is closed (gaze order 1-22). Finally after the additional reminder from operator B (gaze order 23 and later), the subject starts to check the level of RPV (indicated with square)

Occasionally, there is no reaction to the verbally given information. In most cases in which there is no reaction, the addressee actually disregards the given information. This is often observed, if the addressee concentrates on his/her own task (especially with certain active control handling) or if the speaker and addressee speak simultaneously. Due to the limited resources for information processing, the information perception from outside is difficult in such situations. This effect is, as mentioned above, possibly similar to the delays found in laboratory based dual task studies. Figure 12.13 shows an example of the eye movement in such cases. The subject is busy confirming if the TH14 pump is closed, and operator B's question about the current RPV level is incongruent with operator A's track of attention. After operator B's question, he/she continues searching on the screen for further information that confirms that the TH14 pump is closed (illustrated by gaze order 1-22 in Figure 12.13). His/her eye movement is not initially influenced by the question regarding the RPV. Only after confirmation from operator B that the pump is closed and an additional reminder to check the RPV level, does operator A finally start to work on this issue and gaze at the RPV value (gaze order 23 and later in Figure 12.13, with closing the screen for the procedure 'Module F'). In comparison with the case of immediate reaction, the required eye movement is much longer. In this example it takes 21 seconds for the subject to verbally react to the given information.

In several cases, operator A expresses no reaction to the given information, although he/she acknowledges the relevant information. Figure 12.14 shows one example of such 'seeming disregard.' After operator B stated that the steam line isolation was done, the subject shifted his/her gaze point from the measure table of Module F to the relevant information such as the value of differential pressure (gaze order 8, 10, 12 in Figure 12.14) or trend diagram of it (gaze order 14 in Figure 12.14). However, during this process he/she gave no comment about this. After this, he/she began to check the current RPV level (gaze order 16 and later in Figure 12.14) and reported about that

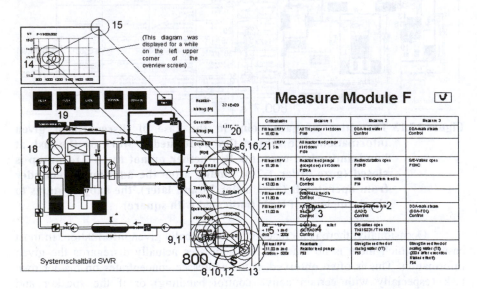

Figure 12.14 **Transition of gaze point in case of *seeming disregard*. The subject regards the measure table on the right display first. As operator B says that the steam line isolation is done, the subject regards the relevant information, namely, observes the value of differential pressure (gaze order 8, 10, 12) and its trend diagram (gaze order 14). However, no comment is given. Afterwards, he/she observes the current level of RPV and reports on it (gaze order 16 and later)**

In such cases, the difference in the priority between the given information and the control task at hand plays an important role. As new incongruent information is given through communication, the subject perceives the verbal information and regards the relevant information on the screen. In a next step, he/she compares it with the current task at hand. If the top priority is given to the control task at hand, this task is completed and the reaction to the verbal information is not made. As a result, it is impossible for operator B to confirm whether the sent information is perceived but not taken into account for subsequent actions or if this has not even been perceived.

Type of Messages Exchanged through Communication

What kind of messages the speaker sends and how the addressee reacts to the message is the fundamental point in the analysis of the whole communication process. The extent to which the communication process is dynamically changed depends on each utterance.

In the above-mentioned NPP simulation study, various types of reactions to the incongruent information are observed. Frequently, the operators understand the given information correctly and react immediately with corresponding utterance and handling. At other times he/she utilizes speaking to react. Many of these reactions can be classified as speech acts. For example, in the case of asking, operator B typically <u>asks</u> for certain information such as the RPV level or the next measure to initiate. Operator A <u>answers</u> by <u>stating</u> the requested information. The <u>suggestions</u> to check the important system variables with the checklist or to deal with the skipped measure are also frequently observed. In these cases, operator A, who is questioned by operator B, sometimes expresses explicit <u>agreement</u> or <u>acknowledgement</u> and then concentrates on the suggested task. In the case of delayed handling, operator A sometimes <u>refuses</u> operator B's <u>suggestion</u>. By <u>providing a reason</u> for his/her <u>refusal</u>, operator A may introduce an <u>alternative suggestion</u> for the next step. Then operator B should <u>acknowledge</u> operator A's argument and consider the next communicative behaviour. The next communicative behaviour may be different from operator B's initial intention (underlined terms: speech act types).

The analysis of protocol data in flight simulation (*Linguistic Factors Group*) shows the relationship between certain speech act types and crew performance. For instance, frequent explicit acknowledgement indicates that communication has been heard and understood. Additionally, speech acts can seek reassurance or correlate with good performance. Good aviation crews tend to have more questions and, in particular, more answers to questions. Greater coherence is also a key for good crew performance. Continued prepositional content in utterance sequences, reference to previous utterances, explicit acknowledgements and request/report/acknowledgement triples are strongly related to good crew performance.

Summary

In real life communication, the congruency of the information provided by communication with the task at hand plays an important role. If the given information is congruent with the task at hand, the reaction is made immediately without complications. However, if the given verbal information is incongruent with the current control task, this information can be regarded as an additional task.

The influence of the additional task is manifested on the observable level as a delay in the reaction to the given information. This is in agreement with the results from the laboratory setting studies (*Microstructure Group* and *Question Answering Group*) and suggests that this phenomenon is due to the limited resources for the communicational and procedural behaviour. On the other hand, the *Process Control Group* further revealed that the priority of each task could also cause communication problems in the NPP simulator study. If the priority of the control task at hand is higher than the priority of the additional task given through communication with other operators, the control task is accomplished first. After finishing the control task, the additional communication task is addressed. In this case, the reaction to the given information is further delayed and, in some cases, there is no reaction at all.

Conclusion and Practical Implications

In this chapter a number of experimental investigations into communicative processes under different forms of task load were described. A common characteristic of these studies is that the communicative task is to be performed simultaneously with some other task. The different research groups focused on increasingly complex scenarios, which increased in complexity from a classical dual task situation with an emphasis on language perception, to question answering while performing different additional tasks and a simulator situation in which the communication task and the additional task of supervising and controlling a nuclear power plant were directly related to one another. A common finding in all of these situations was a delay in the communicative task when additional load was imposed. At least at low task load levels, the delay was not necessarily accompanied by a higher risk for errors. However, a number of conditions could be specified that degraded task performance, e.g. when there was also excessive working memory load or when the communication had to be performed in an operator's second language. In addition, the simulator study from *Process Control Group* showed, first, that delayed responses eventually evoked the need for additional communication and, thereby, further increased multiple task load. Secondly, it showed that interruptions to ongoing tasks due to a need to communicate could cause additional problems, such as a shift of attention. This was reflected by the fact that eyes moved toward the element, which was relevant to the given information.

In conclusion, some practical implications will be discussed. The dual task experiments of the *Microstructure Group* demonstrated that neither time pressure nor five hours of practice were able to truly dissolve existing central processing bottlenecks. These experiments were primarily conducted to provide a basis for the language perception experiments. However, the findings strongly argue against the view that performance can be perfected in multiple task work places by extensive training or special instructions alone. Rather, these work places need to be re-designed in a way that makes it possible to avoid multiple simultaneous decision requirements whenever possible.

The language perception experiments of the *Microstructure Group* showed language perception to be delayed when there is a close overlap with another task. In addition, a difficult overlapping task increases language perception errors when a second language, rather than the native language, has to be processed. This finding has practical implications for work places such as the cockpit or air traffic control in which operators have to use a non-native language. In such cases, care should be taken in designing standardized communication in a way that the operator has only minimal communicative duties. In addition, if possible, operators should be allowed to use their native language.

The results from the *Microstructure Group* help to identify sources of interference that affect communication in operational environments. First, communication impediments may be aggravated by the difficulty of the operations required in the additional task. For example, based on the present results, it is conceivable that simple incompatible arrangements of levers and buttons on a dashboard may impede communication because of interference between the stimulus-response assignment and language perception. Therefore, if simultaneous task performance cannot be avoided, the non-communicative tasks should be designed as simply as possible, by using spatially compatible arrangements, for example. Second, the involvement of language-related elements in the non-communicative tasks may be detrimental, as was the case in the experiments in which subjects had to respond to letters as an additional task. Consequently, performing operations such as deciphering verbal messages on a display leads to an interference with communication in operational environments. For this reason, operational arrangements should use language-like displays as sparingly as possible.

The results from the *Question Answering Group* indicate that answering yes/no-questions is advantageous to answering wh-questions. However, if one extrapolates these results to ecological contexts of high risk workplaces, questions almost always refer to more complex knowledge structures (than those tested here); information uptake of completely new items is seldom necessary, and questions perhaps always focus on possible propositions that mix up elements from existing true propositions. Therefore, the usage of yes/no-questions should be preferred, because answers to yes/no-questions are usually faster and sometimes even more accurate than answers to wh-questions. This interpretation is supported, in particular, by the observation that broad focused yes/no-questions prompt memory retrieval processes that are more robust against additional task load than others. It is fundamentally important to note that any attempt to diminish working memory load, e.g. with short questions or remarks and with standardized communication, as well as with intensive communication training, can reduce the risk of communication errors in high workload situations. This is because the better one knows what to say, the less disturbing the other unrelated tasks are.

Concerning the practical implications of the results of the *Process Control Group*, the influence of temporal overlap of the communicative task and the procedural task on operator behaviour should be systematically considered in the design of systems. If the operator concentrates on his/her task, communication with the other operators is not always properly accomplished. In order to secure proper communication, such overlap should be avoided as often as possible. This fact is often not addressed in system design. Finally, communication requires a certain protocol in order to be effective: in particular, one should not speak when the other operator is speaking. In addition, it is recommended that it be explicitly acknowledged when communication has been heard and understood. The importance of acknowledgement is revealed both in the NPP simulator study and in the speech act analysis of the data from the cockpit in the flight simulation (cf. Chapter 11).

Appendices

Appendix I: The GIHRE Projects and Researchers

Project	Institution/ Location	Project Head	Principle Researchers
Group Interaction under Threat and High Workload	The University of Texas at Austin, Department of Psychology	Robert L. Helmreich	J. Bryan Sexton
The Effects of Different Forms of Co-ordination in Coping with Workload	Swiss Federal Institute of Technology (ETH), Zurich, Switzerland, Institute of Work Psychology	Gudela Grote	Patrick Grommes Enikö Zala-Mezö
Group Interaction in High Risk Environments: Aviation	Swiss Federal Institute of Technology (ETH), Zurich, Switzerland, Institute of Work Psychology Former Swissair Training Centre	Werner Naef	Andrea Amacher Ruth Häusler Barbara Klampfer

Group Interaction in High Risk Environments: Linguistic Factors	University of Texas at Austin Humboldt University, Berlin Institute for German Language and Linguistics	Manfred Krika	Carrie Clarady Silka Martens Florian Schwarz
Language Processing	Humboldt University, Berlin Institute for German Language and Linguistics	Rainer Dietrich	Katja Kühn Sascha Neuper Dagmar Silberstein
Task Load and the Microstructure of Cognition	Humboldt University, Berlin Institute of Psychology	Werner Sommer	Annette Hohlfeld Jörg Sangals
Communication in Nuclear Power Plants	Technical University, Munich Kernkraftwerk Gundremmingen GmbH	Oliver Sträter Ryoko Fukuda	
Central Services	Humboldt University, Berlin Institute for German Language and Linguistics	Rainer Dietrich	Traci Michelle Childress Kateri Jochum

Appendix II: Glossary Terms as Defined within the GIHRE Project[43]

Boiling water reactor (BWR) A certain type of nuclear power plant (NPP).

Communication An interaction intended to change the knowledge state of the other participants. GIHRE is specifically interested in communication that is used in problem solving.

Co-operation An interaction that serves a common goal. This is the type of interaction in which the GIHRE project is most interested. Co-operation and problem solving are closely tied together. Additionally, co-operation is defined as joint task fulfillment, and therefore, also includes a willingness and attentiveness towards working together. Attitudinal factors therefore play a role in the difference in goal and task definitions.

Co-ordination (implicit/explicit) *Explicit co-ordination* is considered necessary when an agreement must be arrived at about how an action should be organized. It typically occurs during new tasks and new situations or when a new group of people makes up a team to accomplish a job. People have to devote extra resources (very often communication) in order to organize the activities. *Implicit co-ordination ordination* occurs when every one in a team knows his/her job; the actions harmonize with each other based on some kind of shared understanding and therefore little noticeable effort for co-ordination is required.

Cued recall Retrieval of facts from memory with the help of other, somehow related, facts called cues. Contrary to this, free recall is retrieval of facts without cues.

Cultural factors Cultural factors label not only the values, beliefs and educational norms of the team, but also national cultural variables, i.e. whether the group is mono- or multi-cultural, the organizational culture, the professional culture and, in many cases, the safety culture within the group and its working environment.

Discourse knowledge In any given conversation the relevant knowledge needed to talk coherently is a part of the knowledge a person has. In authentic situations this knowledge steadily changes, although it may be focused, as in co-operative problem solving. For experimental purposes, it must be held constant or controlled.

Event-based procedures Operational procedures that start with the cause of a system disturbance to guide the user (operator, pilot, doctor, controller) through the required mitigating actions. In this case, the cause has to be diagnosed beforehand by the user (e.g. using symptom-based procedures or his/her expertise).

---

[43] Many thanks to all project members who helped to generate these definitions, and thanks to Kateri Jochum, whose careful guidance and notetaking in Zurich 2000 and Berlin 2001, helped to create and fine-tune many of these definitions.

Event-related potential (ERP) Brain activity in relation to external events, cognitive processes and actions, extracted from the electroencephalogram. Different components of the ERP signify distinct processing stages (--> Lateralized Readiness Potential, -->N400 component, -->P300 component).

Gaze point The point at which the subject is looking / fixating on.

Heedful interrelating Deliberate efforts by all actors in a team to constantly re-consider effects of his/her own actions in relation to the goals and actions of others.

INES (International Nuclear Event Scale) Scale used to classify the severity of nuclear events.

Interaction A global topic defined as a specific activity that is functionally related to the actions of other actors or single acts, such as utterances, for example.

Lateralized readiness potential (LRP) An ->ERP reflecting the brain activation specific for the preparation of manual (or foot) responses. The LRP is already measurable prior to response onset and occurs specific to the response side, thereby distinguishing correct from incorrect response tendencies. Its size reflects the degree to which the preparation has proceeded; it's time course makes it possible to distinguish between the duration of early (e.g. perceptual) processing stages and later ones. The LRP is computed as the difference potential between electrodes over the motor cortex ipsi- vs. contralateral to the hand (or foot) being prepared.

N400 Electrically negative wave in the --> ERP appearing about 400 milliseconds after the onset of a visually or acoustically presented word. N400 amplitude increases when the presented word does not fit into the semantic context, which has been established by previous stimuli (e.g. a lead-in sentence or a prime word).

P300 component (of the --> ERP) Electrically positive wave appearing 300 milliseconds or later after the onset of a significant event. P300 amplitude increases as events become less frequent and more meaningful to the observer and latency increases when perceptual processes are more time consuming.

Performance The qualitative and quantitative outcome of the group process relevant to the task.

Performance Shaping Factor (PSF) All factors having an influence on human performance.

Precueing Paradigm An experimental setting for the analysis of movement preparation and its modularity. Participants have the task to specifically respond to different response signals, e.g. to flex the right finger when the letter 'r' appears and to extend the left finger when shown the letter *L*. Some time before each response signal, a so-called 'precue' is shown that informs of some or all aspects of the forthcoming response, e.g. the direction or the finger. This advance information reduces reaction time, even if it cues only parts of the latter response, and evokes ->ERPs, e.g. the ->LRP.

Psychological Refractory Period (PRP) Term coined in analogy to the refractoriness of nerve cells to explain the delay in reaction times to a second stimulus when presented shortly after a first stimulus. Although the term is still in use, the explanation has been replaced by effects of --> resource sharing or --> bottlenecks in processing.

Quaestio a) Communicative task that guides any speaker's speech production by setting preferences for the linguistic realization of references to abstract entities speakers and hearers may perceive in a given situation. b) (abstract, implicit) question guiding speech/text production; it is understood as the cognitive representation of an information processing task that the speaker him/herself sets, be it in reaction to an actual question the speaker asked or a self developed communicative purpose. c) Communicative task as a consequence of actual or desired changes of a situation. According to recent psycholinguistic models, this task can be seen as the mental representation of an abstract question, which the speaker is setting out to answer.

Question semantics The meaning of a question depends on proper answers to it. In a similar fashion answers cannot be understood completely without the question. This interdependence was used to logically classify several question types in the field of linguistic semantics.

Reactor pressure vessel (RPV) The vessel that contains the fuel elements of an NPP; it is where the thermal heat is produced.

Recognition An act of judgement: perceiving an item as being well known.

Resources Subsumes what a human organism needs in order to process a given task, particularly referring to neural systems for attention, decision, memory, etc. Resources are assumed to be limited and shareable. Conflicts due to the simultaneous allocation of shared insufficient resources by different processes are assumed to cause performance deficits such as delays and errors, particularly in multiple tasks.

Risk One way of defining risk: risk = damage frequency x damage amount, whereby damage amount can be determined by costs involved, level of contamination or lives taken. However, it is important to distinguish what is meant by risk in each case, as the risk of one piece of the entire system might not be enough to define a setting as a risk in general. Risk can play a role on different levels: system, human factors and technical system. Risk does not necessarily signalize danger. Threat factors increase risk. A single part of a system may become a risk to the safety of the whole system.

Second language perception Processing of verbal input in a second, non-native language, which could have been acquired early or late in life (early vs. late bi-lingualism).

Seeming disregard A communication-situation in which the sender requests the receiver to accomplish a certain task and to give him/her feedback on accomplishment. Seeming disregard exists, if the receiver complies with the task but is not providing feedback on accomplishment.

Semantic processing Processing of conceptual knowledge (meaning), either to be put into a verbal message during language production or to be derived from a verbal message during language perception.

Symptom-based procedures Operational procedures that start with the observable symptoms of a system disturbance to guide the user (operator, pilot, doctor, controller) through the required mitigating actions. The user is guided from symptoms to the causes of a disturbance in this case.

Team There are two main types of teams: primary team and extended team. The primary team can be open or closed, must be located in the same place and members must share a common function or work towards the achievement of a common task. An open primary team is one that changes composition, whereas a closed team remains in the same composition. An extended team includes or involves outside individuals for a certain length of time.

Utterance Something uttered such as a statement. Vocal expression. Speech. Recorded utterance data is very important for the analysis of verbal communication.

Workload Mental *workload* is defined as factors that may lead to performance decrements. Task related factors that contribute to mental workload include time pressure, numbers of decisions per time and the overlap between concurrent tasks. Subjective workload refers to the amount of strain experienced by the individual subject that takes the intervening variables that index the tuning between demands on the environment and the subject into account, i.e. external influences and internal resources are set against one another. In this sense, the term *workload* does not describe scenario per se, but the demands experienced by the subject within the scenario/setting.

Appendix III: Percentage of Flights in which the Behavioral Indicator was Observed

Behavioral Indicator	Phase of Flight			
Marker Name	Predept	TO/Clmb	Cruise	Des/Land
Leadership	79.8	69.5	67.4	76.4
Team Environment	91.7	76.6	71.9	82.9
Briefing Content	90.1	47.3	37.2	84.6
Effective Inquiry	49.4	43.8	43.4	57.5
Assertion	27.5	22.2	22.2	33.2
Decisions Stated & Acknowledged	72.7	67.4	64.5	77.2
Workload and Task Distribution	80.8	62.5	62.5	72.5
Tasks Prioritized	59.2	43.9	56.5	60.2
Vigilance	67.2	76.3	70.3	77.6
Stay Ahead of Curve	62.5	51.6	53.3	78.1
Sterile Cockpit	92.9	93.1	NA	94.4
Altitude	74.6	84.7	72.9	86.5
Checklist Compliance	95	93.7	82.4	94.3
Overall Observations				
Overall Crew Effectiveness		98.7		
Overall Technical Proficiency		98.9		

Appendix IV: Behavioral Markers Group

Video analysis

For each of the three scenarios behavioral markers were rated for every flight phase and for the overall flight (cf. Figure IV.1). For reasons of comparability not only LOSA was rated like this, but also NOTECHS, for which observers usually give only overall ratings for the four categories at the end of the flight. Ratings were only given if the respective behavioral markers could actually be observed.

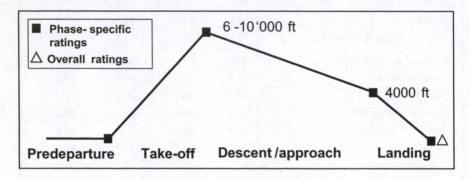

Figure IV.1 Rating procedure for CRM

As shown in Figure IV.1, the scenarios do not include a 'cruise' phase, which is generally the longest phase in normal flight operation. However, for training purposes this phase of low rate of change is considered to be less relevant.

Three project observers with aviation and psychology background (one of them being a captain) served as external observers for the video analysis by means of LOSA and NOTECHS. They had received formal training for both instruments and showed good inter-rater agreement (for both instruments average r_{wg} was above .80). To assure the quality of the CRM judgments several inter-rater calibrations were run and regular expert consultations were scheduled. In addition subject matter experts reviewed all crews that were rated *poor* or *very poor* on overall ratings. In order to reduce possible rater biases, each scenario was observed for LOSA and NOTECHS by a different rater, and a systematic variation of raters and scenarios was applied.

Impact of High Task Load on CRM Performance

Table IV.1 shows t-tests for the comparison of means in subjective workload between two scenarios.

Table IV.1 Comparison of perceived mental workload across scenarios

	Pair	Mean Difference	Std. Deviation	t	df	Sign.
Capt.	S1 – S2	1.95	23.90	.523	40	.604
	S1 – S3	17.09	23.00	4.874	42	.000
	S2 – S3	15.00	28.66	3.352	40	.002
F/O	S1 – S2	-6.31	16.86	-2.425	41	.020
	S1 – S3	6.79	25.99	1.692	41	.980
	S2 – S3	12.84	23.61	3.608	43	.001

Paired-samples t-Test (two-tailed)
Mean differences for the subscale mental demands of the NASA Task Load indeX (ranging from 0 to 100)

[a] Mean differences may deviate from the difference of the means reported in Table 2.4 because of missing data

Tables IV.2 toIV.4 show comparisons of the proportions of crews with substandard CRM performance in two scenarios regarding their risk index.

Table IV.2 Comparison of team performance in two different high task load conditions (scenario 1 and 2)

		Risk index scenario 2		
		RI = 0	RI > 0	Total
Risk index Scenario 1	RI = 0	17 (38.6%)	5 (11.4%)	22 (50.0%)
	RI > 0	15 (34.1%)	7 (15.9%)	22 (50.0%)
Total		32 (72.7%)	12 (27.3%)	44 (100%)
McNemar Test: p= .041[a]; N=44				

RI: Risk index NOTECHS crew
[a] Binomial distribution used.

Table IV.3 Comparison of team performance in high vs. moderate task load conditions (scenario 1 and 3)

		Risk index scenario 3		
		RI = 0	RI > 0	Total
Risk index scenario 1	RI = 0	22 (50.0%)	1 (2.3%)	23 (52.3%)
	RI > 0	17 (38.6%)	4 (9.1%)	21 (47.7%)
Total		39 (88.6%)	5 (11.4%)	44 (100%)
McNemar Test: p= .000[a]; N=44				

RI: Risk index NOTECHS crew/ [a] Binomial distribution used

Table IV.4 Comparison of team performance in high vs. moderate task load conditions (scenario 2 and 3)

| | | Risk index scenario 3 | | |
		RI = 0	RI > 0	Total
Risk index scenario 2	RI = 0	30 (68.2%)	3 (6.8%)	33 (75.0%)
	RI > 0	9 (20.5%)	2 (4.5%)	11 (25.0%)
Total		39 (88.7%)	5 (11.4%)	44 (100%)
McNemar Test: p= .146[a]; N=44				

RI: Risk index NOTECHS crew/ a Binomial distribution used

Stability of CRM Performance

Tables IV.5 and IV.6 show correlations for behavioral markers, categories and risk indices for trans-situational consistency of CRM performance.

Table IV.5 Stability of LOSA behavioral markers across scenarios

	S1xS2	S1xS3	S2xS3
Briefing	.09 (N=44)	.07 (N=44)	.22 (N=44)
Plans stated	.00 (N=44)	-.05 (N=44)	.15 (N=44)
Workload assignment	.06 (N=35)	.13 (N=17)	-.17 (N=17)
Contingency management	.19 (N=32)	-.14 (N=21)	-.05 (N=19)
Monitoring/cross check	.13 (N=43)	.26* (N=43)	-.01 (N=44)
Workload management	.26* (N=41)	-.15 (N=34)	-.21 (N=37)
Vigilance	.07 (N=43)	.06 (N=43)	-.19 (N=44)
Automation management	.34 (N=12)	.00 (N=14)	-.36* (N=24)
Evaluation of plans	-.06 (N=38)	.20 (N=13)	.07 (N=17)
Inquiry	.00 (N=24)	(N=7)	.00 (N=12)
Assertiveness	-.05 (N=25)	-.11 (N=16)	-.38 (N=19)
Risk Index LOSA[a]	.06 (N=44)	.11 (N=44)	.01 (N=44)

Spearman correlations (one-tailed)
* p<.05 ; [a] Pearson correlations (one-tailed)

Table IV.6 Stability of NOTECHS categories across scenarios

	Captain			First Officer		
	S1-S2	S1-S3	S2-S3	S1-S2	S1-S3	S2-S3
Co-operation	.09	.34*	-.02	-.10	.03	-.01
Leadership	.28*	.13	.25	.11	.15	.06
Situation awareness	.11	.04	.17	-.12	.04	.00
Decision making	-.06[a]	-	-	.21[b]	-	-
Risk Index NOTECHS[c]	-.11	-.07	-.05	.03	-.01	.07

Spearman correlations (one-tailed) N= 41 - 44
* p< .05; ** p< .01
[a] N= 31; [b] n= 19; [c] Pearson correlations (one-tailed)

Comparison of LOSA and NOTECHS

Tables IV.7 to IV.9 show details on the correspondence of ratings with LOSA and NOTECHS for similar constructs.

Table IV.7 Correlations between similar LOSA and NOTECHS constructs

		NOTECHS Leadership	
		Captain	First officer
LOSA Leadership[44]	Scenario 1	.650***	.294
	Scenario 2	.568***	.314*
	Scenario 3	.639***	.332*

N= 44-45
* p< .05; ** p< .01; *** p< .001

Table IV.8 Correlations between similar LOSA and NOTECHS constructs

		NOTECHS Situation Awareness	
		Captain	First officer
LOSA Vigilance	Scenario 1	.564***	.325*
	Scenario 2	.452**	.214
	Scenario 3	.382**	.571***

N= 44-45
* p< .05; ** p< .01; *** p< .001

---

[44] Leadership is defined as 'captain showed leadership and co-ordinated flight deck activities.' Therefore, higher correlations are expected for captains than for first officers.

LIVERPOOL JOHN MOORES UNIVERSITY
LEARNING SERVICES

Table IV.9 Correlations between similar LOSA and NOTECHS constructs

		NOTECHS Co-operation	
		Captain	First officer
LOSA	Scenario 1	.572***	.612***
Communication	Scenario 2	.309*	.352*
Environment	Scenario 3	.473***	.592***

N= 43-45
* p< .05; ** p< .01; *** p< .001

Appendix V: Observational Categories with Examples used by the *Co-ordination Group*

Information Flow

All communication units are coded within this category group.

Explicit co-ordination
Provide Information
A team member provides any kind of information:
'I go back to position zero with the flaps.'
'The manual respiration goes well.'
Request information
A team member asks a question:
'Is it the smallest tubus we have?'
Provide information upon request
A team member answers a question:
'Yes it is the smallest.'
Information containing a summary of a state of affairs or a process
A team member summarizes the situation the team is in:
'So, we are going to make a ILS-approach with a longer final. We take the longest available runway. We will use the autopilot as long as it normally functions…'
Reassurance
A team member provides feedback about comprehension of communication, often closed loop communication:
('Speed is one hundred.') 'Speed is checked.'
Or in normal communication:
'O.k.' 'That is right.' 'I agree.'
Give order
A team member gives a simple instruction to carry out actions:
'Have a look at it!' 'Enter this data, please!'
'Can you give me the ECG cable?'
Ask for help
A team member asks for help:
'You have to watch and tell me if the attitude is too high.'
'Will there be more help from somewhere?'

Discussion
More than one person speaks about a subject almost parallel.

Standard communication (only by aviation)
Predetermined communication, which always has to be carried out in the same way:

Pilot flying: 'Gear up'
Pilot non-flying: 'Gear is up'

Communication with Air Traffic Control
Communication to and from members of Air Traffic control
(not included in the analyses)

Communication with patient (specific for medicine)
Communication to and from patient
(not included in analyses)

Implicit co-ordination

Provide unsolicited information
If a team member anticipates a need for information from another team member and provides it without being asked to do so, e.g. in a difficult landing situation, the pilot non-flying sees the runway and informs the pilot flying about it, without being asked to do so:

'Runway is inside straight ahead.'
'I would adjust the frequency first, because it alters the volume.' (This was advice from an experienced team member, as somebody tried to adjust the respirator and it did not work out.)

Offer assistance
If someone anticipates a teammate's need for help and offers this help:

'Should I enter the data?'
'May I give you the breathing bag?'

Provide unsolicited action
If a tean member anticipates an action required for a smooth work process and takes this action without being asked to do so:

e.g. Handing the waste box for a used needle.

Silence
Nobody speaks but the process continues smoothly.

Chatting
The team talks about non-work related issues but the work process goes on smoothly.

Leadership

<u>Make plans</u> A team member creates a plan that includes several steps of the future work process: 'We go in the holding and prepare the clean approach. We have to inform the ATC and the cabin crew.' 'As soon as they are ready with the preparation we will wheel the patient to the operating theatre.'
<u>Assign task</u> A team member allocates tasks among the team. 'I read the quick reference and you can prepare the FMS and ask how is the weather.' 'If you agree I will give the administer the drugs.'
<u>Give order</u> As above
<u>Make decision</u> A team member announces a decision defining the way or the timing for carrying out an action: 'In this case we will make clean approach.' 'We wait one more minute.'
<u>Initiate an action</u> A team member tries to influence the action but wants to get agreement from the team. It is a sign of thinking together with the other actor(s) actively: 'Should I try to recycle?' 'Allright we are ready. Should we make the approach briefing? ' 'Should we give some more Fentanyl?'
<u>Accept order, decision or initiated action</u> A team member gives verbal affirmation or acts directly as an affirmation: 'Yes, I agree.'
<u>Question a decision</u> A team member expresses doubts about a decision: '(By auto break I would select maximum.) Maximum? I've never heard about it.' ('Probably we could change the position of the head.') 'We could do that but it would not change anything.'
<u>Ignoring initiated action</u> There is a suggestion but nobody reacts to it.

Autocratic behaviour
Someone makes a decision without reaching an agreement with the team: 'We are going to land now and we can discuss it later.'   'We have to do it as it is written in the instructions.'

Heedful interrelating

For the coding of these categories, it is important to decide whether a behavior has a positive influence or not. If somebody does not support the aims of the team with his/her behavior, then it is heedless interrelating: e.g. excessive and superfluous teaching can be interesting for the teacher but not for the team..

Considering others
A team member considers or checks the state of other team members: 'Are you ready? '/ 'Do you have a question? '/ 'Can you do it alone?'   'Do you agree?'
Considering the future   A team member thinks about the consequences of the situation in a timely fashion: 'We will use autopilot as long as it functions normally.'   'We are going to reposition the patient in the operating room, it is better so.'
Considering external conditions   A team member keeps the external conditions influencing the task fulfillment in mind: 'We have to check the weather, particularly the wind.'   'If the table too much up you can hardly lift the patient.'
Initiate an action   See above
Question a decision   See above
Providing unsolicited information   See above
Offering assistance   See above
Correct the behaviour of others   A team member reaffirms the right course of action and thereby points to a mistake made by another team member: 'We did decide for flaps zero position, didn't we? It isn't correct in that way.'   'You can fix the tube better.'

| Teach others |
| A team member explains something in a way that is more than just an answer to a question: |
| |
| 'It is not difficult to land as long as it doesn't get choppy.' |
| 'Try to administer the Venflon step in the skin and afterwards drive it further horizontally.' |
| Give positive feedback about performance |
| A team member provides a supportive evaluation of the performance: |
| |
| 'Congratulation. You have managed the approach really nicely.' |
| 'Yes, the respiration is all right now.' |
| Give negative feedback about performance |
| No observation within this category |

Appendix VI: Linguistic Factors: Speech Acts

In the following, the speech act inventory of STACK is described in greater detail. STACK distinguishes between the following groups of speech acts called *Information, Request, Agreement/Negotiation, Dissent, Question, Expressive* and *Interaction Markers*. Speech acts are conveniently named by a verb stem, like INFORM, or EXPLICATE. They are characterized by certain preconditions that have to hold and by the perlocutionary effects that they intend to achieve (see chapter on *Language and Communicative Behavior* for a discussion of speech act theory). The following list specifies for each speech act type the preconditions, gives a short paraphrase what the speech act is about, and points out typical effects of the speech act for the communication process itself and the future behavior of the addressee.

Information-related Speech Acts

INDICATE. S has factual information that A needs to know which is relevant for the immediate action of A. S focuses attention of A on this fact. Typically, A acknowledges understanding.

INFORM. S has factual information that A most probably does not yet have. S believes that this information could be of interest for A. S focuses attention of A on this fact. Typically, A acknowledges understanding and may evaluate information or ask for its relevance.

POINT OUT. S assumes that A hasn't taken notice of a fact that could be obtained by A himself/herself. S focuses attention on A on this fact. Typically, A confirms or comments on this or thanks A.

EXPLICATE. S feels that additional information is necessary to solve a problem, or was asked by A to give additional information; often 'thinking out loud.' S elaborates on a previous utterance to make it better understandable. Typically, A indicates that he/she has understood, or that he/she still needs more information, or discusses or doubts the content of the information.

DESCRIBE. S knows that A does not know a certain fact, concerning an object or an action that is of potential relevance. S gives a description of the object or action to A. Typically, A indicates that he can follow the description or asks additional questions.

ANNOUNCE. S thinks of a future action by himself that A is probably not aware of but that is relevant. S informs A about this future action. Typically, A acknowledges, or asks further questions for elaboration.

JUSTIFY. S thinks it is helpful to give reasons for a particular action or opinion, perhaps because he was asked to. S specifies such reasons for A to convince A that the action or opinion should be followed. Typically, A indicates that he/she understands and follows this justification, or that he doesn't.

CLAIM. S assumes that A does not know a certain fact or doubts it, and S is not totally sure of it either. S attempts to convince A of the truth of the claim. Typically, A agrees, or A contests the claim or accepts it only with qualifications.

VINDICATE. A reproaches S for acting in a certain way, or S senses this. S defends himself/herself by specifying reasons for why he/she acted in this way. Typically, A accepts the criticized behavior, or still disapproves of it.

DEDUCE. A fact was thematized of which certain consequences can be inferred. S makes A aware of these consequences. Typically, A acknowledges this or expresses agreement.

SUMMARIZE. Some fact was thematized in several previous speech acts. S gives a condensed summary for A. Typically, A acknowledges understanding, or names additional important points.

REMIND. S has the impression that A does not think of a fact that he should known, as part of the background, the situation, or previous communication. S informs A of this fact again. Typically, A acknowledges understanding or thanks S or admits that he did not think of the fact anymore.

SUPPOSE. S is not very certain of a fact of potential importance, but considers it likely. S informs A of the fact and qualifies that by indicating that he is not certain about it. A supports the fact, doubts or denies it or asks for evidence.

Request-related Speech Acts

DIRECT. Typical for didactic environments; S (with authority over A) thinks that the actions of A have to be regulated in a certain way. S directs A to behave in certain ways. A can follow these directions or protest against them.

ORDER. S (with authority over A) wants A to act in a certain way, typically in line with general rules or laws. S orders A to act in this way, by (at least implicitly) appealing to the general rules or laws. Typically, A heeds the command.

SUGGEST. S wants A to act in a certain way. S proposes that A acts in this way. Typically, A indeed acts in this way, or gives reasons for not doing so.

REQUEST. S wants A to act in a certain way and knows that A is not obliged to do so. S asks A to act in a certain way. A acts in this way (perhaps with verbal comment), or gives reasons not to act in this way. Further distinction: S and A have equal status, S has superior status, or A has superior status.

PERMIT. A has asked S to be allowed to act in a certain way, or suggested to act in a certain way. S allows A to act in this way, or agrees to act in this way. Typically, A expresses thanks.

Agreement/Negotiation Related Speech Acts

AGREE. A certain opinion or a plan of action has been uttered and is discussed. S informs A that he goes along with this. Typically, no reaction by A; perhaps A shows that he/she is glad about it.

REPEAT. There was a previous utterance that S thinks might not have been understood or grasped well. S repeats the content of this utterance wholly or in part, trying to make sure that the utterance is understood. Typically, A understands and grasps the utterance now, and reacts in a way typical for the utterance.

DISTINCTION. The previous utterance was made by S himself/herself, or by another participant.

REAFFIRM. S thinks that a previous utterance has to be supported. S increases the validity of this utterance. Reactions depend on the type of the previous utterance. Further distinction: the previous utterance is by S himself/herself, or by another participant.

CONFIRM. A has asked S to act in a particular way. S indicates that he is willing to do so. Typically, no further action by A, or acknowledgement, or A thanks S.

Speech Acts of Dissent

REBUT. A has uttered his opinion about a fact. S informs A that he does not accept this, either verbally or by gestures. Typically, A accepts rejection, or expresses disappointment.

REJECT PROPOSAL. A has made a proposal. A rejects that. Typical reaction: A accepts this, or makes another proposal.

REFUSE. A has asked S to be allowed to perform an action. S does not permit this (and would sanction A if he did it anyway). Typically, A expresses disappointment or demands a justification.

OBJECT. S does not totally agree with some implicit or explicitly uttered opinion. S makes a statement that utters partial disagreement or restricts that opinion. A accepts the objection or argues against it. The opinion objected to can be one uttered by someone else, like A, or by S himself.

CORRECT. A (or S himself) has made a mistake, and S corrects that mistake. Typically, A accepts that correction, shows annoyance about the mistake, or may repeat the correction.

CONTRADICT. A has uttered an opinion that is contrary to what S believes. S expresses his/her opinion clearly. Typically, either A confirms and defends his/her standpoint, or gives it up and follows S.

REJECT ACT. A has performed a speech act that is not appropriate for the situation. S indicates that the speech act is inappropriate. Typically, A expresses disappointment, accepts the rejection, or does not react at all.

Speech Acts of Questioning

QUESTION (INFORMATION). S indicates a particular gap of knowledge that A probably can fill; this can concern the truth of a proposition (yes/no question, like *is there any fuel left*), the values that make an open proposition true (constituent question, like *how much fuel is left*), or a choice of values that make an open proposition true (alternative questions, like *should we approach from the east or from the west*). S asks A to fill this gap of knowledge. Typically, A answers the question, or says that he/she doesn't have the information, or asks a counter question for clarification or rejection.

QUESTION (UNDERSTANDING). S thinks that he has not understood an utterance of A properly. S indicates that to A and asks A to repeat the utterance, at least in part. Typically, A repeats the utterance wholly or partly, or rewords the utterance. The lack of understanding can be purely acoustical, or it can concern the meaning or relevance of the previous utterance.

QUESTION (OPINION). S wants to know what A thinks about a certain issue. S asks A about that. Typically, A expresses his opinion, or says that he/she doesn't have an opinion about this issue or asks a counter question for clarification or rejection.

OFFER. S assumes that A might want S to do something. S asks A whether S should do it. Typically, A accepts the offer or rejects it and may express thanks.

MAKE SURE. A certain speech act was performed or an issue was mentioned before by A or can be inferred. S asks A to confirm that A indeed wanted to have this act performed or has the inferred attitude towards the issue. Typically, A confirms this or does not confirm it.

Expressive Speech Acts

APPEASE. A is concerned, disturbed or angry because of an issue. S attempts to invalidate that by arguing that the reasons for the concern are not so serious as A thinks. Typically, A is convinced by this and is less concerned, or A is not convinced and even utters more points of concern.

EVALUATE (NEGATIVE / POSITIVE). There is an issue that is open for discussion (not the behavior of A, but some content). S utters a positive or negative attitude about it. Typically, A agrees with S, or A disagrees with S.

APOLOGIZE. S has offended A in some way. S expresses regret for the action and may offer compensation. Typically, A accepts the apology or does not accept it.

EXPRESS ASTONISHMENT. S is positively or negatively surprised by a fact. S indicates this to A. Typically, A indicates similar surprise, or that the fact is not surprising for him/her.

INSIST. A has rebutted a previous utterance by S, but did not achieve his/her communicative goal. S affirms his/her previous utterance, often by phrasing it in stronger words, attempting to convince A of his position. Typically, A does not change his/her negative position or changes it in accordance with A.

PRAISE. A has performed action that is very good, relative to some norm. S indicates that A's action was good, and expresses positive feelings about it; in didactic contexts, this makes A familiar with the norm. Typically, A expresses pride, joy or embarrassment.

REPREHEND. As with praise, except that A has performed an action that is bad.

ADVICE. S realizes that A needs help to solve a problem. Typically, S attempts to help A by giving information that S thinks is helpful for solving the problem.

UTTER DISGUST. A has violated some rule. S expresses that he/she is annoyed about that. Typically, A apologizes or attempts to justify his/her behavior.

CONCEDE. S shares the opinion of A only partly. S refers to some utterance of A and agrees with it only partly. Typically, A accepts the willingness to compromise or insists on his/her opinion.

Interaction Markers

THANK. A has done S a favour. S expresses gratitude for that. Typically, A acknowledges that.

ACKNOWLEDGEMENT. A has said something to S (not a question). S indicates that he has understood the utterance. Typically, no further reaction by A.

REPORT BACK. A has said something to S or is saying something to S. S indicates that he/she is following the utterance, often just by nodding or verbal gestures, without wanting to take the floor. A feels reassured in the role of speak.

STRUCTURE. A plans to start (or end) a speech act or sequence of speech acts. S indicates that by short verbal or non-verbal signals. Typically, S (or A) takes the floor, or S (or A) leaves the floor to the other participant.

DELIBERATE. A has asked a question. S attempts to answer, but cannot access the information immediately, and signals that he/she is searching for the answer and does not want to be interrupted. Typically, A waits till S can present the answer, or A gets impatient and asks again.

Bibliography

Chapter 1: Group Interaction under Threat and High Workload

Frankel, A., Graydon-Baker, E., Neppl, C., Simmonds, T., Gustafson, M., Gandhi, T.K. (2003), 'Patient Safety Leadership Walkrounds', *Jt Comm J Qual Safety*, Vol. 29, pp.16-26.

Gregorich, S.E., Helmreich, R.L., Wilhelm, J.A. (1990), 'The Structure of Cockpit Management Attitudes', *Journal of Applied Psychology*, Vol. 75, No. 6, pp.682-690.

Helmreich, R.L. (1984), 'Cockpit Management Attitudes', *Human Factors*, Vol. 26, pp.583-589.

Helmreich, R.L. and Merritt, A.C. (1998), *Culture at Work in Aviation and Medicine: National, Organizational, and Professional Influences*, Ashgate: Aldershot, U.K.

Helmreich, R.L., Merritt, A.C., Sherman, P.J., Gregorich, S.E. and Wiener, E.L (1993), 'The Flight Management Attitudes Questionnaire (FMAQ)', *NASA/UT/FAA Technical Report 93-4*, The University of Texas: Austin, TX.

Itoh, K, Andersen, H.B., Tanaka, H. and Seki, M. (2000), 'Attitudinal Factors of Night Train Operators and their Correlation with Accident/Incident Statistics ', *Proceedings of the 19th European Annual Conference on Human Decision Making and Manual Control*, June, pp.87-96.

Maurino, D.E., Reason, J., Johnston, N. and Lee, R.B. (1995), *Beyond Aviation Human Factors*, Ashgate Publishing: Aldershot.

Pronovost, P.J., Weast, B., Holzmueller, C. et al. (in press), *Evaluating a Culture of Safety. Quality and Safety in Healthcare*, BMJ Publishing Group Ltd and the Institute for Healthcare Improvements: London and Boston.

Pronovost, P.J., Weast, B., Rosenstein, B. et al. (submitted), 'Implementing and Validating a Comprehensive Unit-based Safety Program', *New England Journal of Medicine*.

Roberts, P.R. (2003), *In Pursuit of a Safety Culture in New Zealand Public Hospitals*, Masters Thesis, Victoria University of Wellington: New Zealand.

Romanoff, N. (2003), 'Applying WalkRounds Concepts', Presentation at *Improving Patient safety: From Rhetoric to Reality*, Johns Hopkins University Conference: Baltimore, Maryland, 28 May.

Sexton, J.B. (2002), 'A Matter of Life or Death: Social Psychological and Organizational Factors Related to Patient Outcomes in the Intensive Care Unit', unpublished doctoral dissertation, The University of Texas at Austin.

Sexton, J.B. (2003), 'What is the Climate like Now?' Presentation at the Institute for Healthcare Improvement Spring Learning Session, Boston, MA, 19 June.

Sexton, J.B., Helmreich, R.L., Wilhelm, J.A., Merritt, A.C. and Klinect, J.R. (2001), *The Flight Management Attitudes Safety Survey (FMASS): The University of Texas Human Factors Research Project Technical Report, 01-01*, The University of Texas at Austin: Austin, TX.

Sexton, J.B. and Klinect, J.R. (2001), 'The Link between Safety Attitudes and Observed Performance in Flight Operations', *Proceedings of the Eleventh International Symposium on Aviation Psychology*, The Ohio State University: Columbus, OH.

Sexton, J.B., Thomas, E.J. and Helmreich, R.L. (2000), 'Error, Stress, and Teamwork in Medicine and Aviation: Cross Sectional Surveys', *BMJ*, Vol. 320, pp.745-749.

Shortell, S.M., Denise, M., Rouseau, D.M., Gillies, R.R., Devers, K.J. and Simons, T.L. (1991), 'Organizational Assessment in Intensive Care Units (ICUs): Construct Development, Reliability, and Validity of the ICU Nurse-Physician Questionnaire', *Medical Care*, Vol. 29, No. 8, pp.709-723.

Shteynberg, G., Sexton, J.B. and Helmreich, R.L. (2002), 'ICU Safety: A Taxonomy of Healthcare Provider Recommendations for Patient Safety Improvements', *Hot Topic Presentation to the 2002 American Psychological Society*, New Orleans, Louisiana, 09 June.

Thomas, E.J., Sexton, J.B. and Helmreich, R.L. (2003), 'Discrepant Attitudes about Teamwork among Critical Care Nurses and Physicians', *Crit Care Med*, Vol.31, Nr. 3.

Thomas, E.J., Sexton, J.B. and Helmreich, R.L. (under review), 'Translating Teamwork Behaviors from Aviation to Healthcare: Development of The University of Texas Behavioral Markers for Neonatal Resuscitation', *Quality and Safety in Healthcare Quarterly*.

Uhlig, P.N., Haan, C.K., Nason, A.K., Niemann, P.L., Camelio, A. and Brown, J. (2001), 'Improving Patient Care by the Application of Theory and Practice from the Aviation Safety Community', *Proceedings of the Eleventh International Symposium on Aviation Psychology*, The Ohio State University: Columbus, OH.

Vincent, C.A., Taylor-Adams, S. and Stanhope, N. (1998) 'Framework for Analyzing Risk and Safety in Clinical Medicine', *British Medical Journal;* Vol. 316, pp.1154-1157.

Chapter 2: Behavioral Markers in Analyzing Team Performance of Cockpit Crews

Avermaete, J. & Kruijsen, E. (eds.) (1998), 'NOTECHS. The Evaluation of Non-technical Skills of Multi-pilot Aircrew in Relation to the JAR-FCL Requirements', *Final Report NLR-CR-98443*, Amsterdam National Aerospace Laboratory (NLR): Amsterdam.

Ajzen, I. & Fishbein, M. (1980), *Understanding Attitudes and Predicting Social Behaviour*, Prentice-Hall: Englewood Cliffs, NJ.

Brannick, M.T., Prince, A., Prince, C. & Salas, E. (1995), 'The Measurement of Team Process', *Human Factors,*Vol. 37, No. 3, pp.641-651.

Caldwell, B.S. (1997), 'Components of Information Flow to Support Coordinated Task Performance', *International Journal of Cognitive Ergonomics,* Vol.1, No. 1, pp.25-41.

Campbell, D.T. & Fiske, D.W. (1959), 'Convergent and Discriminant Validation by the Multitrait-multimethod Matrix', *Psychological Bulletin,* Vol.56, pp.81-105.

Eggemeier, F.T. (1988), 'Properties of Workload Assessment Techniques', in P.A. Hancock & N. Meshkati (eds.), *Human Mental Workload*, North-Holland Publishers: Amsterdam, pp.41-62.

Hart, S.G. & Staveland, L.E. (1988), 'Development of NASA-TLX (Task Load indeX): Results of Empirical and Theoretical Research', in P.A. Hancock & N. Meshkati (eds.), *Human Mental Workload,* Elsevier: Amsterdam, pp.139-183.

James, L.R., Demaree, R.G. & Wolfe, G. (1984), 'Estimating Within-group Interrater reliability with and without Response Bias', *Journal of Applied Psychology*, Vol. 69, pp.85-98.

James, L.R., Demaree, R.G. & Wolfe, G. (1993), 'An Assessment of Within-group Interrater Agreement', *Journal of Applied Psychology*, Vol. 78, pp.306-309.

Klampfer, B., Flin, R., Helmreich, R.L., Haeusler, R., Sexton, B., Fletcher, G., Field, P., Staender, S., Lauche, K., Dicckmann, P. & Amacher, A. (2001), *Enhancing Performance in High Risk Environments: Recommendations for the Use of Behavioural Markers* [Brochure], Gottlieb Daimler- und Karl Benz Stiftung, Collegium 'Group Interaction in High Risk Environments': Berlin, Germany.

Klampfer, B., Haeusler, R. & Naef, W. (in press), 'CRM Behavior and Team Performance Under High Workload: Outline and Implications of a Simulator Study', in P. Pfister (ed.), *Innovation and Consolidation in Aviation*.

Klinect, J.R., Wilhelm, J.A. & Helmreich, R.L. (1999), 'Threat and Error Management: Data from Line Operations Safety Audits', in *Proceedings of the Tenth International Symposium on Aviation Psychology*, The Ohio State University: Columbus, OH, pp.683-688.

Nygren, T.E. (1991), 'Psychometric Properties of Subjective Workload Measurement Techniques: Implications for Their Use in the Assessment of Perceived Mental Workload', *Human Factors*, Vol. 33, No.1, pp.17-33.

Prince, A., Brannick, M.T., Prince, C. & Salas, E. (1997), 'The Measurement of Team Process Behaviors in the Cockpit: Lessons Learned', in M.T. Brannick, E. Salas & C. Prince (eds.), *Team Performance Assessment and Measurement. Theory, Methods, and Applications*, Lawrence Erlbaum Associates: Mahwah, NJ, pp.289-310.

Svensson, E.A.I. & Wilson, G.F. (2002), 'Psychological and Psychophysiological Models of Pilot Performance for System Development and Mission Evaluation', *The International Journal of Aviation Psychology*, Vol. 12, No. 1, pp.95-110.

Wickens, C.D. (1992), *Engineering Psychology and Human Performance* (2nd ed.), Harper Collins: New York.

Wierwille, W.W. & Eggemeier, F.T. (1993), 'Recommendations for Mental Workload Measurement in a Test and Evaluation Environment', *Human Factors*, Vol. 35, No. 2, pp.263-281.

Yerkes, R.M. & Dodson, J.D. (1908). 'The Relation of Strength of Stimulus to Rapidity of Habit-formation', *Journal of Comparative Neurology of Psychology*, Vol. 18, pp. 459-482.

Chapter 3: The Effects of Different Forms of Co-ordination on Coping with Workload

Avermate van, J.A.G. & Kruijsen, E.A.C. (eds.) (1998), *NOTECHS The Evaluation of Non-technical Skills of Multipilot Aircrew in Relation to the JAR-FCL Requirements. Final Report*.

Bowers, C., A., Braun, C., C. and Morgan Ben, B. (1997), 'Team Workload: Its Meaning and Measurement', in Brannick, M.T., Salas, E. and Prince C. (eds.), *Team Performance Assessment and Measurement. Theory, Methods and Applications*, LEA: Mahwah, New Jersey, London, pp.85-108.

Clark, H.H. (1996), *Using Language*, Cambridge University Press: Cambridge.

Goguen, J.A., and Linde, C. (1983), *Linguistic Methodology for the Analysis of Aviation Accidents. Technical Report, Structural Semantics*, NASA Contractor Report 3741, Nasa Ames Research Center, National Aeronautics and Space Administration: Palo Alto, California.

Grommes, P. (in preparation), *Prinzipien kohärenter Kommunikation*, Dissertation, Humboldt-Universität zu Berlin: Berlin, Germany.

Grommes, P. and Dietrich, R. (2002), 'Coherence in Operating Room Team and Cockpit Communication. A Psycholinguistic Contribution to Applied Linguistics' in Alatis, J.E., Hamilton, H.E. and Ai-Hui Tan (eds.), *Georgetown University Round Table on Languages and Linguistics 2000 – Linguistics, Language, and the Professions: Education, Journalism, Law, Medicine, and Technology*, Georgetown University Press: Georgetown, pp.190-219.

Grote, G. (1997), *Autonomie und Kontrolle - Zur Gestaltung automatisierter und risikoreicher Systeme*, vdf Hochschulverlag: Zürich.

Grote, G., Zala-Mezö, E. & Grommes, P. (2003), 'Effects of Standardization on Coordination and Communication in High Workload Situations', *Linguistische Berichte*, Sonderheft 12, pp.127-155.

Hale, A. R. and Swuste, P. (1998), 'Safety Rules: Procedural Freedom or Action Constraint?', *Safety Science*, Vol. 29, pp.163-177.

Helmreich, R.L., Wilhelm, J.A., Klinect, J.R. and Merritt, A.C. (1999) 'Culture, Error and Crew Resource Management', in: Salas, E., Bowers, C.A. and Edens, E. (eds.), *Applying Resource Management in Organizations: A Guide for Professionals*. Erlbaum: Hillsdale, NJ.

Kanki, B.G. and Palmer, M.T. (1993), 'Communication and Crew Resource Management', in Wiener, E.L., Kanki, B. and Helmreich, R.L. (eds.), *Cockpit Resource Management*, Academic Press: San Diego.

Kerr, S. and Jermier, J.M. (1978), 'Substitutes for Leadership: Their Meaning and Measurement', *Organizational Behavior and Human Performance*, Vol. 22, pp.375-403.

Kieser, A. and Kubicek, H. (1992), *Organisation*, de Gruyter: Berlin.

Leplat, J. (1998), 'About Implementation of Safety Rules', *Safety Science*, Vol. 29, pp.189-204.

Levelt, W.J.M. (1989), *Speaking. From Intention to Articulation*, MIT Press: Cambridge, Massachusetts.

Matieu, J.E., Heffner, T.S., Goodwin, G.F., Salas, E. and Cannon-Bowers, J. (2000), 'The Influence of Shared Mental Models on Team Process and Performance', *Journal of Applied Psychology*, Vol. 85, No. 2, pp.273-283.

Norman, D.A. and Bobrow, D.G. (1975), 'On Data-limited and Resource-limited Processes', *Cognitive Psychology*, Vol. 7, pp.44-64.

Orasanu, J.M. (1993), 'Decision-making in the Cockpit', in Wiener, E.L., Kanki B. and Helmreich, R.L. (eds.), *Cockpit Resource Management*, Academic Press: San Diego, pp.137-172.

Perrow, C. (1984), *Normal Accidents. Living with High-risk Technologies*, Basic Books: New York.

Rasmussen, J. (1997), 'Risk Management in a Dynamic Society: A Modelling Problem', *Safety Science*, Vol. 27, pp.183-213.

Salas, E., Dickinson, T.L., Converse, S.A. and Tannenbaum, S.,I. (1992), 'Toward an Understanding of Team Performance and Training', in Swezey, R.W. and Salas, E. (eds.), *Teams: Their Training and Performance*, Ablex Publishing: Norwood, NJ, pp.3-29.

Serfaty, D., Entin, E.E. and Johnston, J.H. (1998), 'Team Coordination Training', in Cannan-Bowers, J.A. and Salas, E. (eds.), *Making Decisions under Stress*, American Psychological Association: Washington, pp.221-245.

Stutterheim, C. von (1997), *Einige Prinzipien des Textaufbaus. Empirische Untersuchungen zur Produktion mündlicher Texte*, Niemeyer: Tübingen.

Stutterheim, C. von and Klein, W. (1989), 'Textstructure and Referential Movement', in Dietrich, R. and Graumann, C.F. (eds.), *Language Processing in Social Context*, North Holland: Amsterdam, pp.39-76.

Thompson, J.D. (1967), *Organizations in Action*, McGraw-Hill: New York.

Van de Ven, A.H., Delbecq, A. L., and Koenig, R. (1976), 'Determinants of Coordination Modes within Organizations' *American Sociological Review*, Vol. 41, pp.322-338.

Weick, K.E. and Roberts, K.H. (1993), 'Collective Mind in Organizations: Heedful Interrelating on Flight Decks', *Administrative Science Quarterly*, Vol. 38, pp.357-381.

Zaccaro, S.J., Rittman, A.L., and Marks, M.A. (2001), 'Team Leadership', *The Leadership Quarterly*, Vol. 12, pp.451-483.

Chapter 4: Communication in Nuclear Power Plants

Bassing, G. (1999), 'Zur Praxis des betreibereinheitlichen VGB-Human Factors Systems im Kernkraftwerk Phillipsburg', Jahrestagung Kerntechnik des Deutschen Atomforums, Karlsruhe, Deutschen Atomforum: Bonn.

Drøivoldsmo, A., Skraaning, G. Jr., Sverrbo, M., Dalen, J., Grimstad, T. and Andresen, G. (1998), 'Continuous Measures of Situation Awareness and Workload', *OECD Halden Reactor Project*, HWR-539.

Eisgruber, H. and Janssen, G. (1999), 'VGB Human Factors System: HF-Maßnahmen der Kernkraftwerksbetreiber zur Optimierung der Mensch-Machine Schnittstelle', *BFS KT-22/99*, BFS: Salzgitter.

Fleishman, E.A. and Buffardi, L.C. (1999), 'Predicting Human Error Probabilities from the Ability Requirements of Jobs in Nuclear Power Plants' in Misumi, J., Wilpert, B. and Miller, R. (eds.), *Nuclear Safety: A Human Factors Perspective*, Taylor & Francis: London, pp.221-241.

Folleso, K., Drøivoldsmo, A., Kaarstad, M., Collier, S. and Kirwan, B. (1995), 'Human Error – The Third Pilot Study', *OECD Halden Reactor Project*, HWR-430.

Fukuda, R., Voggenberger T., Sträter, O. and Bubb, H. (2003), 'Measuring the Quality of Group Interaction in Nuclear Power Plant Environments by using Eye Movement Behavior', IEA 2003: Korea.

Fukuda, R. and Voggenberger, T. (in press), 'Analysis of Group Interaction in High Risk Environments using a Task Oriented Eye Tracking Approach', GRS final report on the GIHRE project, GRS: Cologne.

Furuta, K. and Kondo, S. (1993), 'An Approach to Assessment of Plant Man-machine Systems by Computer Simulation of an Operator's Cognitive Behavior', *International Journal of Man-Machine Studies*, Vol. 39, pp.473-493.

Guerlain, S. and Bullemer, P. (1996), 'User-Initiated Notification: A Concept for Aiding the Monitoring Activities of Process Control Operators', *Proceedings of the Human Factors and Ergonomics Society 42nd Annual Meeting*, pp.283-287.

Hansen, J.P. (1991), 'The Use of Eye Mark Recordings to Support Verbal Retrospection in Software Testing', *Acta Psychologica*, Vol. 76, pp.31-49.

Hauland, G. (1996), 'Building a Methodology for Studying Cognition in Process Control: A Semantic Analysis of Visual and Verbal Behavior', unpublished master's thesis, Norwegian University of Science and Technology (NTNU), Department of Psychology: Trondheim.

Hyöna, J., Tommola, J. and Alaja, A.M. (1995), 'Pupil Dilation as a Measure of Processing Load in Simultaneous Interpretation an Other Language Tasks', *The Quarterly Journal of Experimental Psychology*, Vol. 48A(3), pp.598-612.

IAEA/NEA (1998), *IAEA/NEA Incident reporting System (IRS) Reporting guidelines – Feedback from Safety Related Operating Experience from Nuclear Power Plants*, IAEA: Vienna.

Kaarstad, M., Follesoe, K., Collier, S., Hauland, G. and Kirwan, B. (1994), 'Human Error – The Second Pilot Study', *OECD Halden Reactor Project*, HWR-421.

Kirwan, B., Kaarstad, M., Hauland, G. and Follesoe, K. (1995), 'See No Evil, Hear No Evil, Speak No Evil: Verbal Protocol Analysis, Eye Movement Analysis, and Nuclear Power Plant Diagnosis', in Robertson, S.A. (ed.), *Contemporary Ergonomics 1995*, Taylor & Francis: London, pp.249-254.

Low, I. (2003), *Assessment of the Impact on Mental Workload from Advanced Air Traffic Management Systems: A Diagnostic Tool*, IEA 2003: Seoul/Korea.

Mumaw, R.J., Roth, E.M., Vicente, K.J. and Burns, C.M. (2000), 'There is More to Monitoring a Nuclear Power Plant than Meets the Eye', *Human Factors*, Vol. 42, No.1, pp.36-55.

Neisser, U. (1976), *Cognition and Reality*, W.H. Freeman: San Francisco.

Rasmussen, J. (1986), *Information Processing and Human-machine Interaction*, North-Holland: New York.

Rößger, P., Rötting, M. and Unema, P. (1993), 'Experimentelle Untersuchung zum Einfluß von Leuchtdichteveränderungen und mentaler Beanspruchung auf den Pupillendurchmesser', *Zeitschrift für Arbeitswissenschaft*, Vol. 47 No. 19, pp.141-147.

Roth, E.M., Lin, L., Thomas, V.M., Kerch, S., Kenney, S.J. and Sugibayashi, N. (1998), 'Supporting Situation Awareness of Individuals and Teams using Group View Displays', *Proceedings of the Human Factors and Ergonomics Society 42nd Annual Meeting*, pp.244-248.

Sassen, J.M.A., Buiel, E.F.T. and Hoegee, J.H. (1994), 'A Laboratory Evaluation of a Human Operator Support System', *International Journal of Human-Computer Studies*, Vol. 40, pp.895-931.

Sträter, O. (1997), 'Beurteilung der menschlichen Zuverlässigkeit auf der Basis von Betriebserfahrung', *GRS-138*, GRS: Köln.

Sträter, O. (2002), 'Group Interaction in High Risk Environments – Communication in NPP', *GRS Report*, No. A-302, GRS: Cologne.

Sträter, O. (2003), 'Investigation of Communication Errors in Nuclear Power Plants', *Linguistische Berichte*, Special Edition 12, Helmut Buske Verlag: Hamburg.

Sträter, O. and Bubb, H. (1999), 'Assessment of Human Reliability Based on Evaluation of Plant Experience: Requirements and Implementation', *Reliability Engineering & System Safety*, Vol. 63, pp.199-219.

Sträter, O. and Bubb, H. (2003), 'Design of Systems in Settings with Remote Access to Cognitive Performance', in Hollnagel, E. (ed.), *Handbook of Cognitive Task Design*, Erlbaum: New Jersey, p. 333ff.

Takano, K., Sunaoshi, W. and Suzuki, K. (2000), 'Total Simulation of Operator Team Behavior in Emergencies at Nuclear Power Plants', *Aviation, Space, and Environmental Medicine*, Vol. 71, No. 9, Section II, pp. A140-A144.

Van Orden, K.F., Limbert, W., Makeig, S. and Jung, T.P. (2001), 'Eye Activity Correlates of Workload During a Visuospatial Memory Task', *Human Factors*, Vol. 43, No. 1, pp.111-121.

Vicente, K.J., Mumaw, R.J. and Roth, E.M. (1998), 'More About Operator Monitoring under Normal Operations: The Role of Workload Regulation and the Impact of Control Room Technology', *Proceedings of the Human Factors and Ergonomics Society 42nd Annual Meeting*, pp.229-233.

Vicente, K.J., Roth, E.M. and Mumaw, R.J. (2001), 'How do Operators Monitor a Complex, Dynamic Work Domain? The Impact of Control Room Technology', *International Journal of Human-Computer Studies*, Vol. 54, pp.831-856.

Yarbus, A.L. (1967), 'Eye Movements and Vision', Plenum Press: New York.

Chapter 5: Linguistic Factors

Chidester, T.R., Kanki, G.G., Foushee, H.C., Dickinson, C.L. and Bowles, S.V. (1990), 'Personality Factors in Flight Operations. Volume 1. Leader Characteristics and Crew Performance in a Full-mission Air Transport Simulation' (NASA Technical Memorandum 102259), NASA-Ames Research Center: Moffett Field, CA.

Cushing, S. (1994), *Fatal words: Communication Clashes and Aircraft Crashes*, University of Chicago Press: Chicago.

Diegritz, T. and Fürst, V. (1999), *Empirische Sprechhandlungsforschung. Ansätze zur Analyse und Typisierung authentischer Äußerungen*, Universität Bilbiothek: Erlangen.

Fischer, U. and Orasanu, J. (1999), 'Say it Again, Sam! Effective Communication Strategies to Mitigate Communication Errors', *Proceedings of the 10th International Symposium on Aviation Psychology:* Columbus, Ohio.

Grommes, P. and Dietrich, R. (2000), 'Coherence in Operating Room Team and Cockpit Communication: A Psycholinguistic Contribution to Applied Linguistics', *Round Table on Languages and Linguistics*, Georgetown University: Georgetown.

Helmreich, R.L. (1997), 'Managing Human Error in Aviation', *Scientific American*, May, pp.62-97.

Hutchby, I. and Wooffitt, R. (1998), *Conversation Analysis*, Polity Press: Cambridge.

Krifka, M., Martens, S. and Schwarz, F. (2004), 'Group Interaction in the Cockpit: Some Linguistic Factors', *Linguistische Berichte*, Vol. 12.

Linde, C. (1988), 'The Quantitative Study of Communicative Success: Politeness and Accidents in Aviation Discourse', *Language in Society*, Vol. 17.3, pp.375-399.

Nevile, M. (2001), 'Knowing Who's Who in the Airline Cockpit: Pilot's Pronominal Choices and Cockpit Roles', in McHoul, A. and. Rapley, M. (eds.), *How to Analyze Talk in Institutional Settings. A Casebook of Methods*, Continuum: London and New York.

Orasanu, J. and Fischer, U. (1992), 'Distributed Cognition in the Cockpit. Linguistic Control of Shared Problem Solving', in *Proceedings of the Fourteenth Annual Conference of the Cognitive Science Society*, Erlbaum: Hillsdale, NJ, pp.189-194.

Sacks, H. (1992), *Lectures on Conversation*, Basil Blackwell: Oxford.

Sbisà, Marina (2001), 'Illocutionary Force and Degrees of Strength in Language Use', *Journal of Pragmatics*, Vol. 33, pp.1791-1814.

Searle, J. (1968), *Speech Acts. An Essay in the Philosophy of Language*, Cambridge University Press: Cambridge.

Searle, J. (1975), 'A Classification of Illocutionary Acts', *Language in Society*, Press: Location.

Selting, M., e.a. (1998), 'Gesprächsanalytisches Transkriptionssystem' *Linguistische Berichte*, Vol. 173, pp.91-122.

Sexton, J.B. and Helmreich, R.L. (2000), 'Analyzing Cockpit Communication. The Links Between Language, Performance, Error, and Workload', *Human Performance in Extreme Environments*, Vol. 5, pp.63-68.

Silberstein, D. (2001), 'Final Report of the Subproject "Initiating Crew Resources under High Cognitive Work Load"', Humboldt University: Berlin.

Vanderveken, D. (1990), *Meaning and Speech Acts*. Vol. 1: *Principles of Language Use*. Vol. 2: *Formal Semantics of Success and Satisfaction*, Cambridge University Press: MA.

Wiener, E., Kanki, B. and Helmreich R.L. (eds.) (1993), *Cockpit Resource Management*, Academic Press: San Diego, CA.

Chapter 6: Language Processing

Blackwell, A. and Bates, E. (1995), 'Inducing Agrammatic Profiles in Normals: Evidence for the Selective Vulnerability of Morphology under Cognitive Resource Limitation', *Journal of Cognitive Neuroscience*, Vol. 7.2, pp.228-257.

Clark, H. (1996), *Using Language*, Cambridge University Press: Cambridge.

Cushing, S. (1994), *Fatal words: Communication Clashes and Aircraft Crashes*, University of Chicago Press: Chicago and London.

Davis, D. (2002), 'Case Studies of Command. Fire Commander', in Flyn, R. and Arbuthnot, K. (eds.), *Incident Command: Tales from the Hot Seat*, Ashgate: Aldershot, pp.88-104.

Dietrich, R. (ed.) (2003), 'Communication in High Risk Environments', *Linguistische Berichte*, Special Issue 12, Helmut Buske Verlag: Hamburg.

Foushee, H.C. and Manos, K. (1981), 'Information Transfer within the Cockpit: Problems in Intro-cockpit Communictations', in Billings, C.E. and Cheaney, E.S. (eds.), *Information Transfer Problems in the Aviation System*, NASA Technical Paper 1875, NASA-Ames Research Center: Moffettfield, CA.

Grommes, P. and Dietrich, R. (2002), 'Coherence in Operating Room Team and Cockpit Communication: A Psycholinguistic Contribution to Psycholinguistics', *Roundtable on Languages and Linguistics 2000*, Georgetown University Press: Washington, D.C., pp.190-219.

Helmreich, R.L. (2000), 'On Error Management: Lessons from Aviation', in *British Medical Journal*, Vol. 320, 18 March, pp.781-785.

Helmreich, R.L. and Foushee, H.C. (1993), 'Why Crew Resource Management? Empirical and Theoretical Bases of Human Factors Training in Aviation', in Wiener, E.L., Kanki, B.G. and Helmreich, R.L. (eds), *Cockpit Resource Management*, Academic Press: San Diego, pp.3-45.

Helmreich, R.L. and Schaefer, H.G. (1994), 'Team Performance in the Operating Room', in Bogner, M.S. (ed.), *Human Error in Medicine*, Lawrence Erlbaum: Hillsdale, New Jersey, pp.225-253.

Howard, S.K., Gaba, D.M., Fish, K.J. et al. (1992), 'Anesthesia Crisis Resource Management. Teaching Anesthesiologists to Handle Critical Incidents', *Aviation, Space, and Environmental Medicine*, Vol. 63, No. 9, pp.763-770.

Kanki, B.G. and Palmer, M.T. (1993), 'Communication and Crew Resource Management. Cockpit Resource Management', in Wiener, E.L., Kanki, B.G. and Helmreich, R.L (eds.), *Cockpit Resource Management*, Academic Press: San Diego, CA, pp.98-135.

Kanki, B.G, Palmer M.T. and Veinott, E. (1991), 'Communication Variations Related to Leader Personality', *Proceedings of the Sixth International Symposium on Aviation Psychology*, Ohio State University: Columbus, Ohio, pp.253-259.

Krifka, M., Martens, S. and Schwarz, F. (2003), 'Group Interaction in the Cockpit: Some Linguistic Factors', in Dietrich, R (ed.), *Communication in High Risk Environments Linguistische Berichte*, Special Issue 12, Helnur Buske Verlag: Hamburg, pp.75-101.

Pashler, H. and Johnston, J.C. (1998), 'Attentional Limitations in Dual Task Performance', in Pashler, H. (ed.) *Attention*, Psychology Press: Hove, pp.150-190.

Sexton, J.B. and Helmreich, R.L (1999), 'Analyzing Cockpit Communication: The Links Between Language, Performance, Error and Work Load', in *Proceedings of the Tenth International Symposium of Aviation Psychology*, Ohio State University: Columbus, Ohio, pp.689-695.

Chapter 7: Task Load and the Microstructure of Cognition

De Sanctis, P.-F. (2002), 'Informationsübertragung bei eindimensionalen Reizen: Eine Überprüfung des asynchron-diskreten Kodierungsmodells', unpublished dissertation, Humboldt-University: Berlin, Germany.

Hohlfeld, A., Mierke, K. and Sommer, W. (in press a), 'Is Word Perception in a Second-Language more Vulnerable than in One's Native Language? Evidence from Brain Potentials in a Dual Task Setting', *Brain & Language*.

Hohlfeld, A., Sangals, J., and Sommer, W. (in press b), 'Effects of Additional Tasks on Language Perception: An ERP Investigation', *Journal of Experimental Psychology: Learning, Memory, & Cognition*.

Kutas, M. and Van Petten, C.K. (1994), 'Psycholinguistics Electrified: Event-related Brain Potential Investigations', in Gernsbacher, M.A. (ed.), *Handbook of Psycholinguistics*, Academic Press: San Diego, pp.83-144.

Leuthold, H., Sommer, W. and Ulrich, R. (1996), 'Partial Advance Information and Response Preparation: Inferences from the Lateralized Readiness Potential', *Journal of Experimental Psychology-General*, Vol. 125, pp.307-323.

Meyer, D.E., Osman, A.M., Irwin, D.E. and Yantis, S. (1988), 'Modern Mental Chronometry', *Biological Psychology*, Vol. 26, pp.3-67.

Osman, A., Loub, L., Müller-Gethmann, H., Rinkenauer, G., Mattes, S. and Ulrich, R. (2000), 'Mechanisms of Speed-accuracy Tradeoff: Evidence from Covert Motor Processes', *Biological Psychology*, Vol. 51, pp.173-199.

Sangals, J., Sommer, W. and Leuthold, H. (2002), 'Influences of Presentation Mode and Time Pressure on the Utilisation of Advance Information in Response Preparation', *Acta Psychologica*, Vol. 109, pp.1-24.

Sommer, W., Ulrich, R., and Leuthold, H. (1996), 'Das Lateralisierte Bereitschaftspotential als psychophysiologischer Zugang bei der Untersuchung kognitiver Prozesse', *Psychologische Rundschau*, Vol. 47, pp.1-14.

Stürmer, B., Leuthold, H., Soetens, E., Schröter, H. and Sommer, W. (2002), 'Control Over Location-Based Response Activation in the Simon Task: Behavioral and Electrophysiological Evidence', *Journal of Experimental Psychology-Human Perception and Performance*, Vol. 28, pp.1345-1363.

Chapter 8: Setting the Stage: Characteristics of Organizations, Teams and Tasks Influencing Team Processes

Amalberti, R. (1999), 'Risk Management by Regulation', 19th Myron B. Laver International Postgraduate Course *Risk Management*, Dept. of Anaesthesia, University of Basel: Switzerland.

Cox, S. and Flin, R. (1998), 'Safety Culture: Philosopher's Stone or Man of Straw?', *Work and Stress*, Vol. 12, pp.189-201.

Crichton, M. and Flin, R. (1999), 'Training of Non-technical Skills for Emergency Management – UK Nuclear Power Industry Experience', Proceedings of the 2nd International Disaster and Emergency Readiness Conference, Andrich International: The Hague, NL, October.

Dedobbeleer, N. and Beland, F. (1991), 'A Safety Climate Measure for Construction Sites', *Journal of Safety Research*, Vol. 22, pp.97-103.

Dekker, S. (2003 a), 'Failure to Adapt or Adaptations that Fail: Contrasting Models on Procedures and Safety', *Applied Ergonomics*, Vol. 34, pp.233-238.

Dekker, S. (2003 b), 'Illusions of Explanation: A Critical Essay on Error Classification', *International Journal of Aviation Psychology*, Vol. 13: pp.95-106.

Emery, F.E. (1959), *Characteristics of Socio-technical Systems*, Tavistock: London, Document No. 527.

Federal Aviation Administration (1991), *Advanced Qualification Program. Advisory Circular AC120-34*: Washington, DC.

Glendon, A.I. and Stanton, N.A. (2000), 'Perspectives on Safety Culture', *Safety Science*, Vol. 34, pp.193-214.

Grote, G. (1997), Autonomie und Kontrolle - Zur Gestaltung automatisierter und risikoreicher Systeme, vdf Hochschulverlag: Zürich.

Grote, G. (2001), 'Planen in Organisationen: Forschungserfordernisse und – ansätze', in Silbereisen, R.K. and Reitzle, M. (eds.), *Psychologie 2000: Bericht über den 42. Kongress der Deutschen Gesellschaft für Psychologie*, Lengerich, Pabst: Jena, pp. 576-586.

Grote, G. and Künzler, C. (1996), 'Safety Culture and its Reflections in Job and Organizational Design: Total Safety Management', in Gheorghe, A.V. (ed.), *Integrated Regional Health and Environmental Risk Assessment and Safety Management. International Journal of Environment and Pollution*, Vol. 6, pp.618-631.

Grote, G. and Künzler, C. (2000), 'Diagnosis of Safety Culture in Safety Management Audits', *Safety Science*, Vol. 34, pp.131-150.

Grote, G., Ryser, C., Wäfler, T., Windischer, A. and Weik, S. (2000), 'KOMPASS: A Method for Complementary Function Allocation in Automated Work Systems', *International Journal of Human-Computer Studies*, Vol. 52, pp.267-287.

Hackman, R.J. and Morris, C.G. (1975), 'Group Tasks, Group Interaction Process, and and Group Performance Effectiveness: A Review and Proposed Integration', in Berkowitz, L. (ed.), *Advances in Experimental Social Psychology*, Academic Press: New York, pp.45-99.

Hale, A.R. and Swuste, P. (1998), 'Safety Rules: Procedural Freedom or Action Constraint?' *Safety Science*, Vol. 29, pp.163-177.

Helmreich, R.L. and Merritt, A.C. (1999), *Culture at Work in Aviation and Medicine: National, Organizational and Professional Influences*, Ashgate: London.

Helmreich, R.L., Klinect, J.R. and Wilhelm, J.A. (2001), 'System Safety and Threat and Error Management: The Line Operations Safety Audit (LOSA)', *Proceedings of the 11th International Symposium on Aviation Psychology*, The Ohio State University: Columbus, OH, pp.1-6.

Helmreich, R.L. and Musson, D.M. (2000), 'The University of Texas Threat and Error Management Model: Components and Examples', *British Medical Journal* [Online], http://www.bmj.com/misc/bmj.320.7237.781/sld001.htm.

Helmreich, R.L. and Sexton, J.B. (2004), 'Managing Threat and Error to Increase Safety in Medicince' in Dietrich, R. and Jochum, K. (eds.), *Teaming Up: Components of Safety under High Risk*, Ashgate Publishing: Aldershot, pp.117-132.

Hofmann, David A. and Stetzer, A. (1996), 'A Cross-level Investigation of Factors Influencing Unsafe Behaviors and Accidents', *Personnel Psychology*, Vol. 49, pp.307-339.

Hofstede, G. (1990), *Culture's Consequences*, Sage: London.

Hollnagel, E. (1998), *Cognitive Reliability and Error Analysis Method - CREAM*, Elsevier: New York, Amsterdam.

Hopkins, A. and Hale, A. (2002), 'Issues in the Regulation of Safety: Setting the Scene', in Kirwan, B., Hale, A. and Hopkins, A. (eds.), *Changing Regulation – Controlling Risks in Society*, Pergamon: Amsterdam, pp.1-12.

IAEA (2001), *IRS Study on Incidents Caused by Loss Of Corporate Knowledge And Memory (Phase II - In depth analysis of selected events)*, IAEA-J4-CS-04/01, IAEA: Vienna.

INSAG (1991), *Safety Culture. Safety Series*, No. 75-INSAG-4, International Atomic Energy Agency: Vienna.

Kanse, L. and van der Schaaf, T. (2000), 'Recovery from Failures - Understanding the Positive Role of Human Operators during Incidents', in de Waard, D., Weikert, C., Hoonhout, J. and Ramaekers, J. (eds.), *Human System Interaction: Education, Research and Application in the 21st Century*, Maastricht, Shaker Publishing: Netherlands.

Kieser, A. and Kubicek, H. (1992), *Organisation*, de Gruyter: Berlin.

Klinect, J.R., Murray, P., Merrit, A. and Helmreich, R.L. (2003), 'Line Operations Safety Audit (LOSA): Definitions and Operating Characteristics', *Proceedings of the 12th International Symposium on Aviation Psychology*, The Ohio State University: Columbus, OH, pp.663-668.

LaPorte, T.R. and Consolini, P.M. (1991), 'Working in Practice but not in Theory: Theoretical Challenges of High-reliability Organizations', *Journal of Public Administration Research and Theory*, Vol. 1, pp.19-47.

Larsson, T.J. (2002), 'New Technologies and Work. Pulverization of Risk – Privatization of Trauma?', in Kirwan, B., Hale, A. and Hopkins, A. (eds.), *Changing Regulation – Controlling Risks in Society*, Pergamon: Amsterdam, pp.15-28.

Leplat, J. (1998), 'About Implementation of Safety Rules', *Safety Science*, Vol. 29, pp.189-204.

Neal, A., Griffin, M.A. and Hart, P.M. (2000), 'The Impact of Organizational Climate on Safety Climate and Individual Behavior', *Safety Science*, Vol. 34, pp.99-109.

Niskannen, T. (1994), 'Assessing the Safety Environment in the Work Organization of Road Maintenance Jobs', *Accident Analysis and Prevention*, Vol. 26, pp.27-39.

NUREG-1624 (2000), *Technical Basis and Implementation Guidelines for A Technique for Human Event Analysis (ATHEANA), Rev. 1*, NRC: Washington DC.

Pasmore, W., Francis, C., Haldeman, J. and Shani, A. (1982), 'Sociotechnical Systems: A North American Reflection on Empirical Studies of the Seventies', *Human Relations*, Vol. 35, pp.1179-1204.

Perrow, C. (1984), *Normal Accidents. Living with High-risk Technologies*, Basic Books: New York.

Rasmussen, J. (1986), *Information Processing and Human-machine Interaction*, North-Holland: New-York.

Rasmussen, J. (1997), 'Risk Management in a Dynamic Society: A Modelling Problem', *Safety Science*, Vol. 27, pp.183-213.

Reason, J.T. (1990), *Human Error*, Cambridge University Press: Cambridge, U.K.

Reason, J.T. (1993), 'Managing the Management Risk: New Approaches to Organisational Safety', in Wilpert, B. and Qvale, T. (eds.), *Reliability and Safety in Hazardous Work Systems*, Lawrence Erlbaum: Hove, pp.7-22.

Reason, J.T. (1997), *Managing the Risks of Organizational Accidents*, Ashgate Publishing: Aldershot, UK.

Reimann, T. and Norros, L. (2002), 'Regulatory Culture: Balancing the Different Demands of Regulatory Practice in the Nuclear Industry', in Kirwan, B., Hale, A. and Hopkins, A. (eds.), *Changing Regulation – Controlling Risks in Society*, Pergamon: Amsterdam, pp.175-192.

Roessingh, J. and Zon, R. (in press), *Measurement and Validation of the Influence of Automation on Teamworking*, Eurocontrol: Brussels.

Schein, E.H. (1992), *Organizational Culture and Leadership (2nd Ed)*, Jossey-Bass: San Francisco.

Schuler, H. (1995), (Hrsg.) Lehrbuch Organisationspsychologie, Huber: Bern.

Sexton, J.B. and Klinect, J.R. (2001), 'The Link Between Safety Attitudes and Observed Performance in Flight Operations' in *Proceedings of the Eleventh International Symposium on Aviation Psychology*, The Ohio State University: Columbus, OH.

Shorrock, S. and Sträter, O. (in press), *Managing System Disturbances in ATM: Background and Contextual Framework*, Eurocontrol: Brussels.

Sträter, O. (2000), *Evaluation of Human Reliability on the Basis of Operational Experience. GRS-170*, GRS: Köln/Germany (ISBN 3-931995-37-2), www.grs.de/grs170.htm

Sträter, O. (2002), 'Group Interaction in High Risk Environments – Communication in NPP', *GRS Report*, No. A-3020, GRS: Cologne.

Sträter, O. (in press), 'Zuverlässigkeit menschlicher Handlungen und Systemgestaltung' in Zimolong, B. and Konradt, U. (eds.), *Ingenieurspsychologie. Enzyklopädie der Psychologie*, Hogrefe: Göttingen.

Suchman, L.A. (1987), *Plans and Situated Actions: The Problem of Human-machine Communication*, Cambridge University Press: Cambridge.

Susman, G.I. (1976), *Autonomy at Work. A Sociotechnical Analysis of Participative Management*, Praeger: New York.

Trist, E.L., Susman, G. and Brown, G.R. (1977), 'An Experiment in Autonomous Working in an American Underground Coal Mine', *Human Relations*, Vol. 30, pp.201-236.

Ulich, E. (1994), *Arbeitspsychologie (3rd Ed)*, Zürich: Verlag der Fachvereine, Poeschel: Stuttgart.

Vermersch, P. (1985), 'Données d'observation sur l'utilisation d'une consigne écrite: L'atomisation de l'action', *Le Travail Humain*, Vol. 48, pp.161-172.

VGB (1998), *Human Factors Benutzerleitfaden*, put together by RWE Energie AG on behalf of the VGB, RWE: Essen.

Weick, K.E. (1987), 'Organizational Culture as a Source of High Reliability', *California Management Review*, Vol. 29, pp.112-127.

Woods, D.D. and Shattuck, L.G. (2000), 'Distant Supervision-local Action given the Potential for Surprise', *Cognition, Technology & Work*, Vol. 2, pp.242-245.

Zohar, D. (1980), 'Safety Climate in Industrial Organizations: Theoretical and Applied Implications', *Journal of Applied Psychology*, Vol. 12, pp.78-85.

Chapter 9: Structural Features of Language and Language Use

Baker, C.L. (1999), 'The Quality of Medical Textbooks: Bladder Cancer Diagnosis as a Case Study', *The Journal of Urology* Vol. 161, pp.223-229.

Beaver, D. (1997), 'Presupposition', in Benthem, J. van and Meulen, A. ter (eds.), *Handbook of Logic and Language* MIT Press: Elsevier and Cambridge, MA, pp.939-108.

Beaver, D. (2003), 'The Optimization of Discourse Anaphora', *Linguistics & Philosophy* Vol. 26.

Bergmann, J. (1994), 'Ethnomethodologische Konversationsanalyse', in Fritz, Gerd and Hundsnurscher, Franz (eds.), *Handbuch der Dialoganalyse*, Niemeyer: Tübingen, pp.3-16.

Blum-Kulka, S., House, J. and Kasper, G. (1989) (eds.), *Cross-cultural Pragmatics: Requests and Apologies,* Ablex, Norwood, NJ.

Brown, P. and Levinson, S.C. (1987), *Politeness: Some Universals in Language Usage*, Cambridge UP: Cambridge.

Cannon-Bowers, J.A., Salas E. and Converse, S. (1993), 'Shared Mental Models in Expert Team Decision Making', in Castellan Jr., N. J. (ed.), *Individual and Group Decision Making: Current Issues*, Lawrence Erlbaum: Hillsdale, NJ, pp.221-246.

Dien, Y. (1998), 'Safety and Application of Procedures, or How Do 'They' Have to Use Operating Procedures in Nuclear Power Plants?', *Safety Science*, Vol. 29, No. 3, pp. 179-187.

Fischer, U. and Orasanu, J. (1999), *Cultural Diversity and Crew Communication*, www.lcc.gatech.edu/~fischer/

Fischer, U. (1999), *Cultural Variability in Crew Discourse*, http://www.lcc.gatech.edu/~fischer/communication-final.pdf

Garfinkel, H. (1967), *Studies in Ethnomethodology*, Englewood Cliffs: Prentice Hall.

Gass, S.M. and Neu, J. (1996) (eds.), *Speech Acts Across Cultures: Challenges to Communication in a Second Language*, Mouton de Gruyter: Berlin.

Geis, M.L. (1995), *Speech Acts and Conversational Interaction*, Cambridge University Press: Cambridge.

Groenendijk, J. and Stokhof, M. (1999), 'Dynamic Semantics', in Keil, F. (ed.), *The MIT Encyclopedia of the Cognitive Sciences*, MIT Press: Cambridge, MA.

Grommes, P. (2000), 'Contributing to Coherence. An Empirical Study of OR Team Communication' in Minnick-Fox (ed.), *Proceedings of the 24th Penn Linguistics Colloquium*, University of Pennsylvania Working Papers in Linguistics 7.1, pp.87-98.

Grommes, P. and Grote, C. (2001), 'Coordination in Action. Comparing Two Work Sitations with High vs. Low Degrees of Formalization', in Kühnlein, Newland and Rieser (eds.), *Proceedings of the Workshop on Coordination and Action*, ESSLLI Summer School: Helsinki.

Grosz, Joshi and Weinstein (1995), 'Centering. A Framework for Modeling the Local Coherence of Discourse', *Computational Linguistics* Vol. 21, pp.203-226.

International Atomic Energy Agency (IAEA) (1998), *Good Practices with Respect to the Development Plant Procedures*, IAEA-TECDOC-1058, International Atomic Energy Agency: Vienna.

Kamp, H. and Reyle, U. (1993), *From Discourse to Logic*, Dordrecht: Kluwer.

Krifka, M. (2002), 'Be Brief and Vague! And How Bidirectional Optimality Theory Allows for Verbosity and Precision', in Restle, D. (ed.), *Sounds and Systems: Studies in Structure and Change,* Mouton de Gruyter: Berlin, pp.439-485.

Krifka, M., Martins, S. and Schwarz, F. (2003), 'Group Interaction in the Cockpit: Some Linguistic Factors', *Linuistische Berichte*, Vol. 12.

Levinson, S. (1983), *Pragmatics*, Cambridge University Press: Cambridge, MA.

Levinson, S. (2000), *Presumptive Meanings*, MIT Press: Cambridge, MA.

Linde, C. (1988), 'The Quantitative Study of Communicative Success: Politeness and Accidents in Aviation Discourse', *Language in Society*, Vol. 17, pp.375-399.

Mann, W. and Thompson, S. (1988), 'Rhetorical Structure Theory. Towards a Theory of Text Organization', *Text*, Vol. 8, pp.243-281.

Matthews, E. (2003), 'Proposed ICAO Language Proficiency Requirements', Conference at *World Airline Training Conference and Tradeshow*.

Nevile, M. (2002), 'Coordinating Talk and Non-talk Activity in the Airline Cockpit', *Australian Review of Applied Linguistics*, Vol. 25, pp.131-146.

Orasanu, J. and Fischer, U. (1992), 'Distributed Cognition in the Cockpit: Linguistic Control of Shared Problem Solving', *Proceedings of the 14th Annual Conference of the Cognitive Science Society*, Erlbaum: Hillsdale, NJ, pp.189-194.

Pierrehumbert, J. and Hirschberg, J. (1990), 'The Meaning of Intonatinal Contours in the Interpretation of Discourse', in Cohen, P. (ed.), *Intentions in Communication*, MIT Press: Cambridge, MA, pp.271-311.

Roth, E.M., e.a. (1998), 'Supporting Situation Awareness of Individuals and Teams using Group View Displays', *Proceedings of the Human Factors and Ergonomics Society 42nd Annual Meeting*, pp.244-248.

Sacks, H. (1992), 'The Relating Power of Adjacency; Next Position', in Jefferson. G. (ed.) *Lectures on Conversation*, Vol. II, Blackwell: Oxford, pp.545-560.

Sacks, H., Schegloff, E.A. and Jefferson, G. (1978), 'A Simplest Systematics for the Organization of Turn-Taking for Conversation', in Schenkein, J. (ed.) *Studies in the Organization of Conversational Interaction*, Academic Press: New York, pp.7-55.

Schiffrin, D. (1988), *Discourse Markers*, Cambridge University Press: Cambridge.

Selting, M., (1998) (ed.), 'Gesprächsanalytisches Transkriptionssystem', *Linguistische Berichte*, Vol. 173, Cambridge, pp.91-122.

Sexton, J.B. and Helmreich, R.L. (2000), 'Analyzing Cockpit Communication. The Links Between Language, Performance, Error, and Workload', *Human Performance in Extreme Environments*, Vol. 5, pp.63-68.

Sibas, M. (2001), 'Illocutionary Force and Degrees of Strength in Language Use', *Journal of Pragmatics*, Vol. 33, pp.1791-1814.

Taylor, T.J. and Cameron, D. (1987), *Analysing Conversation: Rules and Units in the Structure of Talk*, Pergamon Press: Oxford.

Van der Sandt, R. (1988), *Context and Presupposition*, Croom Helm: London.

van Rooy, R. (2003), 'Being Polite is a Handicap: Towards a Game Theoretical Analysis of Polite Linguistic Behavior', in Tennenholtz, M. (ed.), *Proceedings of TARK 9*.

von Stutterheim, C. and Klein, W. (1989), 'Text Structure and Referential Movement', in Dietrich, R. & Graumann, C.F. (eds.), *Language Processing in Social Context*. Elsevier Science Publisher: Amsterdam, pp.39-76.

Wierzbicka, A. (1991), *Cross-cultural Pragmatics. The Semantics of Human Interaction*, Mouton de Gruyter: Berlin.

Zahavi, A. and Zahavi, A. (1997), *The Handicap Principle*, Oxford University Press: Massachusetts.

Zipf, P. (1949), *Human Behavior and the Principle of Least Effort*, Addison Wesley: Cambridge, MA.

Chapter 10: Leadership and Co-ordination

Ayman, R. and Chemers, M.M. (1983), 'Relationship of Supervisory Behavior Ratings to Work Group Effectiveness and Subordinate Satisfaction among Iranian Managers', *Journal of Applied Psychology,* Vol. 68, pp.338-341.

Bcach, E.L. (1946), *Submarine: A Personal Account of War Beneath the Sea*, Holt, Rinehart and Winston: Canada.

Bond, M.H. and Hwang, K.K. (1986), 'The Social Psychology of Chinese People', in Bond, M.H. (ed.), *The Psychology of the Chinese People*, Oxford University Press: Hong Kong.

Brannick, M.T. and Prince, C. (1997), 'An Overview of Team Performance Measurement', in Brannick, M., Salas, T.E., & Prince, C. Mahwah (eds.), *Team Performance Assessment and Measurement. Theory, Methods and Applications*, LEA: New Jersey, pp.3-16.

Chemers, M.M. (1993), 'An Integrative Theory of Leadership', in Chemmers, M.M. and Ayman, R. (eds.), *Leadership Theory and Research: Perspectives and Directions*, Academic Press: San Diego, California, pp.293-319.

Chemers, M.M. and Ayman, R. (1993), 'Directions for Leadership Research', in Chemmers, M.M. and Ayman, R. (eds.), *Leadership Theory and Research: Perspectives and Directions*, Academic Press: San Diego, California, pp.321-332.

Cooper, G.E., White, M.D. and Lauber, J.K. (1980) (eds.), *Resource Management on the Flightdeck: Proceedings of a NASA/Industry workshop,* NASA CP-2120, NASA-Ames Research Center: Moffett Field, CA.

Dickinson, T.L. and McIntyre, R.M. (1997), 'A Conceptual Framework for Teamwork Measurement', in Brannick, M., Salas, T.E., & Prince, C. Mahwah (eds.), *Team Performance Assessment and Measurement. Theory, Methods and Applications*, LEA: New Jersey, pp.19-43.

Dietrich, R. and Grommes, P. (2003), 'The Organization of Coherence in Oral Communication', in Dietrich, R. (ed.), *Communication in High Risk Environments. Linguistische Berichte Sonderheft*, Helmut Buske Verlag: Hamburg, pp.103-125.

Farris, G.F. and Butterfield, A. (1972), 'Control Theory in Brazilian Organizations', *Administrative Science Quarterly,* Vol. 17, pp.574-585.

Frankel, A., Graydon-Baker, E., Neppl, C., Simmonds, T., Gustafson, M. and Gandhi, T.K. (2003), 'Patient Safety Leadership Walkrounds', *Joint Commission Journal of Quality and Safety,* Vol. 29, No. 1, pp.16-26.

Flin, R. and Martin, L. (1998), *Behavioral Markers for Crew Resource Management*, CAA Civil Aviation Authority (Technical Paper 98005): London.

Ginnett, R.C. (1987) 'First Encounters of the Close Kind: The Formation Process of Airline Flight Crews', doctoral dissertation, Yale University: Connecticut.

Grommes, P. and Dietrich, R. (2002), 'Coherence in Operating Room Team and Cockpit Communication. A Psycholinguistic Contribution to Applied Linguistics', in Alatis, J.E., Hamilton, H.E. and Ai-Hui Tan (eds.), *Georgetown University Round Table on Languages and Linguistics 2000 – Linguistics, Language, and the Professions: Education, Journalism, Law, Medicine, and Technology,* Georgetown University Press: Georgetown, pp.190-219.

Grommes, P. and Grote, C. (2001), 'Coordination in Action. Comparing Two Work Sitations with High vs. Low Degrees of Formalization', in Kühnlein, P., Newlands, A. and Rieser, H. (eds.), *Proceedings of the Workshop on Coordination and Action*, ESSLLI Summer School: Helsinki.

Grommes, P., Grote, G. and Zala, E. (2003), 'Approaches to Coordination. An Interdisciplinary Study of Interaction in High Risk Environments', Paper presented at the 8th IPrA-Conference, to Panel: *L'analyse des actions et des discours en situations de travail*, organised by Jean-Paul Bronckart and Laurent Fillietaz: Toronto, July.

Hackman, J.R. (1998), 'Why Teams Don't Work', in Tindale, R. S., Edwards, J. and Posavac, E. J. (eds.), *Applications of Theory and Research on Groups to Social Issues*, Plenum: New York.

Hackman, J.R. (2002), *Leading Teams: Setting the Stage for Great Performances*, Harvard Business School Press: Boston.

Helmreich, R.L. and Merritt, A.C. (1998), *Culture at Work in Aviation and Medicine: National, Organizational, and Professional Influences*, Ashgate Publishing: Aldershot, U.K.

Hines, W.E. (1988), 'Teams and Technology: Flight Crew Performance in Standard and Automated Aircraft', Unpublished doctoral dissertation, The University of Texas at Austin: Texas.

Kerr, S., and Jermier, J.M. (1978), 'Substitutes for Leadership: Their Meaning and Measurement', *Organizational Behavior and Human Performance*, Vol. 22, pp.375-403.

Kieser, A. and Kubicek, H. (1992), *Organisation*, de Gruyter: Berlin.

Matieu, J.E., Heffner, T.S., Goodwin, G.F., Salas, E.A., Cannon-Bowers, J. (2000), 'The Influence of Shared Mental Models on Team Process and Performance', *Journal of Applied Psychology*, Vol. 85, No. 2, pp.273-283.

McIntyre, R.M. and Salas, E. (1995), 'Measuring and Managing for Team Performance: Emerging Principles from Complex Environments', in Guzzo, R. and Salas, E. (eds.), *Team Effectiveness and Decision Making in Organizations*, Jossey-Bass: San Francisco, pp.149-203.

Misumi, J. (1985), *The Behavioral Science of Leadership: An Interdisciplinary Japanese Research Program*, University of Michigan Press: Ann Arbor, MI.

Morgan, B.B., Jr., Glickman, A.S., Woodard, E.A., Blaiwes, A.S. and Salas, E. (1986), *Measurement of Team Behaviors in a Navy Environment*, NTSC Technical Report 83-014, Naval Training Systems Center: Orlando, FL.

Murphy, M.R. (1980), 'Analysis of Eighty-four Commercial Aviation Accidents: Implications for a Resource Management Approach to Crew Training', *Proceedings of the Annual Reliability and Maintainability Symposium*, pp.298-306.

National Transportation Safety Board (1994), *Safety Study: A Review of Involved-involved, Major Accidents of U.S. Air Carriers, 1978 through 1990*, PB94-917001, NTSB/SS-94/01: Washington, DC.

Orasanu, J.M. (1993), 'Decision-making in the Cockpit', in Wiener, E.L., Kanki, B., and Helmreich, R.L. (eds.), *Cockpit Resource Management*, Academic Press: San Diego, pp.137-172.

Pronovost, P., Weast, B., Rubin, H., Rosenstein, B., Sexton, J.B. and Holzmueller, C. (under review), 'Implementing and Validating a Comprehensive Unit-based Safety Program'.

Reason, J. (1997), *Managing the Risks of Organizational Accidents*, Ashgate: Aldershot, U.K.

Romanoff, N. (2003), 'Applying Walkrounds Concepts', Talk Presented at the Johns Hopkins Conference on *Improving Patient Safety: From Rhetoric to Reality*, Baltimore, Maryland, 28 May.

Schneider, C.E. and Goktepe, J.R. (1983), 'Issues in Emergent Leadership: The Contingency Model of Leadership, Leader Sex, Leader Behavior', in Blumberg, H.H., Hare, A.P.,

Kent, V. and Davies, M.F. (eds.), *Small Groups and Social Interaction Vol. 1*, Wiley: Chichester, UK, pp.413-421.

Selting, M., e.a. (1998), 'Gesprächsanalytisches Transkriptionssystem', *Linguistische Berichte*, Vol. 173, Cambridge, pp.91-122.

Serfaty, D., Entin, E.E. and Johnston, J.H. (1998), 'Team Coordination Training', in Cannon-Bowers, J.A. and Salas, E. (eds.), *Making Decision under Stress*, American Psychological Association: Washington, pp.221-245.

Sexton, J.B. and Helmreich, R.L. (2000), 'Analyzing Cockpit Communications: The Links between Language, Performance, Error, and Workload', *Human Performance in Extreme Environments*, Vol. 5, No. 1, pp.63-68.

Sexton, J.B. and Helmreich, R.L. (2002), 'Using Language in the Cockpit: Relationships with Workload and Performance', *Linguistische Berichte Sonderheft*, Vol. 12, Buske Verlag: Hamburg, pp.57-74.

Sexton, J.B., Helmreich, R.L., Thomas, E.J., Rowan, K., Boyden, J., Roberts, P. and Nielands, T.B. (under review), *The Safety Attitudes Questionnaire: A Validation Study*.

Sinha, J.P.B. (1981), *The Nurturant Task Manager: A Model of the Effective Executive*, Humanities Press: Atlantic Highlands, NJ.

Stout, R.J., Cannon-Bowers, J.A., Salas, E. and Milanovich, D.M. (1999), 'Planning, Shared Mental Models, and Coordinated Performance: An Empirical Link is Established', *Human Factors*, Vol. 41, pp.61-71.

Weick, K.E. and Roberts, K.H. (1993), 'Collective Mind in Organizations Heedful Interrelating on Flight Decks', Administrative Science Quarterly, Humanities Press Vol. 38, pp.357-381.

Zaccaro, S.J., Rittman, A.L. and Marks, M.A. (2001), 'Team Leadership', *The Leadership Quarterly*, Vol. 12, pp.451-483.

Chapter 11: Determinants of Effective Communication

Cushing, S. (1994), *Fatal Words: Communication Clashes and Aircraft Crashes*, University of Chicago Press: Chicago.

Daneman, M. & Carpenter, P.A. (1980), 'Individual Differences in Working Memory and Reading', in *Journal of Verbal Learning and Verbal Behavior*, Vol.19, pp.450-466.

Dietrich, R. (2003) (ed.), 'Communication in High Risk Environments', *Linguistische Berichte*, Special Issue 12, Buske: Hamburg.

Foushee, H.C., Lauber, J.K., Baetge, M.M. and Acomb, D.B. (1986), *Crew Performance as a Function of Exposure to High Density, Short Haul Duty Cycles. NASA Technical Memorandum 88322*, NASA-Ames Research Center: Moffet Field, CA.

Frankel, A. et al. (2003), 'Patient Safety Leadership WalkRounds™', *Joint Commission Journal on Quality and Safety*, Vol. 29, No.1, pp.16-26.

Grote, G., Zala-Mezö, E. and Grommes, P. (2003), 'Effects of Standardization on Coordination and Communication in High Workload Situations', *Linguistische Berichte*, Special Issue 12, Buske: Hamburg, pp.127-154.

Krifka, M., Martens, S. and Schwarz, F. (2003), 'Group Interaction in the Cockpit: Some Linguistic Factors', *Linguistische Berichte*, Special Issue 12, Buske: Hamburg, pp. 75-102.

Matthews, E. (2003), Proposed ICAO Language Proficiency Requirements Conference at World Airline Training Conference and Tradeshow, http://www.halldalemedia.co.uk/wats2003/pilotstream.htm.

LIVERPOOL
JOHN MOORES UNIVERSITY
AVRIL ROBARTS LRC
TEL. 0151 231 4022

Robertson, S.P. (1994), 'Simultaneous Understanding, Answering, and Memory Interaction for Questions', *Cognitive Science*, Vol. 18, pp.51-58.

Salvucci, D.D. (2002), 'Modeling Driver Distraction from Cognitive Tasks', *Proceedings of the 24ᵗʰ Annual Conference of the Cognitive Science Society.*

Searle, J. (1968), *Speech Acts. An Essay in the Philosophy of Language,* Cambridge University Press: Cambridge.

Sexton, B. and Helmreich, R.L. (2003), 'Using Language in the Cockpit: Relationships with Workload and Performance', *Linguistische Berichte*, Special Issue 12, Buske: Hamburg, pp.57-73.

Shteynberg G., Sexton, J.B. and Helmreich, R.L. (2002), 'ICU Safety: A Taxonomy of Healthcare Provider Recommendations for Patient Safety Improvements', *Hot Topic Presentation* to the American Psychological Society, 09 June 2002, New Orleans: Louisiana.

Silberstein, D., Dietrich, R. (2003), 'Cockpit Communication under High Cognitive Workload', *Linguistische Berichte*, Special Issue 12, Buske: Hamburg, pp.9-56.

Waller, M.J., Giambatista, R.C. and Zellmer-Bruhn, M. (1999), 'The Effects of Individual Time Urgency on Group Polychronicity', *Journal of Managerial Psychology,* Vol.14, pp.244-256.

Chapter 12: Task Load Effects on Language Processing

Allopenna, P.D., Magnuson, J.S. and Tanenhaus, M.K. (1998), 'Tracking the Time Course of Spoken Word Recognition Using Eye Movements: Evidence for Continuous Mapping Models', *Journal of Memory and Language*, Vol. 38, pp.419-439.

Bourke, P.A., Duncan, J. and Nimmo-Smith, I. (1996), 'A General Factor Involved in Dual-Task Performance Decrement', *Quarterly Journal of Experimental Psychology,* Vol. 49A, pp.525-545.

Bower, G.H. (2000), 'A Brief History of Memory Research', in E. Tulving and Craik, F.I.M. (eds.), *The Oxford Handbook of Memory,* Oxford University Press: New York, pp. 3-32.

Broadbent, D.E. (1958), *Perception and Communication*, Pergamon Press: London.

Broadbent, D.E. (1991), 'Recall, Recognition, and Implicit Knowledge', in Kessen, W. (ed.), *Memory, Thoughts and Emotions: Essays in Honour of George Mandler*, Erlbaum: New York, pp.125-34.

Cushing, S. (1994), *Fatal Words: Communication Clashes and Aircraft Crashes*, University of Chicago Press: Chicago.

Dahan, D., Magnuson, J.S. and Tanenhaus, M.K. (2001), 'Time Course of Frequency Effects in Spoken-Word Recognition: Evidence from Eye Movements', *Cognitive Psychology*, Vol. 42, pp.317-367.

De Jong, R. (1993), 'Multiple Bottlenecks in Overlapping Task Performance', *Journal of Experimental Psychology: Human Perception and Performance*, Vol. 19, pp.965-80.

Dylan, J. and Farmer, E. (2001), *Applying the Cognitive Streaming Theory to Air Traffic Management: A Preliminary Study,* Eurocontrol: Brussels.

Fereirra, V.S. and Pashler, H. (2002), 'Central Bottleneck Influences on the Processing Stages of Word Production', *Journal of Experimental Psychology: Learning, Memory and Cognition*, Vol. 28, No. 6, pp.1187-1199.

Fukuda, R. and Bubb, H. (2003), 'Analysis of Web Use of Elderly People Using Eye Tracking', *Proceedings of the 15ᵗʰ Triennial Congress of the International*

Ergonomics Association and the 7th Conference of Ergonomics Society of Korea / Japan Ergonomics Society, CD-ROM.

Gopher, D. (1986), 'Energetics and Resources', in Hockey, G.R.J., Gaillard, A.W.K. and Coles, M.G.H. (eds.), *Adaptation to Stress and Task Demands. NATO Advanced Research Workshop*, Plenum Press: New York.

Harley, T. (2001), *The Psychology of Language: from Data to Theory*, Psychology Press: Hove, East Sussex.

Heuer, H. (1991), 'Motor Constraints in Dual-Task Performance', in Damos, D.L. (ed.), *Multiple-Task Performance*, Taylor & Francis: London, pp.173-204.

Hoffman, J.E., Houck, M.R., MacMillan, F.W., Simons, R.F. and Oatman, L.C. (1985), 'Event-related Potentials Elicited by Automatic Targets: A Dual-Task Analysis', *Journal of Experimental Psychology: Human Perception and Performance*, Vol. 11, pp.50-61.

Hohlfeld, A., Mierke, K., Sommer, W. (in press a), 'Is Word Perception in a Second-Language more Vunerable than in One's Native Language? Evidence from Brain Potentials in a Dual Task Setting', *Brain and Language*.

Hohlfeld, A., Sangals, J. and Sommer W. (in press b), 'Effects of Additional Tasks on Language Perception: An ERP Investigation', *Journal of Experimental Psychology: Learning Memory, Cognition*.

Jäncke, L. (1994), 'Horizontal Pursuit Right-arm Movements and Dual-tasks Interferences: A Replication and Extension', *Cortex*, Vol. 30, pp.695-700.

Kahneman, D. (1973), *Attention and Effort*, Prentice Hall: Englewood Cliffs, NJ.

Kok, A. (1997), 'Event-related-potential (ERP) Reflections of Mental Resources: A Review and Synthesis', *Biological Psychology*, Vol. 45, pp.19-56.

Kutas, M. and Federmeier, K.D. (2000), 'Electrophysiology Reveals Semantic Memory Use in Language Comprehension', *Trends in Cognitive Sciences*, Vol. 4, pp.463-470.

Kutas, M. and van Petten, C. (1988), 'Event-related Potential Studies of Language', in Ackles, P.K., Jennings, J.R. and Coles, M.G.H. (eds.), *Advances in Psychophysiology*, JAI Press: Greenwich, CT, pp.285-314.

Kutas, M., Federmeier, K.D., Coulson, S., King, J.W. and Münte, T.F. (2000), 'Language', in Cacioppo, J.T., Tassinary, L.G. and Berntson, G.G. (eds.), *Handbook of Psychophysiology*, Cambridge University Press: Cambridge, pp.576-601.

Levelt, W.J.M. (1989), *Speaking: from Intention to Articulation*, MIT Press: Cambridge.

Low, I. (2003), 'Assessment of the Impact on Mental Workload from Advanced Air Traffic Management Systems: A Diagnostic Tool', *Proceedings of the 15th Triennial Congress of the International Ergonomics Association and the 7th Conference of Ergonomics Society of Korea / Japan Ergonomics Society*, CD-ROM.

McLeod, P. (1977), 'A Dual Task Response Modality Effect: Support for Multiprocessor Models of Attention', *Quarterly Journal of Experimental Psychology*, Vol. 29, pp.651-667.

Meyer, D.E. and Kieras, D.E. (1997), 'A Computational Theory of Executive Cognitive Processes and Multiple-Task Performance: Part 2. Accounts of Psychological Refractory-Period Phenomena', *Psychological Review*, Vol. 104, pp.749-791.

Navon, D.A. and Gopher, D. (1979), 'On the Economy of the Human-Processing System', *Psychological Review*, Vol. 86, pp.214-255.

Navon, D.A. and Miller, J. (2002), 'Queuing or Sharing? A Critical Evaluation of the Single-Bottleneck Notion', *Cognitive Psychology*, Vol. 44, pp.193-251.

Neuper, S. (2003), 'Language Processing under Conditions of High Workload', in de Waard, D., Brookhuis, K.A., Sommer, S.M. and Verwey, W.B. (eds.), *Human Factors in the Age of Virtual Reality*, Shaker Publishing: Maastricht, pp. 273-277.

Osman, A. and Moore, C.M. (1993), 'The Locus of Dual-Task Interference: Psychological Refractory Effects on Movement-Related Brain Potentials', *Journal of Experimental Psychology: Human Perception and Performance*, Vol. 19, pp.1292-1312.

Osterhout, L. and Holcomb, P.J. (1995), 'Event-related Potentials and Language Comprehension', in M.D. Rugg and M.G.H. Coles (eds.), *Electrophysiology of Mind. Event-related Brain Potentials and Cognition*, Oxford University Press: Oxford, pp.171-215.

Pashler, H. (1994), 'Dual-Task Interference in Simple Tasks: Data and Theory', *Psychological Bulletin,* Vol. 116, pp.220-244.

Pashler, H. and Johnston, J.C. (1989), 'Chronometric Evidence for Central Postponement in Temporally Overlapping Tasks', *Quarterly Journal of Experimental Psychology*, Vol. 41A, pp.19-45.

Robertson, S.P. (1994), 'TSUNAMI: Simultaneous Understanding, Answering, and Memory Interaction for Questions', *Cognitive Science,* Vol. 18, pp.51-85.

Rohrer, D. and Pashler, H.E. (2003), 'Concurrent Task Effects on Memory Retrieval', *Psychonomic Bulletin & Review*, Vol. 10 (1), pp.96-103.

Sangals, J., Sommer, W. and Ross, L. (under revision), 'Time Pressure Effects on Information Processing in Overlapping Tasks: Evidence from the Lateralized Readiness Potential', submitted to *Acta Psychologica.*

Sangals, J., Sommer, W. and Wilwer, M. (in preparation), 'Practice Effects on Dual Task Performance.'

Schumacher, E.H., Seymour, T.L., Glass, J.M., Fencsik, D.E., Lauber, E.J. and Kieras, D.E. (2001), 'Virtually Perfect Time Sharing in Dual-Task Performance: Uncorking the Central Cognitive Bottleneck', *Psychological Science*, Vol. 12, pp.101-108.

Searle, J.R. (1969), *Speech Acts,* Cambridge University Press: Cambridge.

Singer, M. (1985), 'Mental Operations of Question Answering', in Graesser, A.C. and Black, J.B. (eds), *The Psychology of Questions,* Erlbaum: New York, pp.121-156.

Singer, M. (1986a), 'Answering Wh-questions about Sentences and Text', *Journal of Memory and Language,* Vol. 25, pp.238-254.

Singer, M. (1986b), 'Answering Yes-no Questions about Causes: Question Acts and Question Categories', *Memory and Cognition,* Vol. 14, pp.55-63.

Sommer, W., Leuthold, H. and Schubert, T. (2001), 'Multiple Bottlenecks in Information Processing? An Electrophysiological Examination', *Psychonomic Bulletin & Review,* Vol. 8, pp.81-88.

Sperber, D. and Wilson, D. (1995), *Relevance: Communication and Cognition,* Blackwell: Oxford.

Spivey, M.J., Tanenhaus, M.K., Eberhard, K.M. and Sedivy, J. (2002), 'Eye Movements and Spoken Language Comprehension: Effects of Visual Context on Syntactic Ambiguity Resolusion', *Cognitive Psychology*, Vol. 45, pp.447-481.

Sternberg, S. (1969), 'Memory Scanning: Mental Processes Revealed by Reaction-time Experiments', *American Scientist*, Vol. 57(4), pp.421-457.

Sträter, O. (2003), 'Investigation of Communication Errors in Nuclear Power Plants', *Linguistische Berichte*, Special Edition 12, Helmut Buske Verlag: Hamburg.

Sträter, O. and Bubb, H. (2003), 'Design of Systems in Settings with Remote Access to Cognitive Performance', in Hollnagel, E. (ed.), *Handbook of Cognitive Task. Design*, Erlbaum: New Jersey, p.333ff.

Strayer, D.L. and Kramer, A.F. (1990), 'Attentional Requirements of Automatic and Controlled Processing', *Journal of Experimental Psychology: Learning, Memory and Cognition,* Vol. 16, pp.67-82.

Takeda, M. (1993), 'Eye Movements and Problem Solving', in Osaka, R., Nakamizo, Y. and Koga, K. (eds.), *Experimental Psychology of Eye Movements*, Nagoya University Press: Nagoya (in Japanese).

Tanenhaus, M.K., Spivey-Knowlton, M.J., Eberhard, K.M. and Sedivy, J.C. (1995), 'Integration of Visual and Linguistic Information in Spoken Language Comprehension', *Science*, Vol. 268, pp.1632-1634.

Vatikiotis-Bateson, E., Eigsti, I.M., Yano, S. and Munhall, K.G. (1998), 'Eye Movement of Perceivers During Audiovisual Speech Perception', *Perception & Psychophysics*, Vol. 60, No. 6, pp.926-940.

Welford, A.T. (1952), 'The "Psychological Refractory Period" and the Timing of High Speed Performance - A Review and a Theory', *British Journal of Psychology*, Vol. 43, pp.2-19.

Wickens, C.D. (1984), 'Processing Resources in Attention', in R. Parasuraman, R. Davies and J. Beatty (eds.), *Varieties of Attention*, Academic Press: New York, pp.63-102.

Yarbus, A.L. (1967), *Eye Movements and Vision*, Plenum Press: New York.

Index

LIVERPOOL
JOHN MOORES UNIVERSITY
AVRIL ROBARTS LRC
TITHEBARN STREET
LIVERPOOL L2 2ER
TEL. 0151 231 4022

LIVERPOOL
JOHN MOORES UNIVERSITY
AVRIL ROBARTS LRC
TITHEBARN STREET
LIVERPOOL L2 2ER
TEL. 0151 231 4022